Slightly
PERFECT

A LAKE DISTRICT LOVE STORY

'If you can't actually be at Gilpin Hotel in
the Lake District, then being transported
there is the next best thing.

Instead of a dry, official history, owner John Cunliffe's
memoir charts how idyllic memories of holidaying
at Gilpin with his grandmother just after the war
turned into a slightly eccentric passion,
and finally a thriving business.

Many visitors have been called back to this
enchanting spot, but none so powerfully as that small
boy, who, following a career in the hotel business
spanning New York, Jamaica and the City of London,
could eventually, with his wife Chris, buy back
Gilpin and create something truly special.

Honest, funny and always clear-eyed about
the sheer hard work that goes into this kind
of obsession, and full of insights into the unique
challenges of sustaining that rarest of spots
– a great family-run hotel – *Slightly Perfect* does
justice to Gilpin and a life in hospitality.'

OLIVIA COLE
Literary Editor, British GQ

Slightly
PERFECT

A LAKE DISTRICT LOVE STORY

One family's endeavours to create the
perfect hotel in an imperfect world

JOHN ANTHONY C. CUNLIFFE

gilpin
Lake House Books

First published in the United Kingdom in 2020
by Gilpin Lake House Books Ltd,
Crook, Kendal, LA8 8LN

www.slightlyperfect.co.uk
www.johncunliffe.co.uk

A CIP catalogue record for this book is available from the British Library.

ISBN: 978-1-5272-5428-2

Designed and edited by Richard Eccles, Great Lakes Books

Illustrations by Sara Mulvanny/agencyrush.com
Copyright © Sara Mulvanny

Printed in the EU by Latitude Press Limited

gilpin
Lake House Books

In order to be slightly perfect,
you have to be slightly imperfect.

CONTENTS

CONTENTS

ACKNOWLEDGEMENTS

Xiá. My granddaughter.
For being herself and for the title of this book.

Christine. My wife.
For encouragement. Gentle bullying.
For sharing my life. For making Gilpin.

Barney and Zoë. Our elder son and his wife.
For creating Xiá. For joining us in making Gilpin what it has become.
For huge marketing input to Slightly Perfect.

Ben and Rachel. Our younger son and his wife.
For creating Alice and Freddie: their two children and
our grandchildren. For Ben's input to Gilpin: architectural
and in every sense.

Richard Marriott. For being part of the fabric of
Gilpin for more than 30 years.

Sarah. For looking after our guests and upholding our
values for more than 25 years.

Paula, Suzi and Gill for being 'long sufferers'
for more than 20 years each.

Anna. For technical, administrative and marketing input.

Richard Eccles. A most congenial, professional and
dedicated editor and project manager.

INTRODUCTION

You may understandably wonder what sort of book this is. Please read on and make up your own mind. It doesn't really fit into a traditional category. Although I have to accept responsibility for it (and lay claim to years of planning and writing) *Slightly Perfect* almost wrote itself. By that I mean that there was no plot to conceive; no finale for which to aim and above all no characters to sculpt. The good, the bad and the inconsequential existed. And indeed continue to do so because Gilpin is not history. It thrives.

Certain events have been excluded and a few names changed in order to avoid pointless hurt or unpleasantness. Otherwise, it happened. If accuracy is lacking in any part of the book, it is accidental.

I can, however, reveal what this book is not. It is not an autobiography nor a biography. It is not a cookery book – I have no qualification to write one. Above all else, it is not a textbook on hotel management. Indeed the management of Gilpin, which I hope and believe is deeply steeped in professionalism, is about as distant from textbook orthodoxy as you could get. Caesar Ritz and Peter Drucker would squirm. Charles Forte (of whom Chris and I are protégés) might too, but then I hope and suspect he would have added, in what always seemed to me such a surprisingly deep voice for such a small man, a voice accented with a whiff of Scotland and a soupçon of Italy, 'Well! It's not quite how I would have done it but they're trying!'

I have indulged in a bit of "background" – a flavour of pre-Gilpin days. The reason is simple: earlier experiences shaped our route to Gilpin and what we have done there.

I'm John, by the way. My wife's name is Christine; in fact she was christened Christina. But I have always called her Chris. So Chris she is in this book. We met in 1961 at Battersea College of Advanced Technology (please take note of the advanced) which in the year after our four-year course in Hotel and Catering Management became a part the University of Surrey, based at Guildford. I suspect my motive for making this point is that we were disappointed to miss out on university status. Everyone knows what a degree is, but who's heard of an ACT(Bat)?

On the plus side, we had London at our feet. I state this not in the sense of association with the Swinging Sixties, which completely passed us by, but because in learning about our adopted business we had access to the "grandes dames" hotels including the Savoy, the Dorchester, Grosvenor House and the Ritz.

The debate about the London Hilton on Park Lane overlooking Buckingham Palace was in progress. As far as I recall neither Her Majesty nor the Duke of Edinburgh publicly expressed a view, but to suddenly have one's bathroom overlooked by one's commoners must have been somewhat alarming. The Royal Garden hotel had just opened. Escoffier was the only recipe book worth possessing and nouvelle cuisine had not been invented. Neither "marketing" nor "branding" (as concepts) existed – at least in the hotel industry. There was no minimum wage, so good service (and appropriate rewards) was more the norm than the exception. Computers were really adding machines and the size of houses.

London boasted, as well as exquisite hotels, many fine, unaffordable restaurants and bars. Our lecturers knew the management of these establishments and we came to see the kitchens, the stores, the housekeeping offices, the back of reception and the accounts departments. There were no sales offices. HR was Personnel. Finance was Accounts. Training was at the mercy of experience. There were no Standard Operating Procedures!

The first two years at Battersea College were intensely practical and we became reasonable cooks and competent waiters and waitresses. We wore our whites with pride as we went to the training kitchens and restaurant. Students of chemistry or biology could not boast such a distinguished uniform. We carried our knives without fear of being arrested as potential murderers or terrorists.

Crossing the thresholds of the hotels and restaurants we visited – those elegant palaces of hospitality – either on ventures arranged by Battersea or independently, brought to me an element of confidence. These experiences mitigated the natural nervousness of being in places surrounded by cultures of history, famous people, snobbery, glamour, sex, expense and supposed superior beings (many of whose main aim was to earn tips). Such exposure was a personal and professional bonus to us young things in the Hotel and Catering Management department.

Nonetheless, there remains a part of me that, despite this and subsequent experiences, has never quite lost an awe of hotels and restaurants – even now when I know that it is unlikely (within reason) that my credit card will be declined or that I will under-tip the concierge. Perhaps this respect is a part of my love affair with this industry. Fine creations deserve respect, whether they are hotels, churches, works of art, concertos, mountain ranges, oceans, icebergs, rivers or women!

Slightly Perfect is essentially a love story. A love story in a non-soppy sense. Love of the Lake District, of Gilpin and the Lake House, of hotels as places to be enjoyed, of my own family and of an extended family of people who have helped to make Gilpin – and who still do. And love of a vocation which I truly believe the hotel business is.

No sane person – unless on a mission – would work like so many of us do, with little respite and often for minimal financial reward. Survival certainly comes into it. If you take the bungee jump from the relative security of employment (however dour) into your own business, you probably don't have the option of reversing the process without many years of worry and work to solidify your precarious investment: precarious because of your own abilities (or lack of them), the number of hours in the day, the economy, the weather, the often tragic consequences of decisions made by politicians, dependence on others, the financial seesaws of current times and the fickle attitude of most banks.

Certainly no such alternative was available to us. To combine a flight of clichés (probably not recommended so early on in a book, but I implied above that this one is unconventional), we had to reap what we had sewn, and having jumped from the frying pan into the fire we had well and truly made our bed and had to lie on it. A chance to do so (for very long) would have been a fine thing!

Slightly Perfect is also a tale of sadness. I have described events as they happened and I wish that many of them had not.

The hotel business is a demanding taskmaster, mainly for three reasons. First, our clients are people. And people are very variable. Being at the upper end of the business is undoubtedly easier than other sectors of the industry, and the vast majority of our guests are charming and appreciative. But there are exceptions – and some people with money to throw around can be very difficult.

Secondly, our main tool is again people: staff. Human beings, subject to all the vagaries of life. Prone to headaches, hangovers, loneliness, lovesickness, feelings of inadequacy, exhaustion, depression, sadness, jealousy and illness as well as to the opposites of those conditions.

Thirdly, in this business you can never turn off the lights, lock the door and forget it all until the next day, or on a Friday switch off till Monday. You can never hold a meeting when all those who should be in attendance are. Someone has got to look after the guests. So you have to have another meeting and say all the same things again. Communication is onerous.

Although I was born in exotic Watford on 11th February 1944, the Lake District has always been home. As the end of World War Two approached, my parents sent me and my older sister Elizabeth away from south-eastern England to the safety of the Lakes. Elizabeth and I spent many happy holidays at Gilpin Lodge from babyhood to teens.

My paternal grandmother Harriet, a widow of the so-called Great War, lived at Gilpin Lodge, an Edwardian House in the countryside just over two miles from Windermere. Her husband had in fact survived World War

One, but died just months later from tuberculosis contracted in Flanders. He had been a prominent officer, doctor and administrator in the Royal Army Medical Corps and the family had moved to the Lakes at the end of the war in the hope that the country air would cure him. It didn't. A photograph of him with King George V and Queen Mary inspecting nurses at the RAMC hospital in Manchester hangs on the "family" wall at Gilpin.

These childhood forays to Gilpin were almost invariably without my parents, and Granny did not have much time to entertain us. The days of servants were largely over. But there were loads of toys including dressing-up stuff, a moving picture projector operated by a handle, a rickshaw, a small bicycle (my favourite) and many others. We were probably too young to appreciate the sight of the fells in the distance, the autumn heather, the yellow gorse in springtime or the sunsets.

Our nurse Celia was sometimes with us in the early days. I am vague about her comings and goings in our young lives. Elizabeth became a devotee of Jack Mason the gardener. His daughter Christine was to later work with Chris in the kitchen at Gilpin Lodge when we first bought it.

But this book is not about my boyhood. However, my soul has always bonded with Gilpin Lodge, which I did not in fact inherit. Granny died in the mid-sixties and Gilpin had several owners before Chris and I finally bought it in 1987.

To clarify a potential misunderstanding, Gilpin Lodge is the name of the house. When we turned it into a hotel we called it "Gilpin Lodge Country House Hotel". This is indeed somewhat of a mouthful. The term "country house hotel" had been coined by Francis Coulson and Brian Sack at the renowned Sharrow Bay on Ullswater some years before.

I think it was an appropriate way of describing this genre of establishment. However, the term "lodge" brought with it some problems, particularly with Americans and Australians.

Initially our business was all British so this dichotomy was unimportant. But as our international market grew, as well as motorway lodges and budget hotels – some called lodges – the need grew to drop "lodge" from the name of the hotel. And then in 2010, we opened the Lake House as a part of Gilpin and it was definitely time to rebrand to "Gilpin Hotel & Lake House".

*

Granny was a typical lady of her age, from a large family made prosperous through Lancashire cotton. Reference to "dark satanic mills" in the stirring hymn *Jerusalem* by William Blake still worries me. Driving around Lancashire even these days there are mills aplenty to see – some converted, some ruins. It is not difficult to imagine that they had been both dark and satanic, laboured in for long hours for minimal wages. Tea breaks non-existent. Lard sandwiches for lunch. Toilet visits refused. What else?

Two of Granny's sisters, Gertrude and Adelaide, both spinsters probably denied husbands due to World War One, moved to Windermere at the same time as my grandparents. "Gertie" and "Adgie", as they were always known, had bought a Victorian mansion called Nine Oaks in the village, and Elizabeth and I spent many holidays there too. I retain memories of my fear of its enormousness and its dark corners. Worse were the cavernous cellars accessed via a steep, dark staircase. It was necessary to descend into this miniature hell from time to time in order to fetch items of food stored in the pantry.

I recall Nine Oaks's coldness. Irrespective of the time of year, fires were not lit before 6 p.m. There was of course no central heating. I suspect that had there been, it would not have been switched on till the evening. While the saying "looking after the pennies" is associated mainly with Scotland and Yorkshire, my grandparents' generation were very "careful". The end of that expression "the pounds will look after themselves" has always seemed to me a singularly stupid attitude, and when I look at our accounts for the hotel, my eyes go first to the largest area of cost: salaries and wages. Large amounts of pounds. Never mind the silly little pennies!

Auntie Gertie bought Knipe Tarn – a Norwegian-style bungalow perched on the edge of a small lake three miles south of Windermere – in 1919 as a picnic venue. Yes. How nice! Land and property in the Lake District at that time was very cheap. But that is all Knipe was used for. She never stayed there nor lived there. Knipe Tarn (meaning, I am led to believe, "Place of High Rocks" in Norse) was to become a pivotal place in Chris's and my life, and is still our home today. The hotel part of Knipe Tarn became Gilpin Lake House in 2010.

The Lake District was new to Chris when I first took her there. My father had asked Auntie Gertie if he could make Knipe Tarn habitable and use it for holidays. This was a major labour of love. The house needed everything doing to it and the garden was a jungle. Quite why this undertaking was considered a holiday I am not sure. But much had been achieved before Chris first visited.

Nonetheless, daily chores left little time for outings or relaxation. There was no electricity in those days, no telephone, no flushing toilets and no running water. The daily attendance to fires (for heating and cooking), oil lamps and candles, as well as shopping and cleaning, was a full-time occupation. Amazingly it was fun and very peaceful.

My dad had to touch base with his work almost daily, and visits to the nearest telephone box doubled with visits to the Brown Horse at Winster or the Wild Boar at Crook – which happened to be where the nearest payphones were. When I whinge now (which I do frequently) about mobile phones clanging off all day long, I sometimes recall the inconvenience of lack of communications in those days. These necessary visits to the phone were a good excuse for a few beers or glasses of wine.

Chris adopted the Lake District hook, line and sinker, although that was probably where Knipe Tarn's long-established fishing associations ended as far as she was concerned.

This story will be the worse if it is other than truthful, including in relation to matters which now cause embarrassment. So let me confess that when Chris and I first embarked on finding a hotel to buy in the Lake District, the plan was that this would be semi-retirement.

And just how embarrassed am I to admit this? To imagine, as experienced hoteliers, some forty-something years old and therefore on paper possessed of a modicum of wisdom, that to run a hotel – however small, however simple, however hands-on and therefore devoid of potential for discord – could be in any sense retirement! You can't, at that age, plead senior moments.

We all make mistakes in life – some bigger than others. But sometimes good can come from mistakes – as long as you face up to them sooner rather than later.

*

Because my father was a doctor I got no student grant whereas Chris did. I suppose this was in a sense student loans in reverse; if you were in the right place at the right time you got paid to go to university. My dad never quite "got" this and kept me on a very tight financial rein. Thus I was the pauper in the relationship with Chris.

She was a Yorkshire girl from successful but probably less prosperous roots than me. Her father, Reg, did not believe in further education for women. He was a highly decent, hardworking man but steeped in South Yorkshire attitudes (and attitude actually), which at that time strained relations somewhat between him and me. He was also extremely mean.

In the days when the GPO (oh! General Post Office) was in charge of telecommunications and you had to wait months to get a phone installed, Reg was the only person known to mankind who had the telephone taken out when they moved into their new house on the grounds that it might get used. Chris's mother Audrey was a very different kettle of fish, who I suppose regarded me as a good catch. She lavished affection on me and encouragement on our relationship. Chris has always taken the view that I courted Audrey rather than her. Unkind and untrue!

Chris had left grammar school with a pile of O and A-levels, despite which Reg wanted her to join ICI (which had taken over British Nylon Spinners in Doncaster), and start work immediately in the laboratory. Reg had an excellent job at ICI where he was fulfilled and respected. Chris however, both industrious and determined even at that young age, had done her homework and decided that she wanted to study Hotel and Catering Management in London. Battersea was the place to go.

Audrey had backed her and Reg had called them both snobs. A major row had ensued. Chris had to go before a panel of councillors in Sheffield to justify going to Battersea (out of t' county!). She persuaded them. Audrey was elated. Reg was furious and assured her that he would not part with one penny to finance her extravagant and unnecessary decision. He later relented – although I don't recall a deluge of pennies.

Love between Chris and I had not been at first sight. At the outset of our first lecture at Battersea we were asked to stand and say who we were and why we wanted to go into the hotel business. We all replied that it was because we liked people. With hindsight, we had a lot to learn. There are people and people!

I did notice Chris and clocked a pretty face and good legs. She has since said that she didn't notice me at all…

It all started at the end of the Easter term in the second year. The parents of a friend and fellow student, Di, had a cottage in Glenelg, a to-die-for village on the western coast of Scotland opposite Kylerhea on the Isle of Skye. Somehow, despite our tender ages, eight of us managed to hire and insure a minibus and drive to Glenelg, stopping, late at night, for a break at Chris's parents' house in Yorkshire. The journey from London to Glenelg was a considerable undertaking. This was 1962, with the M1 only on the drawing board, and the A1 meandering through many towns and traffic lights.

This was the first time I met Reg and Audrey. They were probably as nervous as we were. We sat around and made polite conversation. Their grown-up little girl with seven friends from college. I was asked, by Audrey of course, to pour the tea. Chris smiled at me. I think it was the first time I knew that she had noticed me.

We arrived at Glenelg late the following day. It was as wonderful as Di had promised. The sun was shining and the vicious tide was visibly racing through the sound separating the mainland from Skye.

I really cannot remember the sleeping arrangements at Half Croft – the cottage in Glenelg. I suspect that they were very proper.

One of our colleagues turned out to be supremely bossy, attempting to run the holiday like a military operation. He was a Scottish lad called Jock who probably felt that under the circumstances he should be in charge. To avoid an escalation of tension, Chris, her London flatmate Sarah and her boyfriend John, and I hijacked the minibus one day and took off for a little sightseeing. This well-intentioned act backfired in that removal of the party's only transport was deemed by the others as selfish.

It probably was, but I for one didn't care. Chris had actually asked me to join this exclusive little expedition. And that on top of the smile over pouring the tea at her home. Either our love of hotels or of sampling single malt whiskies guided us to the Cluanie Inn where, as chance would have it, the landlord was an expert on malt whiskies and fond of demonstrating his great knowledge. The outcome was an unforgettable day and even before Barbara Castle's drink-drive legislation, the obvious impossibility of driving back to Glenelg.

Although Cluanie was a simple glorified pub, our exposure to it was full of romance. Mists swirled around as did whisky and the fantasy of the Highlands. Robin (our host) undoubtedly fancied his chances with Chris and took her fly fishing in the wee small hours of the morning. Since she and I were not by then an item, I felt unable to protest. I was never advised if there was a bite!

Chris and I didn't live together at college. Oh no, no, noh! I was obliged to live with my parents in a posh house in Hampstead. My mother was a semi-invalid and with my father a busy medic I had to do my bit looking after mother. Chris and Sarah shared various flats in Battersea and Clapham. All were basic, furnished as befitted student flats in the sixties, and the rooms lacked privacy. But to me they were heaven. They were not my home but rather my sanctuary, and after boarding school and compared with the house in Hampstead they were somewhere where I could be myself with the girl I had fallen in love with.

Chris and I spent every waking hour together, including lectures at college and a lot of time in cookery and restaurant practicals. Although some of the hands-on work was spurious (I recall a whole lesson devoted to analysing the difference between a brush and a broom), most of it was invaluable and gave us skills and knowledge which, coupled with lectures on wine, housekeeping, law, business, finance, accounting, economics and reception, turned us into reasonably knowledgeable – albeit inexperienced – hoteliers.

Chapter One

CHILDHOOD

I had rather stumbled into the hotel business, having left Ampleforth College in Yorkshire in 1961 with rather less than the results which would have accessed Oxbridge. My father was a successful Professor of Microbiology in London, and, with hindsight, was too busy to seriously dedicate much time to his children's careers. I say this because the same sort of fate, albeit not in hotelkeeping, befell my sister Elizabeth.

I hated my prep school in Gloucestershire, mainly because I was bullied mercilessly for being the only Catholic in the school. The single break in the clouds started when it became apparent that I played the piano well, hampered by my ability to read music only very slowly. Hence I was able, with much practice, to perfect my pièce de résistance for the end-of-term examination, performed in front of the whole school. And what a nerve-racking business that was. I carried off every first prize for the piano until it was time to leave that school. The prizes were leatherbound copies of English literary classics, and I still have many on the bookshelves in our house.

But there turned out to be other benefits from my piano-playing prowess. One term, the music teacher went ill and there was no-one to accompany the hymns which were sung in assembly every morning. This ceremony was presided over by the senior headmaster, after which it was announced who was to be punished that day for various heinous crimes. I only once got beaten and that was for making "inappropriate" noises in the wake of one huge and smelly lady teacher.

But to return to piano playing. I was told that for the foreseeable future I was to accompany the hymns at morning assembly, and it was conceded that I could spend as much time as I wanted in the music room preparing. For some strange reason this accorded me much kudos in the eyes of fellow pupils, including the erstwhile bullies, and scores of volunteers appeared to turn the pages of the music sheets. I could not see the point in this as I was quite capable of turning the pages myself, but if this was to be the price of peace, I thought so be it. This renaissance of attitude remained with me for the rest of my time at that school.

A priest from the Dominican monastery in nearby Woodstock visited me every Thursday afternoon to instruct me in the Catholic faith. He was a dear man – Father Alphonsus – almost too large for the moped on which he travelled. And on Sundays I walked across Minchinhampton Common to the small Catholic church. There seemed to be no fear in those days of youngsters going about their business alone. Was it a different world or just a different attitude? Also on Sundays, I then had a peaceful hour or two to myself while the remainder of the school walked in crocodile to the Church of England church in Amberley.

During these periods on my own, without supervision from school staff, I took to smoking a pipe. I have no idea why. I made it from a wooden dice shaker with a hole drilled into it, in which was inserted a bicycle pump connector. Tobacco was dried leaves. Matches were readily available.

I particularly remember this because we used them to light candles on occasions when we "climbed Mount Midnight" while boarding at Lime Cottage. This was the house of the headmaster's mother, in Box village, just a few hundred yards from the school. The charming thatched cottage provided two small dormitories, with just four beds in each, to complement the larger rooms in the main school buildings.

Mount Midnight was an exciting, secret adventure undertaken once a term. Lights out was 8.30 so there were three-and-a-half hours to kill in pointless chatter and storytelling before the summit was reached, by which time we were exhausted, frozen and short of oxygen. The flag of achievement was a pair of underpants attached to a pole for opening and closing the higher window!

I have often looked back on these schooldays and wondered what really was the ethos of the school. It was owned and run by a thoroughly well-meaning family, of which the three brothers shared the title of Headmaster, and yet some quite cruel practices were permitted, and bullying, which must have been obvious, was not stamped out.

The physical side of things was overseen by an ex-army sergeant major who seemed to believe that military toughness was appropriate for eight- to twelve-year-olds. One of the "sports" conducted under the misnomer of PE was for the boys to remove their shoes and form two tramlines in between which a "victim" was made to run as fast as he could in order to supposedly minimise the blows from the shoes of the boys in the two lines. This was brutal and inappropriate for all involved. Boxing was compulsory, with serious mismatching of opponents. I recall being pummelled by a boy twice my size and teased for being a coward because I was unable to put up much of a performance under the circumstances.

Work was taken very seriously and included Latin, French, mathematics and sciences from the age of seven or eight. I found Latin particularly difficult, even though I had the advantage of exposure to the Latin Mass. Ridiculously, I recall a rhyme taught to enhance our Latin pronunciation:

Caesar ad sum jam for te.
Brutus aderat.
Caesar sic in omnibus.
Brutus sic in at.

The compulsory purchase of a newspaper every Sunday enabled us to keep up with what was going on in the world. None of it made much sense.

Yet there were many kind and generous instances. Whenever a boy was awarded a scholarship to public school, a half-day's holiday was given to the whole school. We all knew in advance that someone had won a scholarship and bets were taken (for items of tuck) for which day would be the half-holiday. This was never announced until the morning of the selected day and even then the announcement was not made until the assembly hymn had been sung and the punishments announced. These latter were a fait accompli because they were assigned on a points system and everyone knew how many order marks they had been given in a week. So anticipation was high on potential half-holiday days – somewhat diminished for those in for a thrashing first! Summer half-holidays were often spent in a (with hindsight) charming wooded area containing a lake. Picnic tea was provided. I recall (strangely) one such day when a gang of us witnessed a grass snake eating a frog. The frog just sat there allowing the snake to pull out and devour its guts.

I was invited to Sunday lunch several times each term by a lady who lived in Box village. She attended the same church as me. These were blissful escapes from school and I hope I showed my appreciation. I hope my parents did too – assuming that they knew of these occasions. I can recall a couple of visits by my parents, but that's all. Poor child.

To illustrate the extent of my neglect (I never regarded it as such) my father was asked, or maybe he volunteered, to go to the USA for a six-month period. My recollection is that this was to share his research into disposable medical products with his American colleagues.

Preparations for this project were immense. The house in Keats Grove in Hampstead (worth a few million now I bet) had to be let, my mother's mother (who lived with us – I never met either of my grandfathers) had to be housed, and Elizabeth and I had to be dealt with – including this period crossing two school terms and the long summer holiday in between. It transpired that the parents of one of my friends at school had a large house in Devon which they operated as a boarding home for children during the school holidays. This was a godsend and not too painful for Elizabeth and me as Mark was a known quantity. The logistics of getting Elizabeth and me from schools in Kent (she was at Benenden) and Gloucestershire and back must have been complex. I recall quite an upset with the matron at my school, who wanted to pack for me for the holidays in Devon. I wanted to pack for myself. My independent self starting to emerge.

The house in Devon, in a village called Shebbear, was heaven. A vast rambling pile with lofts and attics, garages and sheds, lakes and lawns, a treehouse and (of course) segregated dormitories. The girls tended to hang in together, as did the boys. We discovered a loft above the girls' bathroom with many cracks in the floorboards. The girls' bathtimes were popular with us. Dirty little boys!

On the day that my parents returned to Liverpool on the *SS Sylvania*, my maternal grandmother died of a heart attack in Hampstead tube station. My uncle Christopher, one of my father's brothers, was a judge of some sort in Liverpool and he had arranged for Elizabeth and me to be allowed on board the arriving ship to surprise my parents. And it did. But as we arrived at Gilpin, where they were to stay until the tenants at Keats Grove in Hampstead left a week later, the phone rang and the news broke. My mother wailed for days and we all had to return immediately in order for my father to take over the arrangements. We stayed in a squalid pub opposite Hampstead Heath. I was deemed too young to attend the funeral. I think that my mother's raison d'être disappeared with my grandmother's death.

I didn't hate Ampleforth, although the regime was tough and disciplinarian, and I came to respect and even love the ingrained Christianity – which was hardly to be unexpected in a school and abbey run by Benedictine monks. Underlying the work, sport and character-building ethos was a deeply rooted fairness and sense of care for the wellbeing of the boys and their souls. Needless to say, there were no girls at the school in those days. In my case, this exposure to beliefs which I came to accept as good and right have stayed with me all my life, and often supported me in both good times and bad.

I was under the influence of, almost but not totally without exception, intelligent, sincere, religious, dedicated men, and in times throughout life of doubt about faith, God, goodness and associated matters, I have always reflected that such people could not have made it all up either for themselves or for us boys at the school.

Most renowned of these men was Basil Hume, later to become Cardinal Hume. He tried to make me into a rugby player and failed miserably. But as an example of leadership, scholasticism, holiness and love of mankind he remains for me an inspiration. There is little doubt that we now largely live in a religious vacuum, and with that has come a void in leadership and understanding of how to live. What the rules are. By and large there aren't any. And what a pickle that has led society into. I suspect that people would now sneer at one of the school's maxims at that time, which was that an education at Ampleforth was a preparation for life and for death. Perhaps I won't risk my readers' scorn by proceeding with that line of thought. This attitude was illustrated through the one and only prescribed item of uniform – a black tie.

Another monk, one of many, who influenced my faith was Father Wilfred. I was in his class for religious instruction, for which year I don't recall. We loved his sessions because he tended to sidestep the syllabus and stray into real-life stories. Some of these accounts concerned the fact that he was psychic. I use the word "fact" intentionally because that was how he regarded it. While it might be thought that this subject would be regarded as mysterious, even shrouded in suspicion, there was no doubt nor reticence as far as Father Wilfred was concerned. And this situation was known throughout the monastery. For this reason he was usually chosen by the Abbott to undertake exorcisms when requests were made for this activity. He regarded such a function as completely practical and a logical job for a priest to undertake.

He told the story of one occasion when he had been asked to see what he could do for an old Amplefordian called Gregory Steele, who had bought a rundown golf course near Fort William. With the golf course came a dilapidated clubhouse which Gregory and his wife wanted to upgrade as a facility for golfers and as a bed and breakfast. For some reason which no-one could explain, the house was known as The Manse, although it had never served as a vicarage.

During the renovation process an unnaturally large number of accidents happened, even though the work was under contract to a respected building company. A wall supporting the roof collapsed with no explanation and with it the roof, trapping one of the builders who had to have a leg amputated. A strut on a new metal ladder broke causing another builder to fall to the ground, breaking a leg. One of the contractor's lorries, while parked and unattended, mysteriously plunged down a bank and crashed into a wall. Gregory's beagle dog was found dead on the site. The vet could find no cause. There were other incidents.

A part of the building, a newer wing, was not part of the contract and the Steeles lived in it. But they were becoming spooked. Neighbours hinted that the place had been haunted since memory began. Gregory had asked the local Catholic priest for advice, but while sympathetic, he had declined to go near the place. So Father Wilfred was dispatched from Ampleforth. He liked the occasional game of golf and took his clubs.

Benedictine monks take a vow of poverty and don't actually own anything, but the school and monastery had a pool of cars and one was allocated for the job. Father Wilfred left very early having said his daily Mass in one of the many chapels in the crypt of the abbey. He arrived at lunchtime and after a sandwich and a beer, he and Gregory decided to play nine holes. They talked about the strange events that were going on while they played. Gregory told the priest that his main purpose in seeking help was that his wife was running very scared and was unhappy about living at the Manse, and unhappy in general about the whole situation.

The three of them dined together that evening and Father Wilfred drank only water. He left his hosts early, explaining that he wanted to prepare for the night ahead.

At this point a voice from the back of the classroom asked, 'Sir. Were you afraid?'

'Not at this point. Not in the slightest. You see, because of my condition, I live with spirits and the souls of the dead all the time. It is my cross. And also my privilege. I am armed with the sword of the Father, the courage of our Saviour and the armour of the Holy Spirit. Let me continue and I will explain that answer.

'My preparations were of course prayers. Prayers to an extent for my hosts but above all for myself. I knew as soon as I stepped into the Manse that there was evil there. Powerful evil. And let no-one be fooled that evil is not powerful. It is the work of Satan. And I am but a man. A weak mortal.

'I knew that the Evil was as aware of me in the Manse as I was of it. There was to be conflict that night. My prayers probably kept the Evil at bay. But at some point I had to allow the conflict to begin.

'It was not the so-called bewitching hour. The wind did not howl. Branches did not whip across the windows. There was no thunder nor lightning. The perceived appendages to ghost stories were not apparent.

It was very dark and very still. I held my Crucifix in front of me. Then it began.

'The moon disappeared although it had been bright as a button a few minutes before. The pressure started slowly and built up. Pressure from behind me and in front of me – from my head to my feet. There was no sound apart from my own intensifying breathing. The pain was extreme. You see I was the meat in the sandwich – the two slices of bread being the power of Good and the power of Evil. I didn't know whether the Good was in front of me or behind me.

'Then I saw it. The face was like an X-ray, barely visible in the total darkness. The outline of the bone structure glowed. It was a cruel face, full of malice. It was only a face. There was no body. But now I knew that Evil was in front of me. I lifted my Crucifix and holding it in both hands I thrust it in the direction of the face. I shouted as loudly as my crushed lungs would permit "in the name of the Father and of the Son and of the Holy Spirit depart from this place now never to return".

'There was a hideous scream like a cat being tortured but at a volume more like a dozen cats. The face dimmed and disappeared. Then there was a crash from outside my bedroom window.

'The moon shone again. The pressure from in front of me ceased. The pressure from behind became a gentle warmth. I started to shake violently. The warmth at my back calmed me. I looked out of the window – I had not drawn the curtains. A chimney stack had fallen on my car which was crushed. There were no more incidents at The Manse.'

Could this clever, sincere, charming, spiritual man have made all this up? And if so for what? I think not.

The school was run on "house" lines and while classes and sports were in-dependent of house, we were quite clannish about our house association. My housemaster, Father Benedict, was another good man, although I fell foul of him towards the end of my time at Ampleforth because I became part of a gang of cigarette smokers. Smoking was seriously forbidden and our circle designed a complex game of cat and mouse to avoid detection. I regret it now.

Despite this misconduct, I did get made a house monitor. Responsibilities were not very onerous but the power to hand out lines was wicked, and the tie with silver stripes on a black backdrop was a proudly worn icon. The house monitors were invited to an annual binge in the form of an evening barbecue at Gilling Lake. It was an elitist, grown-up summer party at which half a bottle of wine per person could be consumed. I managed to exceed this on one occasion and back at the house, the "big white steering wheel" in the bathroom was essential throughout the night.

I don't recall regular parental visits at Ampleforth either. But they must have happened from time to time, and half-terms became associated with hotels and food, which without doubt surpassed the meals at school, although fine dining at that time had certainly not been invented in Gloucestershire or Yorkshire. The establishments that provided these treats became fixed in my mind as places associated with the good life in so far as I knew it.

The Bear at Woodstock was the prep school bolthole. Low oak beams, log fires, warmth and an illusory freedom from fear were the principal delights. The Black Swan at Helmsley was the later equivalent. Being older and much more content with life, visits here were more hedonistic and as time went on came to include small quantities of beer and certainly a growing admiration of fellow pupils' sisters. Good. Very good.

The question of girls, needless to say, grew in importance. I had some idea what they were for.

The Headmaster's "Golden Lecture" on the last day at prep school covered this topic, albeit in a slightly embarrassed and smoothed-over vein. Their physical attractions, well-disguised long before miniskirts and skimpy tops, were obvious. Why they caused both pleasure and confusion was a mystery, and this took eons before I came to understand – or probably failed to understand – how complicated they were. I had a fair idea of what I wanted to do with them.

It was going to be a long time before this was put to the test. The Catholic attitude to sex or anything approaching it (avoiding "occasions of sin") is unequivocal.

Chapter Two

BATTERSEA

C hris and I finally married in February 1966 after a far from easy courtship in which at times I felt like a soloist playing in a duet. The match was encouraged by Reg and Audrey in almost exact proportion to the opposition posed by my parents. The effect of the latter on Chris was far greater, so she subsequently told me, than I had imagined.

There's no doubt that my mother was a snob without a cause. There is also no doubt that she adored me, although she was not a very good mother. Despite the fact that she achieved little herself, she was critical of my father's professional progress (although he was, in fact, an eminent medical scientist) and she hated my going into the hotel business. She saw me in the Foreign Office. Chris was, in her eyes, not only another hotel student, but from Yorkshire to boot. A place where they had coal mines and spoke with a funny accent. Chris was not welcomed into the bosom of the family and I should have done something about it.

The attitude of my parents undoubtedly made Chris's and my relationship harder. I was far too young and inexperienced to understand my mother and I knew little of her background. Her father was originally from Cork in Ireland and rose to become Harbour Master in the important port of Liverpool. She was undoubtedly given one hell of a ride by my father's family (the Lancashire cotton lot) who, as I came to realise later, had a bit of a bee's knees complex. She met my father because she taught dancing in London and he became one of her pupils. I suspect that this was also frowned upon. A bit close to the wrong side of the street! Serious careers for women had certainly not come into being and I suspect that Ma was neglected and very lonely. Who in their right mind would buy a house in Hampstead and work in Denmark Hill? At least an hour each way. Additionally, success does not come without effort and therefore sacrifices – for all concerned.

My first exposure to live (as opposed to student) hotel work was as a commis waiter at Le Grand Hotel de la Plage et d'Angleterre in Royan – not a million miles from Bordeaux. Battersea required us to find our own position and work in a hotel or restaurant for eight weeks in the summer at the end of the second year. Having failed A-level French at Ampleforth, I thought that working in France would make amends. I perceived glamour in this atonement. The name of the hotel, chosen from an ancient *Guide Michelin*, caused me to believe that it would be Brit-friendly. My letter in bad French was rewarded with an invitation to arrive on an appointed date. No mention was made of terms of employment. Stupidly, or perhaps just naively, I let that go.

It wasn't Brit-friendly, nor was there any glamour. The cold and unceremonious lack of welcome has caused me at Gilpin to always try to do better by new and inexperienced staff arrivals, particularly from abroad.

My error in reporting to the reception desk and attempting to explain my purpose in being there (a speech I had rehearsed in the latter hours of the arduous train journey from Paris), was rewarded by being requested to about turn and leave through the front door of the hotel and seek the staff entrance at the back. I was shown to a room with six small beds and told which was mine. I was to report for duty to the restaurant at 5.30 p.m. The room smelt of sweaty feet. The whole idea was becoming incredibly bad. I was frightened and lonely. What would I be required to do in the restaurant? Speak fluent French to sophisticated guests? Cook crêpes Suzette? Know the wine list backwards?

For at least the second time in my life I experienced the pain of being in a minority of one. An English boy in a room with five French boys and a language problem. Initial shyness all round soon gave way to something not far short of persecution. They were the majority in nationality, language, knowledge of the hotel and of the ropes of how the restaurant worked. I was the alien. I was also the unknown quantity as far as waiting was concerned.

I was assigned a station next to the kitchen and furthest from the windows, which overlooked the beach and the sea. This contained the least desirable tables in the entire room, and consequently my guests were the least content – a fact which was not infrequently made obvious. It was also where the owners ate breakfast, lunch and dinner. They were a sour triplet consisting of Monsieur, Madame and an older woman – presumably the mother of one or the other. They were my first guests that evening.

The maître d'hôtel was a cheerless individual who directed the dining room with extravagant gestures and broad smiles – grins even – to favoured guests. Those escorted to my section were clearly not favoured, so smiles were infrequent. I was not introduced to the owning family and they made no attempt to greet the new member of staff. No procedures were explained to me nor instructions given. So I did my best, attempting to be professional and pleasant despite my huge anxiety and feeling of isolation.

My almost insuperable desire to run away was hampered only by the fact that I had no money. Nor did I receive any until my final day at work 56 days later. Duties consisted of serving breakfast, lunch and dinner, with cleaning in between, seven days a week, with no days off. A two-hour break in the afternoon was made available on alternate days only. On the others I was responsible for washing the salads.

This thankfully brief introduction to hotel life was inopportune and might have been terminal had I not realised that it was untypical in several ways. Even to my inexperienced eyes this hotel was inferior and poorly operated. I also came to learn quite early on that the English were not popular in that particular part of France, having extensively shelled the area during World War Two – then barely twenty years before.

I find it interesting to reflect on the contrast between staff welfare now and then. We now give a great deal of thought and money to retaining our staff. Our latest staff house in Windermere (we now have three) comprises

12

single or double bedrooms with en-suite shower rooms and a television in every room, a common room with a pool table, transport to and from work and a cleaning service. Lunch and dinner are provided in the canteen at Gilpin. Barney (our elder son and now the Managing Director of Gilpin – much more of him later) is fanatical about "work-life balance". In Royan we worked an eighty-hour week and did nothing else except sleep when possible. There was no leisure. What a change in just over fifty years.

One benefit only accrued: to survive I had to speak and understand French. I learned quickly and it has been a great benefit personally and professionally ever since. Many happier times have been spent in France – a country that all my family enjoy and love.

Two incidents jump out from this job. The restaurant floor was wooden parquet and as such hard and somewhat noisy. The tables were laid out in neat rows like some canteen, which is not far off what it was.

One evening when the room was full of guests I tripped on an uneven bit of floor and dropped the large round stainless steel tray I was carrying. It had been full of empty glasses on their way to the wash-up. The crash was in itself spectacular. A showstopper – or at least a conversation stopper. Silence fell – just as the tray had done. But greater humiliation was to follow. Fate dictated that the tray fell onto its rim with a slight spin towards the far side of the room. The tray, as if self-possessed, commenced its noisy journey in a precisely straight line. It veered not one inch to right or left, which might have stopped it. It slowed as it approached the window and commenced a circular accelerating descent to the floor: whoooomph... whoooomph... whoooomph... whoooomph with increasing speed and noise till it came to rest upside down. Total silence broken only by the maître d'hôtel shouting "idiot". I certainly felt one. The cost of the glasses was deducted from my pay.

The staff food was inadequate by any standards. Some representations to the chef by the maître d'hôtel (not inspired by me) brought no change. One early evening, a particularly fatty, grisly, tough, thin stew made of goodness knows what was plonked on the table in the staff room. Discontent was rife and the waiters decided that this must be brought to the attention of the owners, who would, as usual, be down for dinner just before the restaurant opened to the guests. It was explained to me in front of all the staff by the oldest of the waiters – still only in his late twenties – that the tradition was that the most junior member of staff (moi of course) must undertake this task. I felt that this tradition was inverted and that the job should be done by the most senior member of staff – if not by the maître d'hôtel himself. I said so.

It was explained to me that I was a dirty, stupid, bastard English shit and that if I didn't do it I would be castrated. I almost believed this.

Monsieur and the ladies took their places as usual. I offered bread and poured their wine – only ever one glass each (which might explain a lot!) – and water, always Badoit. Then I put an empty plate in front of Monsieur and served some of the staff slop onto the plate – most dextrously of course.

There was a painful silence. I vividly remember imagining the indignity of having to tell my father that I had been sacked from my first job. Monsieur tilted his head back from his sitting position to look me in the eye. He said nothing. He picked up a knife and fork and tried to saw a glob of meat into a smaller piece. It wouldn't split. He gave up and, bravely I have to admit, put the whole piece into his mouth.

He chewed. And chewed. And chewed. And swallowed. And gagged. And chewed. And swallowed again. The muscles in his throat visibly distorted. He took a massive swig of wine and slowly returned the glass to the table. He shrugged and said, 'Il manque peutêtre un peu de percil' – it could do with a bit of parsley perhaps. I cleared the plate. No more was said of the incident by anyone. The staff food did not improve. My chances of promotion to a demi chef de rang had evaporated.

Chris's summer was spent altogether more glamorously – if with no less hard work. Obviously I can only tell this second hand. She elected to be a stewardess on Union Castle's RMS *Transvaal Castle*, and our parting at Southampton before she sailed and I set out for France was poignant. She made two round trips calling at Madeira, Cape Town, Port Elizabeth and Durban.

Hours of work seem to have been similar to mine in France. Probably the biggest difference between her work experience and mine was the crew's after-work parties. Probably enough said. She relates harrowing tales of apartheid South Africa and inhuman battles in port to salvage scraps from the ship's bins by starving and impoverished Africans.

I wrote long letters to Chris to await the ship's arrival in her various ports of call. I never received replies. This was a difficult phase in our relationship, hampered no doubt by such widespread separation. I empathised with the words of a then-popular song, *it's going to be a long, lonely summer.* I don't think either of us learned much about hotelkeeping from these jobs, but I believe we both learned a good deal about management, determination and humanity.

The third year at Battersea was spent in industry. Chris and I were both assigned to J. Lyons & Co. This was an organisation well ahead of its time in identifying its market and running its operations with clarity and precision. The training department was purposeful, dedicated and focused.

During the first few months, life was "underground" and no job in the kitchens or wash-up was too menial. We even had to spend one night working with the man specifically employed to shoot rats. Why they were shot rather than poisoned I don't recall. But you never felt like a cheap pair of hands. You knew you were heading for the white coat and then the morning suit via the restaurant. And we got paid! Five pounds and three shillings a week.

The three Lyons Corner Houses at the Strand, Coventry Street and Tottenham Court Road proudly offered five themed restaurants with tightly controlled standards for each. Nothing was left to chance. We management trainees were monitored every step of the way. From my point of view, and I believe Chris felt the same, our experiences the year before were now counterbalanced by professionalism and pride in what we did.

We learned and we learned, and if I was asked what above all else I learned it was – and this was conscious on the part of the company – *attention to detail.* Whichever outlet you were working it, expensive or cheap – and there was quite a range – there was only one right way to do it. All alternatives were wrong. Did this make us zombies? Interestingly, no. It made us disciplined and precise.

At last we made it to the front of the house and became waiters and waitresses. We dressed very traditionally in white shirt, bow tie (made-up ones were forbidden), waistcoat and a long, crisp, white apron. Trousers were encouraged too! Black shoes had to be polished to sergeant major standard. We felt like professionals. Relating to guests was encouraged (within defined boundaries) and my word, tips were a great incentive.

Skills now rarely seen were commonplace, the most demanding of which was filleting a Dover sole in front of the guest – fast enough to get it in front of them while still hot. Restaurant supervisors regularly slunk items off our tables or skewed our tablecloths to see if we noticed and took corrective action. Noticing became an obsession. I think my love of restaurant work began at J. Lyons and certainly my understanding of training, standards and detail. It wasn't fancy stuff and the icing was later to be put on the cake.

Then came the morning suit – the ultimate badge, and as junior management we were treated as such. The "M-word" applied. Erstwhile colleagues (mentors), who a few weeks before had been Emily and Daniel, were still Emily and Daniel. But we were "Sir" or "Madam". Ecstasy!

Chris at some stage was selected to take charge of one of the J. Lyons satellite restaurants in Kensington High Street. This was a singular achievement and she accepted the challenge with massive pride and dedication.

We returned to college for the final year much more grown up, accomplished and focused. Restaurant fashions change of course and whatever brought about the eventual demise of J. Lyons & Co is a mystery to me.

The next thirty weeks or so were intense. Exams loomed. The ACT (Bat) was to be achieved or not, and with it automatic full membership of the Hotel, Catering and Institutional Management Association – then an important ticket to the best jobs.

Cooking and waiting were put on the back burner and accounts, law, economics, management studies, wine and reception featured large. Some of the terms now in use in our industry were not in use then: marketing, room yield, brand, even occupancy, but the concepts were in use, albeit greatly simplified due to the infancy of computing.

As this year progressed I found myself particularly determined to obtain good qualifications. Although my decision, made three years before, to study hotel management had been a somewhat casual one, I now felt that it had been right and that I flourished in the environment of looking after guests, and I obtained great satisfaction from feeling that I had contributed to a pleasing experience. Chris I know felt the same, although, by her own admission, she did not work as hard as I did and she often borrowed my notes to catch up on missed lectures. In the first two years at Battersea, full-time attendance was compulsory and students were required to sign in to all lectures. Some of our colleagues felt this was too much like school and resented this requirement. However, in the final year, attendance was not mandatory. Whether this was part of the testing process or not I don't know.

Chris in fact, in the final year, flew by the seat of her pants to such a degree that she was nearly expelled. This threat did not go down well with me and some of her other friends, not to mention the Students' Union.

Our relationship was by this time common knowledge and we became engaged on my 21st birthday in February of that year, so it was perhaps not as odd as it might otherwise have seemed that I sought an appointment with the Director of the Hotel and Catering Management department to plead for Chris. Patronising it may have been, but I agreed to ensure a better attendance record and brought to his attention (he didn't know individual students that well) that she was a natural hotelier and extremely intelligent. Due to whatever influence she was allowed to stay on, and the shock of such a narrow escape did lead to better attendance. I suspect that a further motivation was not to allow Reg to be proved right in his perception that further education for women was a waste of time.

In the weeks leading up to the final exams Chris and I agreed to see little of each other and to concentrate on studies. I prepared for the exams with demonic single-mindedness, swotting far into the night.

And then it was all over. We were grown up and set free in the big wild world in the summer of 1965.

Chris and my situation as an engaged couple then became complicated. Due principally to my mother's opposition to our relationship, it was not practical for her to stay at my parents' home in Hampstead and the alternatives for my future employment seemed then to lie in the south.

So we were again separated by circumstances.

Chapter Three

NEW YORK

I t quickly became apparent that opportunities for female hotel and catering graduates were not as great as for males. The situation may have
been further influenced by the fact that Reg's position on this was to
get out and earn a wage. Chris was of course living back with her parents, and Reg was not a man to keep his opinions to himself. We had both
passed our final exams, and at a ceremony at Battersea certificates were
presented, goodbyes were said, commitments to stay in touch were made
and too many drinks were drunk. It was also announced that I had been
awarded the prize of a year's postgraduate training at the Waldorf Astoria
Hotel in New York City. This was for achieving the highest marks in the
final exams. Chris outwardly mocked me among our friends as a swot, but
was, I know, inwardly proud.

This award was not something on which one could have depended in
planning for the future and so other applications had been made.

I clearly remember two. One was with British Rail Hotels, who then
owned and operated the great station hotels in London, Manchester, Edinburgh, York, Glasgow, Sheffield, Birmingham and elsewhere. I attended an interview in offices at St Pancras station. Never having attended

an employment interview before, I was very nervous. People (including Chris) have usually perceived me as confident, but underlying this exterior shield, which I probably generated on purpose, has always been apprehension. Without getting too introspective, I think this stemmed from a somewhat unstable childhood at home as well as the bullying to which I was subjected at prep school.

Enough of that. I was escorted into the interview room to be faced by five middle-aged men in very formal attire. I was asked to sit in a single chair facing the interview panel. There was no preamble nor welcome.

The gentleman sitting in the middle introduced himself and his colleagues. He then turned to me, cleared his throat and said, 'Mr Cunliffe. If you were to be offered a position with this company, what do you think you could contribute?'

My already numbed brain virtually closed down. In those days there was no internet on which to research prospective employers. Unless you were lucky enough to be privy to inside information, you pretty much knew what you knew – and in my case this was not a great deal. How could I possibly know what I could contribute without considerably greater knowledge of what I was to contribute to? Older and more experienced, one could have done a fair job of bullshitting. I was neither. I could think of no answer at all.

Eventually one of the other gentlemen took pity on me and coaxed me out of my paralysis. I have no recollection of the rest of the interview. I was never given the opportunity to know what my contribution might have been. I was not offered the job.

At Ampleforth I had greatly enjoyed the Combined Cadet Force and had risen to the rank of Sergeant, and then Acting Under Officer. I recall that I had come under scrutiny after one parade for reporting a fellow schoolboy for pocketing several rounds of live ammunition.

As, I imagine, in most sections of society, there were strict codes in place about sneaking. I subscribed, whether from free will or because a code is there to be followed. To snitch on a colleague for smoking or drinking or possessing a sexy magazine would have been unheard of, but in this instance, not only was I in a position of trust as a sergeant, but possession of live ammunition struck me as potentially very dangerous. Possibly even lethal. What the boy intended to do with it was irrelevant, and I did not find the decision to report this act difficult.

What I did find difficult to live with were the unexpected ramifications. The boy was expelled from the school. My actions had not been taken in secret and many others were aware of what I had done. I feared a reaction. But none came. My colleagues, some of whom were friends, appeared to understand.

Later in the day I received a message from my housemaster that the Headmaster wanted to see me in his office that evening. Such a summons was normally an occasion for fear.

There were in those days four rankings for a beating. The minimum was from the Head of House; next up was by the Housemaster; one up from that was by the Head Monitor of the school, but the ultimate thrashing was by the Headmaster, and a summons to his office was usually (or so it was perceived) for this purpose.

Needless to say, corporal punishment no longer exists at Ampleforth, nor elsewhere. But it was an accepted part of life in my schooldays and there is no doubt in my mind that it was an excellent incentive not to screw up too badly. I suspect that it was not good for the senior boys who administered these punishments. My personal experience was that beatings were only for serious misdemeanours and were handed out only after a fair hearing and due consideration. I only got it once from my housemaster and for due cause.

Most, but not all of the teachers were monks, and within the school and monastery they wore black habits, a part of which was a hood, which when not covering the head fell down the back. This was called a cowl and was specifically for privacy during prayer.

A particularly innocent (or so it seemed to us boys) chap taught us history, and these lessons followed the mid-morning break when we could purchase drinks, sweets and biscuits. On the day I was beaten I had decided, I suspect with others, that it would be highly amusing to secretly fill this man's hood with biscuits, with the inevitable hilarious result when he put his hood up at the end of the class.

Hilarious it was too. But the innocent monk turned out to be less guileless than we thought, and as he stood there dripping biscuit crumbs down his face and onto the floor, he demanded to know who was responsible. Owning up was another part of the code. So I did. Neither the monk, nor my housemaster nor I in the end found the consequences very amusing.

Anyway, my summons to the head's office was for more benign purposes and on entering I was greeted warmly by the Headmaster and the Commanding Officer of the CCF, by then back in his monkly habit.

I was commended by the head for reporting the stolen ammunition and told that I had taken the only possible responsible action available to me. I was informed that the expulsion of the thief was, in turn, the only possible action left to the school. I was then advised by the CO that due to the likely long-term illness of my company's Under Officer (a rank held by senior boys) I was with immediate effect to become Acting Under Officer.

In view particularly of the imminent CCF summer camp in Perth, this was a position of real responsibility and one which I enjoyed, to the extent that when I went to Battersea I joined the University of London CCF as an Officer Cadet.

The above diversion is to explain why, on leaving school, I also applied to join the RAF as a catering officer. The process was more straightforward than the Army and I felt more appropriate to my qualifications.

The two-day interview at Biggin Hill was thorough, comprehensive and gruelling, giving the adjudicating panel every opportunity to evaluate leadership, courage, intelligence and all the other stuff that goes with being suitable to being an RAF officer. Unfortunately, in the first one-to-one interview I came up against a Squadron Leader who for some reason disliked me on sight.

He made no attempt to disguise the fact that he did not like boys from private schools and attempted, with some success, to rile me to the point where I had no option but to stand my ground on certain issues. One, interestingly, was the whole question of monks (obviously with military experience from National Service, service in World War Two, or as officers in previous lives before joining the monastery) dressing in military uniforms and participating under actual military conditions in CCF activities.

While this is not an area I want to stray into here, the rationale of this had been discussed in some depth at school, and, suffice to say, the perception was based on the concept of "just war". But this man put me squarely on the back foot and strayed into criticism of perceived privilege, Catholicism and religious belief in general.

At the end of the first day, the applicants were divided into two groups. Those selected to continue with the process were dismissed and told to report the next morning. Those less fortunate were seen individually by a Wing Commander and advised that they had been deemed unsuitable.

I was so advised and asked if I had any questions. I will not pretend to recall the exact words of a conversation held some fifty-plus years ago, but I do recall protesting against the decision and asserting that there had been a personality clash with the interviewing officer. I got the feeling that this was not the first time this had happened and the Wing Commander revisited in some detail the earlier interview. He told me that he was overturning the previous decision and that I should report for further evaluation the next morning.

As fate would have it, the letter offering me a commission in the RAF arrived two days after the offer of the traineeship at The Waldorf Astoria. Chris was enjoying – no tolerating – a rare stay in Hampstead. The dilemma now posed was in a sense encouraging. To actually have a choice between two good options was a positive. But either posed problems for two young people in love. Enquiries of the American Embassy in Grosvenor Square elicited that to get a "Green Card" to work in the States you would have to possess a firm and irrevocable job offer, which Chris did not have. Officer training, on the other hand, would involve a year in single residence for me.

Chris and I were by now very much an entity, and after some somewhat stormy periods were maturely in love. I tried to face this dilemma with us both in mind; not easy in one so young and inexperienced. Chris had to a large extent copped out of the decision, saying it was my job at stake and therefore my decision. This was not hugely helpful. I discussed the situation with my father who was not very helpful either, in part I suspect because either solution involved me leaving him in sole charge of mother.

In the end I decided to accept the position at The Waldorf for three reasons – one about me, one about Chris and one about us both.

First, although the RAF appealed, I felt that hotelkeeping was in my blood. Secondly, I had come to terms with the fact that Chris had quite a rebellious streak in her and I was not sure that she was cut out be a services wife. In truth (although I am not sure that I realised this as such at the time) I was not really certain that I was cut out for the services either. The contretemps at Biggin Hill – and my reaction to what had happened – had caused me to realise that I too had a stubborn side which might not sit comfortably with service discipline. Thirdly, I felt that once I had forged relationships at the Waldorf, I would be able to obtain a job offer for Chris and she would in turn be able to get a Green Card.

Much later, I discussed with Chris the scenario behind my decision. She was flabbergasted at my rationale and felt that she would have made a textbook officer's wife! Who knows?

The decision made and having politely declined the RAF, I felt that the sooner I got on with the matters in hand the better.

My departure for New York on the *SS United States* was a lonely affair and I felt homesick before we even cast off. As usual, my parents were not available to see me off and, as money was very tight, Chris and I decided that for her to come all the way down from Yorkshire to Southampton was an expense we could do without.

The transatlantic crossing (steerage) was, according to the crew, the roughest the *SS United States* – the fastest liner afloat – had experienced. Only a few stalwarts (myself included) continued to enjoy the very reasonable meals and inexpensive drinks.

The YMCA in New York, which the personnel department at the Waldorf had suggested would be a good starting point, was depressingly institutional and did little to boost my nervous and lonely spirits.

I was, however, greeted warmly in the Personnel department where, as it turned out, I spent several months. The traineeship was in truth a bit of a farce. Most jobs in the hotel were unionised and without being a union member they were certainly not available to foreign trainees. This did not bother me and I welcomed an extraordinarily quick absorption into the work of the Personnel department, which consisted mainly of recruiting and hiring staff.

I was also exposed (although thank God not involved in) union negotiations in a very public open-plan office. To a youngster such as myself, the dogfights which were enacted between the senior personnel managers and the union representatives were fascinating, enthralling, eye-opening and rather frightening. It was not clear to me who was in fact in charge of the operation of the hotel and I found it sad that such a magnificent place should be so adversely affected by such deep-rooted controversy – which it was, as I was to discover in greater detail when I was later moved to the banqueting department.

This strained relationship between hotel companies and unions exists in New York to this day and its impact is as tangible now as it was then.

I found an apartment in Williamsburg, Brooklyn – now a fashionable district but then a not totally savoury area. It was all that I could afford.

I wrote to Chris frequently and got no replies. Telephoning was out of the question even if she had had access to one at her end – which she didn't.

I was worried and hurt. I felt that my situation was déjà vu – Royan all over again. All work and no play; loneliness and little else to live for. I had no money for entertainment of any sort and had to telegraph my father for an advance on my wages from the Waldorf to buy crockery, cutlery and household essentials for my dingy flat. It was painted green throughout and furnished with the cheapest necessities. The chief asset was access to the fire escape via the kitchen window. This was the coolest place to sit, tough on the bum though it was.

Then the blow fell. The process for obtaining a Green Card was changed and was to be based on quotas and experience. This was partly I believe to protect the jobs of US citizens serving in Vietnam. So Chris could not join me – unless she was my wife. I didn't need to think. I sent her a telegram:

DARLING, RULES ON GREEN CARDS CHANGED.ONLY WAY
OF BEING TOGETHER HERE IS FOR YOU TO BECOME MY
WIFE.HOW ABOUT SOONEST? WILL YOU?
ALL MY LOVE, JOHN

I received a reply the next day:

DARLING MAN.READY WILLING AND ABLE.ADVISE ETA.
ALL LOVE,CHRIS

I borrowed the money for my fare from a trusting friend who had not known me that long, and I booked the cheapest route available: Icelandic Airways. On the second leg of the journey, from Reykjavik to Prestwick near Glasgow, the heating had broken down and we were issued with blankets and whisky.

I forget how long this flight was but we arrived blue with cold. I went straight to Doncaster. The wedding was all set for just ten days' time so there was much to do.

Only when I got to Chris's home did she tell me that she had had a near-fatal car crash the day I sailed for America, crying while driving to work. She had entered the A1 from a minor road without stopping and caused a multiple pile-up from which, through some miracle, she was the only injured person. Her hands had been particularly badly damaged, as was still evident, and she couldn't write.

Chris's family, and Chris, had decided not to tell me. Little did they know that the absence of letters had caused me far more grief than the truth would have done.

Chapter Four

MARRIAGE AND
NEW YORK WITH CHRIS

A fter a crash course for Chris in Catholicism with Father Gheeny, conducted over sherry, the main thrust of which was that a wife should not deny her husband sex, we were married on 5th February 1966 in Bentley, near Doncaster. My family was badly represented and my mother had said she was not well enough to come.

Before my return to England my father had visited Reg, Audrey and Chris in Doncaster and tried to put them off the wedding. Chris later told me that from her standpoint this was the worst possible thing he could have done.

I had to resist attempts by many of Chris's family, and in particular her brother-in-law to be, Ian, to get me plastered the night before the wedding. This was apparently the tradition. I was partly successful.

The church was well attended but the Catholic rites were foreign to most of the congregation. The wedding breakfast was held in a pub we liked, and Reg was astonished at the proposal that everything should fall on the shoulder of the bride's father – as was usual in those days. He was even more dumbfounded that real champagne should be offered with the cake-cutting and the toasts.

Under the circumstances and given the timescale, it was a pretty good wedding. I was very hurt that my mother could not be bothered to come.

As soon as Chris's Green Card could be processed, we were on our way back to New York – steerage of course – on the original *Queen Mary*. Once again, I – in this instance we – departed Southampton with no send-off from my parents.

The great ship had barely cast off her lines before I began to feel seriously ill. The thought of a ship's doctor's bill was unwelcome but Chris insisted, and eventually the man arrived at our cabin. I was diagnosed with pneumonia and spent the rest of the week-long voyage in bed. I have no recollection of it apart from agonising injections from an evidently blunt needle. We were advised by the crew that I had to appear to be absolutely healthy on arrival or I could be denied admission to the United States.

I complied with great difficulty in the freezing February weather. Flakes of snow were falling and trying to settle. Chris was quickly exposed to New York's speciality breed of rudeness in the form of a taxi driver who did not like the amount of luggage we had. We had decided to bring as much stuff as possible so as not to have to buy it again. Electrical equipment was not included due to the different voltage, but our Wedgwood china, silver cutlery and crystal wine glasses – all wedding presents – were in various suitcases.

We were greeted like royalty by the concierges at the Waldorf, and I felt warmed that so many of the staff remembered me and knew that we had just married. Marriage was of course a big thing then and I think even more revered in America than in England. One colleague Jim, who had leant me the money to fly to England, was quickly on hand to greet us, and was probably pleased to get his bucks back.

Before I had left the USA to marry Chris, the Vice President in charge of the Waldorf, who had the unusual name of Frank G. Wangerman Jnr, and who had made a real effort to get to know me and had given the traineeship some gravitas, had told me that when I returned with my "bride" we could have a week staying in the hotel as a wedding present.

This was truly good news as I had given up the apartment in Williamsburg, which Chris would not have liked. So we settled into a delightful room. Flowers, champagne and chocolates had been arranged. I went straight to bed as I was still feeling quite ill. I knew this was very frustrating and disappointing for Chris, but it wasn't man flu (which anyway had not been discovered then) – it was pneumonia.

The phone rang after only a few hours and I answered it. It was Carl Zimmerman, my then boss who was the food and beverage manager. He was a charming and affable German with a strong accent. 'Hello Chon,' (as he pronounced John), 'velcome back. How are you?'

'Carl,' I replied. 'Actually I'm in bed with pneumonia.'

'Oh! Sorry.' And the phone went dead.

A week or so later, me having recovered, Chris and I were walking down a corridor and Carl was coming towards us.

He rushed towards Chris, hand outstretched and said to her, 'Ah, hello. You must be Pneumonia.'

True story.

Chris was immediately seconded to a job in the Personnel department doing much the same as I had done. I was despatched to other departments to continue my training. The detail of the personnel work suited Chris very well and she came in for much praise. I had my spies by then! She showed a natural aptitude for judging which applicants would be suited to which jobs – a talent she has never lost. These appointments were of course subject to membership of the appropriate union.

We quickly found a pleasant enough apartment in Flushing, Queens, on a direct subway route to Grand Central Station on 42nd Street. Only air conditioning was lacking (this little luxury we could not afford) and was it hot and humid? The apartment's furnishings were minimal and did not include a television, which we had to buy. Our first introduction to hire purchase – or whatever it was called. With it came an enormous aerial which needed to have a code introduced for the various channels. It was that long ago. We did eventually buy a fan which was positioned at the bottom of the bed. Heaven!

Despite our two salaries, the finances were very tight. Two stories come to mind. One was going to the cinema to watch *Doctor Zhivago*, which had just come out. We shared a Coke in the interval, unable to afford two. Violins are permitted at this point!

The second concerns a party to which we had been invited. If my memory serves me well it was given by the International department of Hilton whose offices were opposite the Personnel department of the Waldorf. We came out of the hotel onto Lexington Avenue. Snow was falling in huge bright flakes reflecting the street lights: New York at its most beautiful. Chris, who was tipsy, flew through the revolving doors and dropped the bottle of whisky which we had won in a raffle. It broke. So did my heart! The pristine snow turned golden on the pavement. I sadly collected up the bits of broken glass and deposited them in a bin.

Determined not to let this mishap spoil an otherwise happy evening, we turned back into Oscar's (the Waldorf's coffee shop), and ordered two dry martini cocktails and two Mexican beef dogs – an Oscar's speciality – hot roast beef with a vicious peppery sauce. So what? We had an account! Tomorrow is another day.

We were in New York at an interesting time. Princess Margaret visited and being "limeys", both Chris and I were given jobs of some sort at the dinner she attended. Pope Paul VI also stayed in the Waldorf Towers while we were there.

The transit strike left New York paralysed for 24 hours and all non-unionised staff (many unionised personnel came out in support of the strikers) were seconded to doing our best to make hotel guests stranded without rooms as comfortable as possible. Needless to say, there was not a room of any size, shape or price to be had in the whole city, and no-one could move or get to or from a railway station or airport. Great esprit de corps was shown by the cheerful bunch allocated to these duties and we were well "taken care of", as the saying goes.

There was another occasion when the electricity workers went on strike. We had advance notice of this and candles by the ton were ordered in. These, combined with the emergency lighting, made quite a cosy setup, which most guests appreciated. Some did not. In fairness, the absence of elevators made a climb to say, the 40th floor, no joke, particularly if a room service trolley could not get there either.

We still have (albeit stuffed in a cupboard) an ashtray inscribed with our names, presented by the hotel to all staff on duty that night. Imagine a company presenting an ashtray these days. Tips were astronomical that night.

In a sense, the Personnel department was the hub of the hotel. We (by now Chris) may not have been privy to the grand strategic plans of the Hilton Corporation, but not much went on that we did not know about. The only truly private office in the department belonged to the Vice President in charge of Personnel. This office was invariably empty as the official occupant "lived" on the golf course.

One day Chris was approached by the VP's deputy. There was a crisis. Said VP had to make a presentation the next day to all the Hilton's Personnel people about the corporation's personnel and training policy. The VP had decided (just that afternoon – probably from the golf course) that his presentation would be greatly enhanced if each attendee had before him a copy of the policy manual. This was 89 pages and there were 76 attendees. So 6,764 pages needed to be photocopied, collated and bound before noon the next day. Would Chris and I do it? Was it technically possible? Did we have 14 reams of copy paper? Did the photocopier (about the size of a Rolls Royce) have enough ink? Chris and I were offered an unturndownable amount of money to solve these issues and get the job done. We roped in Mary (thus reducing the sum by a third). We did it. No bed that night! Personnel VP never even said thank you.

Mary. Chris had made friends with a new member of staff in the Personnel department. Mary was as hard up as we were. We became close friends at once. She was American, but with some Scottish blood which was reflected in her accent. She spoke as if she had a permanent frog in her throat. She was tall and blonde and attractive. And very determined.

Somehow we all got invited to work as function waiters at the weekends at the Tarrytown Inn, about 25 miles up the Hudson River in New York State. This property also came under the wing of the golfing Personnel VP.

Mary had a car and we shared the cost of the petrol. The three of us worked lunch and dinner every Saturday and Sunday. Our muscles bulged from carrying trays with ten covers on them – one-handed of course. This took some getting used to. The union's authority did not apparently extend to upstate New York. The money flew in and we hoarded it greedily in our bank account in the hope that it might be the start of a deposit on a house for our eventual return home. We were paid cash daily by the hotel with a share of gratuities paid a week in arrears, and we were young and foolish enough not to worry about tax.

In-between lunch and dinner we were fed leftovers from the function just completed. Sometimes this was sparse fare and sometimes it was a feast complete with as much wine as we could scrounge. Occasionally a half-hour kip in a corner was accommodated. So we were working eighty hours a week but our wages from Tarrytown made our salaries at the Waldorf look like petty cash.

There was an additional perk. The booze on the tables had already been paid for by the host – normally the bride's father. Tarrytown was an affluent area and lavish weddings were the order of the day. Thus the hotel's management were not particularly concerned where the leftover bottles went. Technically it was supposed to go back to the bar. In point of fact, considerable quantities went down the chute provided for dirty linen. The laundry room below was not manned in the evenings – nor was it locked. Thus retrieval of the ill-gotten gains was a piece of cake, albeit it involved sorting through quantities of dirty table cloths and used napkins. The chore was worth it. A further increment to the finances – no need to buy liquor. Some of the less scrupulous staff (after all, we were management at a sister hotel) found other uses for the laundry chute, including leftover wedding presents. One day this included a television set. We drew the line at this activity. Entrepreneurism was one thing. Theft was another.

Sometimes dinner was provided on the same basis as lunch and Mary not infrequently drove back to the city well over the permitted limit. Often we got home after midnight to be back at our desks at the Waldorf by 8 a.m. the following morning.

This had to stop when I was transferred to the banqueting sales office. Bob Dowd, the real head of Personnel, had sent for me. He was a dyed-in-the-wool New Yorker with a drawl to match, and he conducted all the union negotiations for the hotel.

He knew swear words I didn't know existed and used them readily. His

31

background was as a union convener – a poacher turned gamekeeper.

'Jan,' he began (this was New Yorkeese for "John"), 'how's the training scheme going?'

'Fine Mr Dowd,' I lied. He had on a previous occasion told me to call him Bob away from work but Mr Dowd in the office. I was not about to tell him that in reality the scheme was a bit of a sham.

'Lot of pretty girls where you are now.' (I was on the Front Desk which for some reason was not unionised).

'Not interested,' I lied. 'Old married man.'

'Lying bastard,' he parried. 'But talking of marriage, that bride of yours is doing a fine job here. Seems to be able to get inside people's heads.'

'Really?'

'Yeah. Got instinct.'

'Really?'

'Limey bastard. Is "really" all you can say? Well Jan, we figure it's time you did some real work and earned some real dough. Have you met Sig Stanke?'

'No, but I know he's the Banqueting Manager.'

'Hell of a guy. Could sell ice to Eskimos. He's looking for a young man or woman to learn the ropes up there. Jean Scanlan recommended you.'

'The Executive Head Chef?' I asked. 'I didn't know he knew me.'

'He knows everyone and everything. Apparently you did some good work for him when you spent time in the food and beverage control department.' I recalled spending a few weeks in this football pitch of a department where all the food and beverage was delivered. I had been asked to undertake a project on the amount of prime rib of beef consumed by the hotel in a year. Something for a butchery magazine. I had not known that Scanlan was behind it. 'Said you did a thorough job.'

'Very pleased to hear it. I'll thank him when I see him.'

'Sig is expecting you in his office at two. He'll discuss details and money.'

The interview with the Banqueting Manager was brief and to the point. The hours were long, six days a week. The money was mindblowing – three or more times my trainee's salary.

I was again crashed into responsibilities for which I had little training or experience. With over forty function rooms catering for any number between ten and two thousand, with no fixed menus nor price structure, it was a challenge for me. I had a lot of assistance from the other more senior men in the department. Phones rang incessantly and there was competition to avoid answering them because we were all so busy. Prospective clients arrived to discuss functions inevitably without appointments. Many included whole families to research lavish weddings and could they negotiate? Yes they could indeed – in terms of requirements and prices. True New York style.

We worked 8 a.m. to 8 p.m. six days a week. Saturdays and Sundays were different because the phones rang less – there were no secretaries present – but enquiries for weddings in particular were sometimes overflowing from the relatively small interview lounges.

To my surprise, we were not expected to manage functions at all. This was done entirely by the unionised Banqueting Head Waiters' department from detailed written instructions issued by us. A fiercely regimented timetable for the issuance of these instructions was enforced by an equally fearsome lady who was PA to the Banqueting Manager. The big functions, mostly massive charity balls, were arranged by the Banqueting Manager himself. Bedrooms associated with function bookings were co-ordinated by the Sales department, and battles raged over room rates so as to make the overall package as attractive as possible for the client.

Gratuities amounted to percentages varying from 12.5% to 15% of total bills. Vast sums of money sloshed around.

Banqueting waiters – never waitresses – were supplied by the union on demand, thus service staff did not belong to the hotel. This led to a stereotyped style of service throughout the unionised hotels and to an almost total lack of control of standards. Many of the battles fought in the Personnel department were about issues with banqueting service staff who varied between charming and helpful to damned rude, an observation which is incomplete without realising that New York's perception of polite and rude was very different to an interpretation based on English behaviour.

This of course applied to all strata of life in New York and for an English person took some getting used to. One would need to be a sociologist, historian and psychologist to understand why "attitude" was and still is so prevalent. Chris and I anticipated our 50th wedding anniversary by a few months in May 2015 and spent a few days in New York, returning to England on *Queen Mary 2* in a rather better cabin than that of our outbound journey in 1966.

We found that little had changed, certainly in the hotel we stayed in – which I shall not name – and indeed in some of the restaurants in which we ate. However, by way of a major contrast, we dined one night in Thomas Keller's restaurant Per Se and had the experience of a lifetime. Somehow they had found out that we were celebrating a big anniversary and I am sure that the events of the evening were influenced by the fact that the restaurant is a member of Relais & Châteaux. We were greeted as royalty and escorted to the best table overlooking Central Park. No menu was presented. Dom Perignon was served. I remarked to Chris that I suspected that this was going to be an expensive evening. She said she didn't care. Nor did I. Presently, the delightful Maître D' – as they insist on calling these highly skilled people who deserve a much more serious-sounding title – appeared and declared that the champagne was from Chef himself, who had also designed a menu especially for our anniversary. The many courses which followed with accompanying exceptional wines and flawless service were something out of this world. When the bill came at the end it just said: 'Two dinners. $1,000.' Worth it. But the credit card shuddered.

One of the noteworthy distinctions between some New York restaurants (notably not Per Se) and many in the UK is that (I presume) they are leased rather than owned. Hence the decor is not given the attention that it might otherwise be. Alternatively, this theory is completely wrong and maybe Godlike chefs regard fancy surroundings as a distraction from their seraphic food. Akin perhaps to some restaurants not putting salt and pepper on the table – as if to suggest that the seasoning could possibly be less than perfect. A silly affectation. People have different seasoning preferences to each other and to the chef.

My responsibilities in the banqueting department started in a very mundane way. I was a sort of dogsbody to everyone. Then one of the seasoned managers was fired for being drunk on duty. I witnessed the occasion. He could barely walk.

The next day I was, without preamble, given his desk, phone, secretary and workload. Terrifying. By working many extra hours, and seeking a lot of advice from my more established colleagues – advice readily given – I was able to perform to a credible standard.

I believe that I was actually at an advantage when it came to client contact. Function organisers were surprised to be greeted by a young Englishman. In truth, the function organisation was not particularly difficult and the menus tended to follow a theme. Pâté of smoked salmon and roast prime rib of beef featured high on the list of favourites. A key to menu planning is of course (under most circumstances) to play it safe, particularly when the guest list is likely to include a number of Jewish people. Being New York, this applied.

I found the hardest part of the job to be pricing the menus. There appeared to be very few guidelines, and the price, while affected by the (very) estimated ingredients' cost, was by no means dictated by it, as it would be in the UK where food cost is regarded as king. I tended to keep the price down in order to secure the booking. Banqueting in New York was very competitive with at least a dozen luxury hotels vying for the business. Then I was pulled up for not being aggressive enough with pricing and I adopted a new formula. What I had quoted before increased by ten percent, and was then rounded up to the nearest dollar.

While we banqueting sales managers did not run the functions, we were encouraged to greet our clients. My brief tended to include the cocktail parties thrown by major players prior to association banquets. Lawyers did it, bankers, insurance companies, medical bodies and many others. One evening I had thirty-two such cocktail parties to oversee. My little feet barely touched the ground.

The Waldorf banqueting department was a splendid experience for a kid straight from college.

I barely saw Chris but the money rolled in.

The signal to leave New York was as unexpected as it was unwelcome – a summons to attend an army medical. It was 1968 and the Vietnam War was at full tilt. Mature doctors, dentist and professionals from all walks of life were being called up in the panic to bring to a head this foolish war.

And holders of Green Cards were eligible for call up. So this communication was a message to leave.

I never felt bad about this. While it is true that the right to a Green Card was only granted on the understanding that the possibility of this event existed, such an eventuality was something that happened to other people. It was not our war. It transpired, we discovered, that Chris would not have been granted American citizenship whether I survived or not, and I did not feel a responsibility to join the American services or fight in their conflicts. Indeed I felt a far greater responsibility to Chris. My boss Sig Stanke, being German, was very sympathetic to my situation. He agreed to an almost immediate release from my responsibilities.

I felt keenly sorry for my colleagues in the banqueting department who were without notice allocated responsibility for my files. Work pressure was at best punishing and to have it suddenly escalated must have been painful. (Well! I had experienced this). Chris's boss in Personnel was equally understanding and we were sent on our way with glowing references signed by Frank G. Wangemann Jnr.

We were advised by friends to leave the country by bus over the Canadian border. Evading call-up was illegal. Checks by US officials, so we were told, were far less thorough at the border than at airports and seaports and particularly late at night.

Our relief as we passed unchallenged into Canada at about midnight was intense.

Chapter Five

BROWNS HOTEL

P rior to our unexpected and accelerated exit from the US, Chris and
I had discussed our next move on a number of occasions, expecting, however, to be able it implement it in a rather more leisurely
manner. We had made friends with a few people in the personnel office of
Hilton International. It had been suggested that if we felt like a change or
when our Green Cards expired we would be welcome to explore possibilities elsewhere in the multinational company, and Chris had particularly
favoured a posting to Bermuda.

Nothing was decided and events overtook the opportunity to further
this. But I favoured returning to the UK. The forces which had originally
endeared me to the hotel business were tugging at my shirt sleeve, and
while I did not have eyes closed to the advantages and fun of far-off places, I felt the need to pursue the original ambition. Speculation as to what
might have happened under other circumstances is somewhat pointless.

Back in England, Chris's personnel specialisation bore fruit for her in a
job in the head office of Forte & Co in London's Jermyn Street – an opportunity which was later to become important for both of us. I came to know
the people she worked with and for in the personnel department and it

was obvious to me that she was respected and trusted – a situation which did not surprise me.

She was immensely proud of the fact that she came to know "the old man" as Charles Forte was affectionately known, even though he was not particularly old then. The activities within her office were rather more genteel than in New York, although the unions not so long thereafter tried to elbow their way into the Forte empire. Additionally, trade unions were ferociously strong at that time in some places where Forte hotels had sprung up, one being in Cyprus where Chris and I were (although we didn't know it then) destined to wind up later.

Trainee waiting staff had to sit a test before they were let loose on guests and one of Chris's jobs was to administer this process. Sometimes Charles Forte himself handed out the certificates. On one of these occasions he admonished Chris for allowing one of the participants to wear too short a skirt. Chris had to put the girl wise, and pronto!

I became an assistant manager at Browns Hotel in Dover Street. The less said of this the better. After the considerable responsibility and buzz of the Waldorf Astoria this was the ultimate boredom in every sense, and I started to contemplate escape almost before my morning suit had lost its shine. I was conscious, however, that my CV was still in its infancy and that a decent period in the job must be observed. To me, "decent" was a year.

I felt particularly aggrieved because at neither of the two interviews for this job, one with some head office man and one with the General Manager of the hotel, no-one had even bothered to tell me that the assistant managers were required to sleep in the hotel for three nights one week and two nights the next. Indeed, on my very first day at work, it was my turn to stay the night after a mere 13-hour day including an evening shift!

The House Manager who was my immediate boss was as dour as the General Manager and his response to my questioning this rather serious breach of disclosure at two interviews was that it was normal in Trust Houses hotels for assistant managers to sleep in on a shift basis.

I was not altogether surprised at being advised that the fact that this was my first job in a Trust Houses hotel was immaterial. I decided it would be my last.

Chris was not very impressed with this state of affairs either. We had both come to realise from the start that this was a career which called for some sacrifices. But this was too much.

My responsibilities were primarily threefold. At breakfast it was supervising the making of toast in a rotary toaster. During the day, I was responsible for the Goods Received Book and this involved copying (exactly) all invoices into a ledger. I know for a fact that photocopiers had long since been invented. This activity generated in me a severe disgust at this wastage of management time. This revulsion was multiplied by a number of factors, not least by the behaviour of the live-in General Manager's five-year-old son, who was prone to kicking the assistant managers.

The third activity was far more exciting. Indeed terrifying and probably (I think I dare say certainly) was the sort of thing which brought the Health and Safety Executive into being. The lifts – there were two – were old and temperamental. During the day, Monday to Friday, that was not my problem. But from 5.30 p.m. to 8 a.m. daily and all day and night at the weekends, the assistant managers had to deal with any problem with the lifts.

Of course, we were not trained to, nor expected to, repair them. But stuck guests had to be rescued and released. We had to wind the failed lift up or down to the next floor (a breakdown invariably happened between floors) in order to release the guests. This took some time and much shouting and complaining about the rotten elevators (and other choice expressions – the guests were mostly Americans) was audible during the process which involved going to a cage on the roof and holding a wheel while releasing the brake on the lift.

Dependant on the weight of the occupants (which in turn depended to an extent on the nationality thereof) the pressure on the wheel was slight or significant. The wheel was then manually turned to align the lift with the nearest floor. The brake was then reapplied so that the double gates could be opened to release the terrified and angry guests.

I had nightmares about the consequences of forgetting to reapply the brake. It was an astonishingly dangerous process in the hands of untrained and inexperienced young people. And then of course, there was only one lift in use until the maintenance people's next shift. Further grief for guests and assistant managers.

The hotel was run by and for the hall porters or maybe they were called concierges – not by the managers, and no-one cared a damn. Presumably everyone got paid! And certainly tips abounded. The AA and the RAC then had sparse demands for criteria of any sort and the only requirement for food at night was for sandwiches which the kitchen prepared and left (in case needed). They were often needed by me. Our dinner was at a table tucked away in an alcove out of sight at the end of the restaurant.

Every drink we consumed had to be paid for – at full price. I deeply resented this setup. Communication with hotel guests was discouraged. Hospitality of any sort was non-existent. We assistant managers were actually forbidden from making contact with diners in the restaurant – the restaurant manager didn't like it! He exerted far more influence than the head chef. How times have changed.

This hotel, and I rush to emphasise that this was in the late sixties, was the epitome of bad hotelkeeping and bad management. No-one was then to know that a few years later, Forte & Co and Trust Houses Hotels would merge into Trust Houses Forte or THF, (and later renamed Trusthouse Forte). I cannot other than wonder looking back now whether the extremely divergent cultures of the two organisations were not in part responsible for the unhappy marriage of the two companies and the ultimate demise of THF.

Despite my being away five nights out of fourteen, Chris was pronounced pregnant just a few days before I left Browns. We had been living in a small rented basement flat in Hampstead and it had been a pleasure to see something of my parents and to look after my mother from time to time. We also saw a bit of my sister Elizabeth and her husband Roger, who lived down the road in Camden Town.

I recall one evening when we invited my parents to dinner in our little flat. Creative cooking was certainly not then a part of our repertoire. We were doing boeuf Stroganoff, or to be accurate, Chris was. I had been despatched to buy a table cloth. On my return Chris greeted me with an ashen face. 'What's the matter darling?' I asked.

'A daddy-long-legs has flown into the Stroganoff and I can't find it. We'll have to throw it away and start again.'

'But the shops are shut now. And it was made with fillet.'

'I know. But I can't serve my in-laws dead insects.'

'But they'll never know. You said yourself you couldn't find it.'

'But I'll know,' she wailed.

We served the Stroganoff. They never knew. We did and did not enjoy dinner that much.

I had known from day one at Browns that this was not for me and had applied for several jobs.

The Lake District beckoned like a bone to a dog and we had been offered the management of the Beech Hill Hotel on the shore of Windermere lake, south of Bowness. We both itched to put our hospitality skills into action, and this job was particularly exciting as the hotel had been closed for some time and we were to oversee a total refurbishment as well as the addition of several new bedrooms prior to opening.

Chris's condition and its consequences made us a little nervous that this situation would be unacceptable to the owner, but while not exactly delighted, he was anxious for us to start.

Chapter Six

THE BEECH HILL HOTEL

Chris still had to serve her notice with Forte & Co, so I went first to Windermere with Wee Dram. He had not been part of the master plan and was the consequence of a rather daft and immature decision. On a second holiday in Glenelg just before we left college, we happened across a kennel which bred pedigree Skye terriers. Neither of us had heard of the breed and we could not tear ourselves away. This particular puppy adored us on sight. What vanity! Chris's paternal grandparents, then eighty-something, had just lost a dog and we thought a replacement would be a good idea. So we bought him on the spot as well as a dog bed and took him back to Doncaster. He nearly got washed away in a stream near Sterling where we stopped for a picnic.

Chris's grandparents were not impressed. They were a generation more dyed-in-the-wool Yorkshire than even Reg, and made a virtue of calling a spade a spade, irrespective of whether the resultant issue was rude or hurtful. They told us that they felt too old to take on and train a spirited puppy. A few days later they relented and said they would give it a go.

We had already named him Wee Dram for obvious reasons. But as this was a bit of a mouthful when imploring him to desist from chasing sheep or whatever, Dram stuck. When we let it be known that we were going to live in the Lakes, Grandpa and Grandma asked us if we would take Dram. The grandparents and he had not got on, mainly because he had this habit of disappearing for a couple of days at a time (without seeking permission) on what we could only assume was dog's business. No kilt ye ken! He would return in a bedraggled and exhausted condition and without any plausible explanation.

The cottage which went with the job at the Beech Hill was basic but warm and clean, and for the period of refurbishment of the hotel was office as well as home.

While I have always missed Chris to distraction when we are apart, I have found such situations ones in which I can be very selfish about my work. Thus, I threw myself into the project, which I enjoyed, and if I dare say it myself, did it rather well. Opening a new (to all intents and purposes) hotel combined with a new build was no small feat. But I had Dram to help me! Chris joined me soon, looking a little plumper than when I had last seen her.

The Beech Hill was not a happy period for us. While I believe that my organisational skills were responsible for a very smooth opening, I had little experience of 'solo' (as opposed to corporate) man-management, and staff retention was not good. With hindsight (yet again), I was so desperate to get the hell out of Browns that I think I would have accepted any alternative. Also, and as time went on, it became obvious to everyone that not having any kind of an assistant was unworkable.

So I worked for a year with only one day off, which was for Chris's sister Jane's wedding to Ian. Even this was granted begrudgingly by the owner. While I think he may have regarded Chris's pregnancy as not his fault (which indeed it was not!), I felt abused.

The owner was an accountant with a singular lack of knowledge of the hotel business, and while he may have taken the view that he had employed me to inject that, it is fairly obvious that a man in his mid-twenties, who by definition was not very expensive, did not have huge experience. It should also have been obvious that to expect an employee (whatever his status or age) to work seven days a week for a year with only one day off and with no holidays was inhumane and unlikely to produce a euphoric outcome. I blame myself for tolerating the situation which I in fact caused. I do not believe that anyone told me I had to work these hours. I don't think it was ever implied that I would be in trouble if I did not. I just could not see how without an assistant or any sort of qualified back-up, I could leave the hotel at all, except at night.

The overriding problem for me then was strangely not unlike the one which we still have today, nearly fifty years on. A hotel of the size of the Beech Hill then, and Gilpin now, does not generate the revenue nor profitability to employ top-flight managers capable of truly standing in for the owners. This is only partially a financial problem. It is also an organisational issue. We now own Gilpin and as such it would be unfair to expect anyone, irrespective of ability, background or salary, to make the sort of decisions which only an owner can make.

This is, of course, one of the major differences between an owner-run hotel, a privately owned hotel and a corporate business. We have brilliant managers at Gilpin now. Competent, trained, experienced, responsible, motivated and able. But they are not the owners. And as we were to find out many years later (at Gilpin), the question of employing a general manager is fraught with dangers, complications and frustrations.

But at the Beech Hill I had no managers at all. Three receptionists; a senior housekeeper; a head waiter and an assistant; a head chef and an assistant, and probably a dozen staff. So I covered every shift. Very stupid and not fair to Chris.

Even in those days, the Lake District was beginning to shine as a culinary centre. Indeed it is probably true to say that at the time "food" (at any rate provincial hotel food), was just beginning to emerge from a typical menu which included juice as one of the first courses and an omelette as one of the mains. Francis Coulson and Brian Sack at Sharrow Bay were beacons as country house hotels went, and John Tovey was revving up in the wings before making a name for himself at Miller Howe. In fact John dined at the Beech Hill one night and expressed the view that the meal was uninspired. I suspect he may have been right.

The owner, quite understandably, wanted to be involved in decisions about crockery, cutlery, glassware and the like. Before we opened for business, he and I made several sorties together to catering wholesalers and it became apparent that his ideas and mine were somewhat divergent.

Little attention was given to decor, and even in those early days of our careers, Chris (pretty preoccupied with pregnancy) expressed surprise. It was left to the architect – a pretty common state of affairs in those days. I loved the staffing-up period and Chris dragged herself to many of the interviews. What quickly became apparent was that we were woefully short of staff accommodation. Public transport was non-existent and most junior staff did not possess cars. Somehow we opened.

We hosted a grand opening party for everyone we could think of, including all the other hotel owners and managers in the area. One such was Peter Crook, who was manager of the Belsfield Hotel in Bowness-on-Windermere. Peter was to become a lifelong friend and colleague. He opined at the party that the Beech Hill 'did not make him nervous'.

Pompous sod, I thought.

Nor was Barney's birth a bed of roses, particularly for Chris. We went together to Helme Chase (then the maternity department of Kendal hospital, and not to be confused with the current medical practice which operates at that address) late on the Friday evening. I was not even allowed through the door. 'Don't call us, we'll call you,' might have been the actual words, and was certainly the message. The baby was not delivered until Monday 8th July. Over sixty hours in labour for Chris with no support from me. He was a boy, and Barnaby he became. It was of course a wonderful event for us – and a life-changer in every sense.

Chris did her best to help at the hotel and it became quite a ritual in fine weather for Dram to guard Barney in his pram on the terrace outside the hotel, while she helped housekeeping or in the kitchen or in reception.

None of the now taken-for-granted methods of filling hotel bedrooms had been invented. The web did not exist; there was no means of publicising packages and for sure they did not exist; the only guidebooks were the AA and RAC gazetteers. Arguably, reputation was all that counted. We did not have one.

Strangely, the main problems then were, in a way, the same as they are now: chefs and staff accommodation. Several staff lived in the hotel.

Permitting this was a gross act of naivety on the part of both the owner and myself. Disturbance to guests from the staff quarters was a problem I could have done without.

Trading was poor. The budgets prepared by the chartered accountants were hopelessly adrift. I received precious little assistance, encouragement, advice or backup from head office. I was advised that the business could not afford to rent staff accommodation. Where were staff to live?

Even in those long-ago days, all employees were entitled to a contract of employment. I had asked the boss on several occasions for mine. None was forthcoming. I should have seen the writing on the wall.

Finally I got fired. A great disappointment.

More urgently, the bottom line was that Chris and I had a new little baby, no home, no job and no income.

Chapter Seven

RING & BRYMER: ROUND ONE

ortunately, Chris's erstwhile employers at Forte were delighted to take her back. Not only this, but being the Personnel department, they arranged several interviews within the company for me. I was offered the position of Catering Manager at a company called Ring & Brymer. This is worth a little explanation as this move was to become for me the start of thirteen years of employment with Forte & Co and subsequently Trusthouse Forte.

Ring & Brymer was a long-established city-based catering company. Indeed the venture claimed to have been in existence since 1690. It did not fit anywhere into the parent company's portfolio and was therefore (at that time) largely left alone. Its acquisition by Charles Forte was undoubtedly a very clever move in terms of exposure within the City where it was at the time the leading outdoor (a misnomer) catering company.

Its somewhat quaint but very functional offices, central kitchens and depot were in Sun Street, tucked away behind Finsbury Square. The City catering division dealt with the City Livery Halls, the Mansion House, The Guildhall, The London Press Centre, catering at The Royal Courts of Justice (The Old Bailey), Twickenham rugby ground, much of the catering for

10 Downing Street and other government entertaining, as well a plethora of highly varied outdoor catering activities ranging from private weddings to massive undertakings like the Farnborough Airshow. The other division was Racecourse Catering which dealt primarily with Sandown, Kempton, Ascot, Newbury and Epsom. There were also units in Manchester and Newcastle.

City catering operations were deeply steeped in tradition, as were most of the activities and clients for whom we catered. Our very influential chairman was ex-Lord Mayor of London (not to be confused with the new position of Mayor of London) Sir Lindsay Ring.

Apart from Ring & Brymer's uniqueness within Forte & Co, there was another reason why successive directors of operations for the parent company largely left Ring & Brymer alone: they didn't understand it and were I think rather scared of it. Countless attempts over time to adapt Ring & Brymer's ways of doing things to established corporate procedures resulted in spectacular backfires and even departures.

For me, this first venturing into the lions' den (there was, many years later to be a second) was relatively easy, albeit the learning curve was virtually perpendicular. I was given the warmest welcome by a bunch of seasoned Ring & Brymer managers, directors and senior people, who took it upon themselves to immerse me into their operation and the ways of our clients. This was Hospitality with a capital H, and the exponents thereof were Gentlemen with a capital G. Later on a few Ladies were admitted (with a capital L).

I loved it and thrived on it. Chris subsequently suggested that it brought out the snob in me. I think it brought out appreciation of things done well.

My first day at work was that of the Lord Mayor's banquet. Ring & Brymer had done the catering for this annual ritual at the Guildhall since time began, and I was astounded at the complexity and organisation. The numbers I'd been responsible for in New York banqueting were larger, but at the Waldorf Astoria I had not been closely involved in the logistics, and so the detail of a full-blown Guildhall banquet, including the ramifications of the ceremonial, traditions and hierarchy, made any function that I had ever seen look like a tea party.

The so-called "outmesses" were nearly as complex as the main banquet, ranging from an identical meal and wines to the guests for the likes of The Keeper of the Guildhall, the Lord Mayor's secretaries, assistants to guests of honour (the latter might include Royalty, the Prime Minister, the Lord Chamberlain, senior officials from the Foreign Office to ensure the appropriate treatment of foreign dignitaries and the like), down to more simple fare for lesser mortals. Splendid music and fanfares accompanied the procession to their places of the Lord Mayor and Lady Mayoress, the Sheriffs and their Ladies and other dignitaries. A magnificently adorned Toastmaster announced grace which was intoned by a senior cleric from the Church of England. And so on.

Armies of Ring & Brymer waiting staff, chefs and wine waiters performed and the directors and managers oversaw activities and greeted City figures. Head waiters in full evening dress directed the progress of the banquet. I was mesmerised.

Irrespective of rank, we all worked, greeted, took questions, honoured requests, dealt with issues, carried and cleared plates, silver served, topped up glasses, bowed and scraped as appropriate and solved problems. How it should be done.

After the banquet, speeches were made by prominent speakers, the announcement of their titles promulgated by the Toastmaster, amounting to a stocktake of their precedence and rank.

And as the saying goes "after Lord Mayor's banquet cums muck-cart", and we were about the last to leave, taking our muck with us in liveried Ring & Brymer lorries.

I was so sad that Chris was not around that night to tell her all about it. Our lives were very complicated at this time as we had not found a place to live. I based myself at Keats Grove in Hampstead, much to my parents' delight. Chris sort of commuted back and forth to Doncaster, dumping Barney on Audrey or whoever would have him – which certainly excluded my mother! We still had some money from the Waldorf and Tarrytown Inn in the bank, but not the fortune it had once seemed.

We spent every spare minute searching for a place to rent, buy if we could, or lease. Property was scarce and expensive. Mortgages were hard to come by and time-consuming to source. There being no computers, treading the pavement between offices of building societies was the only way to find out which office had cash to lend. Parental assistance was not forthcoming. While Chris's hours were fairly nine to five, mine were obviously going to be very erratic and we were keen to base ourselves not too far from the City.

Then one evening we packed Barney into his carrycot and set off to have dinner in the home of an erstwhile colleague from Browns and his wife. They had a small flat in Beckenham in Kent. We arrived in time to wander around, ever on the lookout for a suitable area in which to live. It felt appropriate. A village. It was further from town than we had hoped but we fell in love with it and bought a maisonette in Apex Close, a new-build just off The Avenue.

It was a complex deal as the ownership was shared with a housing association. But we had a foot on the ladder. The architecture was weird – it looked like a mediaeval castle complete with crenellated staircases. It was home. It was fun. We moved in and bought the essentials. We possessed no furniture. I learned DIY fast: the sideboard I built in the living room contained 1,244 screws – it wasn't even very large!

All the catering managers and directors at Ring & Brymer were flexible but assigned particular responsibilities and functions. I was to look after the Tallow Chandlers Hall in Dowgate Hill, where I was also made most welcome. My office was in Sun Street. John Coomb was the Director of City Catering. He was a convivial man who left the team to do pretty much their own things. But he knew everyone worth knowing in the City and any news – good or bad – would reach him.

A colleague of mine – Tony White, whose Dutch wife Helene ran reception and the switchboard at Sun Street – came to visit us for Sunday lunch one day at Apex Close, and liked the place so much that they bought the next-door maisonette. We shared babysitting and driving to work.

While catering and menus were inclined towards traditional (indeed the banqueting scene has changed so much in the intervening period, not least because of technology and new equipment), the standard was very high and I learned a great deal, particularly in the vital field of culinary practicability in a peripatetic environment.

I was regarded as a particularly useful animal to have on the team as while in the Territorial Army at Battersea I had been taught to drive vehicles of up to, I think it was, seven tons. And I had a licence to do so issued by the MoD. This was before the existence of the DVLA or HGV licences. So if for whatever reason there was a shortage of drivers I was able to deliver the catering requirements, supervise the function and then drive the lot back to Sun Street.

The City was not accustomed to seeing drivers dressed in a three-piece morning suit nor in a dinner jacket, and it caused some amusement. It also gave me some sound ideas which served me well when I came back to Ring & Brymer in a different role some years later.

My driving prowess had not always been successful at the University of London Officers' Training Corps (ULOTC). Rule number one was that you never reversed a vehicle without someone behind you to act as a guide. Rule number two was that you did not even consider reversing without a guide if you were towing a trailer.

We were at a camp somewhere off the A3 in Surrey. The weekly sessions at a barracks in London were fairly boring but the camps were great fun. We worked hard and my word we played hard in the evenings, unless we were on night exercises.

The evening before my fateful accident, someone had introduced me to rum and black. It went down like lemonade because the blackcurrant cordial disguised the rum. I got slaughtered and had to get up in the small hours of the morning to clean up my greatcoat. I felt terrible. The Captain of my company had been a student at Battersea doing hotel management. He was obviously a few years senior to me.

I was seconded to catering duties in the ULOTC – usually a relatively cushy number. We were to leave the camp on exercises the morning after my introduction to rum and black. I felt it unwise (and unmanly – particularly since it was such a girly drink) to admit to anyone that I felt incapable of driving. But I overlooked rules one and two and reversed a trailer containing all the food supplied for the exercises into a ditch. I was stripped of Officer Cadet rank and demoted to Private. Pay was adjusted accordingly.

Chris had meanwhile been promoted to Personnel Manager for International Hotels. She juggled babysitting with friends and neighbours and was a vital part of the company's expansion into international operations.

She became a huge admirer of Charles Forte for a plethora of reasons, but particularly because of his approach to the employment and promotion of women. I don't think there was much pay-off from her employment after travelling costs and paying childminders, but she was fulfilled, successful and happy. She also did a commendable job for her employers.

Barney thrived and was a joy. He particularly enjoyed feeding the ducks in Beckenham Place Park. He started to show signs of stubbornness which friends said was healthy independence.

We missed Dram, who had had to return to the grandparents. All three involved regarded this arrangement with suspicion. Dram told me so personally. The grandparents told Chris.

We were both content and for the first time ever able to open the bank statement without terror.

Chapter Eight

THE CAFE ROYAL

As always, good things don't last forever. I received a call one day from Vincent Franzini, who was the General Manager of the Café Royal in Regent Street. This venerable institution came under the same directorship as Ring & Brymer – a Forte legend called John Longdon. Vincent invited me to meet him at the Café Royal. He was a charming, polite, unassuming Italian who explained to me that while he regarded himself as a restaurateur and caterer par excellence, he struggled with the enormous administrative burden of this huge building comprising nearly thirty banqueting suites, two famous restaurants, two bars and (although this last had to be treated with great discretion) the offices of Charles Forte and the executive board members. It was clearly not an opportunity to be turned down. The position was that of Deputy General Manager.

If Ring & Brymer had been a learning challenge, the Café Royal surpassed it. Not only was it a hallowed and historical star in the galaxy of the London restaurant catering scene (Oscar Wilde had dined in the Grill Room most nights), but it hosted some of the most prestigious functions in the capital.

Of equal if not greater importance, the Old Man operated out of there, lunched there, entertained there, had meetings of supreme importance there and articulated the tentacles of power from there. Additionally, a new complex comprising four new restaurants and three bars was being created in the basement, and this opened six months into my tenure there.

In fairness to the ethos, there was very little creeping. We were all aware that screwing up was out of the question, but because The Café Royal was the jewel in the company's crown, we had the best people to run everything.

We knew that the Old Man liked management to be visible, so between Vincent, Peter Crook (who joined us) and myself, we made sure that we were. Most lunchtimes and early evenings one of us would be in the marbled entrance hall, greeting guests and exuding bonhomie. And what an excellent lesson that was, and one that I have followed and encouraged others to follow ever since.

We also had a very generous budget for most things and since expenditure was by and large my baby, I felt like a cat in a creamery. And Vincent was a joy to work with. He was short, slim and well dressed; a kind and sincere man who felt failures keenly. Whenever we got a letter of complaint he banged his head with his fist and muttered 'a la Madonna Senor poco miserio', the rough translation of which is fairly obvious.

The new catering complex was to be called Mr Fogg, based on Jules Verne's *Around the World in Eighty Days*. It was a clever idea as the menus reflected four very different geographically based food styles. My favourite was called My Apartment and involved the guests cooking their own fillet steak on a gas grill built into the centre of the table. A jacket potato and salad were the only accompaniments available. Very simple and very inexpensive in terms of staff costs. However, the cost of the extraction over the grills turned out to be extortionate and very maintenance intensive.

It had been decided that the waitresses working in My Apartment would wear very brief and tight hotpants (a sexy fashion of the day) and the interviews were fun. Political correctness had not been invented and we saw nothing wrong with sticking out for the attributes which we required, and a part of the interview process was for the interviewees (girls only) to model the uniform. Hell would freeze over before this would be allowed now!

*

My biggest fear on coming to the Café Royal in this relatively senior position was that the old pros would scorn a youngster like me. The opposite was the case and I was treated with respect while being politely put on a better course if I was heading for a precipice. There were many such round every corner. Everyone loved Vincent and I think knew that he needed support in the administrative areas, which I enjoyed dealing with.

There was a very odd organisation structure. Vincent was the General Manager but there was also a General Manager Banqueting, who did not report to Vincent but rather to John Longdon. This was untidy and led to a lot of problems. Of course the General Manager Banqueting's title was a sop to keep this rather smarmy man happy. But the reporting structure enabled him to back out of many responsibilities which should have been his had he been prepared to accept them.

One of these anomalies was that he did not consider himself in charge of the banqueting kitchen, which was completely separate from the kitchens which served the two restaurants. Thus – you guessed it – there were also two Head Chefs. So it was a very grey area as to who was really responsible for banqueting food quality or profitability. I tended to carry the can when things went wrong in these areas. Of course GMB was quite happy to take the credit when a function was a notable success – and most were.

The Waldorf Astoria and Ring & Brymer had taught me about serious banqueting and so-called Outdoor Catering, but the Café Royal gave me an insight into the equally serious world of restaurants. I don't think the term "fine dining" had been coined. "Haute cuisine" was in common use. The Café Royal had two serious restaurants. The Grill Room was a sacred cow – and rightly. It's a strange term "grill" in that (fairly obviously) it implies that the dishes are grilled. Nothing is further from the truth – any more than it is in the Savoy Grill or many other so-named restaurants in cities around the world. The Grill Room was packed for lunch and dinner every day. Carlo Ambrosini presided as Restaurant Manager when I was there, and he could charm the birds out of the trees. He was also a living carbon copy of *Who's Who* and knew everybody worth knowing – and probably quite a few not worth knowing.

I must stray into a little story worth the telling. I don't think Carlo would mind, if he's still around...

While the Grill Room thrived, the other restaurant – imaginatively called The Restaurant, (this name subsequently changed to Le Relais) – was (in my time) an ongoing problem. With hindsight, it did not know what it was – unlike the Grill Room which knew exactly what it was, had been and would be.

Looking back on this, I find it strange that it was not obvious to all concerned (including me) what the problem was. The two restaurants were in competition with each other. One (the Grill Room) was a romantic, historical, richly decorated room, serving the kind of food everyone (then anyway) wanted to eat: the real classics; the true Escoffier. There is an argument for saying that this remains the sort of food that many people would like to eat today. It will probably come back, to the undoubted horror of most chefs and foodies!

The Restaurant boasted red velvet banquettes and served regional French cuisine. John Longdon, whom I liked and admired enormously, made the solution to the Restaurant's problem a cause célèbre. I have in more recent years felt that he was at the root of the epidemic from which we have all suffered for many years, of spoiling chefs. He brought in, at an astronomical salary, a Frenchman to run the kitchen which served both the Grill Room and The Restaurant. This man became untouchable.

Forte managers were entitled to a discount credit card for use in company establishments. The percentage discount varied with seniority. On one occasion Chris and I entertained some neighbours to dinner in The Restaurant. It was not good. The next day I advised the chef accordingly, politely and constructively. He complained to John Longdon who told Vincent to tell me to back off.

Many variations on the menu were tried in Le Relais. None succeeded. Still oblivious to the underlying cause of Le Relais' failure to keep pace with the Grill Room, Vincent and John Longdon decided to promote Carlo and put him in charge of both rooms.

I think Vincent liked working with me and certainly we dealt with many situations together. Our offices were next to each other on the top floor of The Café Royal, and Vincent was forever sticking his head into my cubby hole (I shared the office with Peter Crook and a secretary who looked after all of us) and inviting me to join him in his office to discuss this or that, or participate in a meeting.

Such was the scenario when Carlo was invited to discuss taking over both restaurants. I often got lost in such meetings, because Vincent and Carlo would break off into Italian. I recall this meeting particularly well because of the extraordinary outcome.

'Carlo,' Vincent began, 'the sales figures for The Restaurant continue to be depressing. What are we going to do about it?' Vincent was very good at extracting other people's ideas from them rather than imposing his own.

'I keep telling you Mr Franzini,' (never Vincent), 'put in the same menu as the Grill Room.'

'Then we have two half-empty restaurants,' Vincent replied.

We had had this discussion many times. 'I am looking for a new solution,' he continued. 'Something imaginative. Something creative. Giovani,' Vincent turned to me, 'what do you think?'

Vincent, Carlo and later Ron Zanre were all Italians and all called me Giovani.

'As the new boy,' I said, 'it seems obvious that the Grill Room has some major advantages. First, it is right opposite the front door of the Café Royal. You can even see it from the pavement on Regent Street. The Restaurant will never have this advantage.

'Second, it is a beautiful, interesting room. The Restaurant will never have such ambience without spending what? A hundred thousand pounds? And no-one is going to spend that kind of money on a restaurant which is not successful and which has no guarantee of success.

'I agree with Carlo about the menu, but using the same menu as in the Grill Room would carry huge risks. Yes, OK, you would fill both rooms on a Saturday night, but at other times? Who knows? The main problem with a tangible solution is you Carlo.'

I knew this would evoke a reaction, which was what I wanted.

'How am I the problem, Giovani?' Carlo almost shouted. 'My restaurant is highly successful. I do two sittings most evenings, sometimes three. For lunch you have to book weeks in advance. Well. Unless you know me very well.'

Yes, indeed, I thought.

'You just admitted it, Carlo. The problem with The Restaurant is that you run the Grill Room.'

'So what do you want me to do? Resign from my job in the Grill Room to save The Restaurant?'

'No Carlo,' Vincent interrupted. 'Change your job.'

'What? Move to The Restaurant?'

'No,' Vincent replied.

'A la Madonna,' Carlo muttered.

Clearly this was part of Café Royal lingo.

'You two are something else. Can't you just tell me in plain English what you want me to do?'

'I certainly can't tell you in plain Italian,' I joked. Everyone laughed.

'But to be serious, start promoting The Restaurant instead of stabbing it in the back,' I said.

'I don't stab it in the back,' he protested.

'No? Standing in the hall in front of the Grill Room door dressed to the nines and almost jumping on every guest who comes through the front door to ensure that they go to the Grill Room and don't stray into The Restaurant?

'You may not like the term I used, Carlo,' I said, 'but the effect is that your highly commendable promotion and management of the Grill Room is at the expense of The Restaurant.'

'A la Madonna,' he said again.

'So you want me to escort these guests who I jump on to The Restaurant instead of the Grill Room?'

'No. To both,' I said

'You want me to manage both restaurants?'

'The penny has dropped,' said Vincent. 'What do you think Carlo?'

We all sat very still and said nothing for at least a minute.

'I think it would be good for The Restaurant and for The Café Royal' he said eventually. 'I know I am good at what I do and – yes – I see what you mean about diverting guests to The Restaurant.'

'And looking after them when they are there,' I added.

'Of course. I also do that well. I think Sir Charles would be pleased.'

He knew that the Old Man regarded him as one of the best restaurant managers in town. Carlo usually oversaw functions at the Fortes' house in Chester Square.

'But,' he said, 'I am not sure that it would be good for Carlo. I earn a lot of money. The tips in the Grill Room are very good. Largely due to what I do.'

His modesty was, as usual, second to none.

'You don't think you could continue to have tips if you managed both rooms?' Asked Vincent.

'Definitely not.' Carlo was emphatic. 'That would not be right for my boys.'

'I agree,' said Vincent. He and I had already discussed this just in case the conversation were to veer in that direction. The Grill Room 'boys' were a longstanding team of seasoned professionals who were as happy with a crêpe Suzette as with a tournedos Rossini. The sommeliers could sell a Premier Cru claret to a pauper, although few of the Grill Room's clients fitted into that category.

They all earned a fortune in tips – that much we knew. But the "tronc" payments throughout the building were all handled by the operational managers, who accounted directly to the Inland Revenue. We had no idea of the sums involved.

Vincent stood up and paced around his office with his hands behind his back. 'I think,' he said, 'you should be paid (whatever-it-was) pounds on a salaried basis.'

He named a sum which was many times what I was paid. I had no idea what Vincent was paid. Carlo looked unimpressed.

'Mr Franzini. I earn three times that amount at the moment.'

The promotion never went ahead. As far as I know, The Restaurant remained a problem – certainly for the remainder of my time at The Café Royal.

One of the main board directors, a man famed within the company for expressing the view that smoked salmon should be carved so thinly that you could read your *Financial Times* through it, came up with the bright idea that one of the problems with Le Relais was that there was nowhere to park a car – particularly at lunchtime.

I never subscribed to this concept as the Grill Room was always packed. But I was given the job of sorting out valet parking. This is easier said than done when you don't have a car park.

We had a relationship with a private car park around the corner just off Shaftesbury Avenue where we got a special rate for parking our own cars. This was sometimes necessary if we were going to finish after the last train had gone. I had a meeting with the management of the car park and a satisfactory rate was negotiated. It was however going to be quite a 'hit' for the Café Royal.

The deal was that the parking would be complimentary for Le Relais guests. I thought this very foolish. Clearly the promotion would not work unless it was promoted. So discreet tent cards were produced and put on the tables in the cocktail bar. But the hugely "regular" clients of the Grill Room could understandably see no reason why their cars should not also be parked free of charge. This was a valid argument and I had to bite my tongue.

There was some impact on business in Le Relais. But the hall porters and doormen were rushed off their feet parking and retrieving cars. I regularly had to help. When there was no hall porter available to take coats and direct banqueting guests to their functions, there were further problems and complaints. One day, the Old Man came through the front door for lunch. There were no hall porters, doormen nor management. The shit hit the fan and the valet parking scheme was discontinued forthwith.

Out of the blue, the General Manager Banqueting got fired. No-one could confirm why. I assumed that Vincent must have known but he assured me he did not. The senior assistant banqueting manager was promoted to Banqueting Manager reporting to Vincent. This made the organisation and indeed my own position much tidier.

Peter Crook, whom I had recruited as House Manager, had by now got his feet under the table and it was great to have him around. He had a horrible job, being responsible for all the back of house stuff and non-glamorous jobs. One of his first problems was to stop the wash-up porters from washing their socks in the flight dishwasher! He got stick from everyone for anything that went wrong and no thanks ever.

He and I had been friends since we met in the Lake District and we were close. He was a tall, elegant man and everyone assumed he oozed confidence, but he was in fact quite insecure. He regularly sought my advice, which I found flattering, particularly as he was older than me. He had come to London leaving the Belsfield in Bowness-on-Windermere at about the same time as Chris and I left the Beech Hill. He had joined the London Hilton on Park Lane as an assistant manager and hated it. The Hilton, being American, operated on the model of having assistant managers operating in the lobby. They were mainly there to deal with complaints, principally from Americans who didn't like the floor their bedroom was on or the way the omelette had been cooked at breakfast. An unenviable position.

His other principal activity at the Hilton was keeping non-resident ladies out of the hotel. He found this very difficult. Peter's main failing in managing people or situations was that he was incapable of being nasty to anyone. He was at all times charm personified. This aspect of his nature did not serve him well at the Hilton, the Café Royal or indeed eventually in his own business.

He liked to tell the story of his first encounter at The Hilton with a lady of the night. Apparently, the procedure was that this job must be undertaken by the assistant managers – not by the hall porters or parking attendants, who would certainly have performed the task more easily, coming in the main from a more down-to-earth background than managers. It's the same principal as used in the armed forces. An army sergeant normally acts as a buffer between the troops and an officer. Peter was definitely officer type. On this occasion, resplendent in his dinner jacket, black bow tie and white breast pocket handkerchief, clean-shaven and whiffing of expensive eau de toilette (not that he was what then might have been called a ponce – just a proper gent), he was approached by the doorman on duty.

'Mr Crook,' said the doorman, 'Emily's up to her tricks again. Look over there.' He pointed in the direction of Hyde Park Corner. A willowy woman of an indeterminate age wearing a clingy dress was talking to a smart gentleman. Even Peter, as he tells the story, eager to give the world its space, realised what was afoot. He was numb with indecision.

'What should I do Fred?' he asked the doorman.

'Tell her to fuck off,' suggested Fred.

Peter girded up his loins, as the saying goes (he was a very religious man), and approached Emily and the man.

He bowed to the gentleman and said to him: 'Sir. Would you be good enough to excuse me? I am the assistant manager of this hotel and I need to have a word with the young lady you are talking to.'

The man did not reply but walked off.

'Young lady eh?' said Emily in a strong Cockney accent. 'Isn't the new young manager polite?'

'Now listen Emily,' said Peter quietly, leaning in towards the woman so that he did not need to raise his voice and risk a scene. 'I know what you are and I want you to go away now and stay away please.'

'You've got your job to do and I've got mine and I ain't goin nowhere.'

Peter leaned even closer into Emily, trying to avoid contact with her more than ample breasts. He whispered, 'OK, Emily. If you want it that way, fuck off.'

Emily stood back from Peter, cupped her hands to her mouth and bellowed, 'No. You fuck off mister.' It could be heard at Marble Arch.

Peter retreated inside the hotel. He phoned me the next day to see if we had any vacancies.

Vincent, being another gentleman, took to Peter at once. Peter got more than a job out of The Café Royal as he met Jane, assistant to the sales manager. They later married.

I must move on from the Café Royal. Many books have been written about it and this one is heading in another direction. I would like to think that I straightened out quite a few knots there and I certainly learned a great deal about catering, man-management, administration and accountancy.

My most scary experience was the budgets. While at the Beech Hill I had had to contribute some hopefully intelligent guesses to this process, I had never tackled anything like the Café Royal, and while the restaurant and bars managers and other department heads were smoothies to a tee at what they did, paperwork was not their thing.

To assist me I had a "computer" the size of a television, which, if you wanted to enter ten times ten, you had to enter ten, ten times. It could not multiply nor divide. But it did get the result right at one hundred! Vincent was ill and I had to present the resultant financial plan to the board of the catering division, which included much of the top brass and a bevy of accountants. The process was complicated in that we had just gone through decimalisation (another story) and while now you would not dream of including pence in a budget for a large business, in those days eleven pounds and four pence was a lot of money. The board accepted the budget. I was chuffed beyond measure.

While I was at the Café Royal, the merger between Forte Holdings and Trust Houses took place. It was of course a very tight secret until the deal was announced in the press, but we all knew that something big was afoot. The directors were cloistered in their offices and in meeting rooms for weeks on end, often working at weekends. Demands for coffees and meals in private rooms replaced the usual dining habits in the restaurants. The comings and goings of strangers was most noticeable and the subject of much gossip by the Hall Porters, who had welcomed guests to the Café Royal for yonks and knew everyone in London, including their tipping habits, on being folded into their expensive coats.

After public notification of the merger, the politics became even more intense as the warfare began between the two sides. The power of money and its potential for destruction oozed from the wallpaper.

Christine was pregnant again and the birth of our second child was imminent. Fortunately my dad was the Professor of Microbiology at King's College Hospital in Camberwell, South London, and my cousin Claire was a doctor there, so we had vastly better treatment than in Kendal, including a private room.

I took Chris in and the prognosis was that the birth would happen very quickly. Chris was high as a kite on pethidine and even gave me a whiff. It was not in those days usual for fathers to be actually present at the birth and I had no intention of being so. As I gave Chris a hug and prepared to head for the waiting room, a stern sister rammed me into a white coat, told me not to be a baby and insisted that I stay. After the treatment at Barney's birth, who was I to argue? Chris giggled contentedly. And thus Benjamin arrived in the world. He gave us a big fright almost immediately by turning blue and having to be whisked away to an oxygen tent.

Barney was not well pleased when we got home! Audrey had come to help and it was all a bit crowded as we only had two bedrooms. But Chris and I were elated. Our family was compete. Two beautiful boys.

Vincent was not in the best of health and had asked to be transferred to a position with less responsibility. I wish we had not lost touch but we did. I desperately wanted Vincent's job and had the gall to feel that I might get it. I knew I was young for such a position but also felt that I had got The Café Royal under my skin.

My possible appointment to the General Manager's position was not even discussed with me. I was very disappointed to learn that Ron Zanre was to take over. I barely knew him, but he had grabbed my job. It was felt, or maybe Ron felt, that it would be better if a new team was put together and I was asked to go and see the Personnel Director of the International Division.

Chris and I had discussed a posting abroad, and although we had not made a formal application, she was obviously well placed to talk to the right people. With almost indecent haste I was offered the position of Food and Beverage Director at The Jamaica Pegasus Hotel, which the company was to open in less than a year's time.

Thus I left the Café Royal with mixed feelings of great fondness coupled with sadness. I had loved the place; its grandeur; its history and associations but above all its highly professional people who had made me welcome.

I was given a splendid farewell dinner at The Fairmile Restaurant in Cobham, which Vincent had taken over as general manager. All the senior people from the Café Royal were invited. This was the sort of generosity for which Forte was famed. Work hard, think hard, be loyal, even make mistakes if you have to, but God help you if you got caught cheating or slacking. Vincent had had table arrangements made consisting of two apples with a banana in the middle. Everyone thought this was very funny, except Vincent's wife, who was furious.

The company had just bought three hotels in Paris, including the famed George V. A strenuous effort was instigated to encourage bonding between the management of the French hotels and their English counterparts. Both the Café Royal and the George V had football teams. The match was to be hosted in Paris and I was invited, coincidental with my last day at the Café Royal, to go (along with Chris) as the official photographer.

I had been given my first movie camera as a farewell present from the Café Royal. I knew nothing about photography, and as we boarded the plane at Heathrow did not even know how to switch the blessed camera on. I learned fast. Goodness knows who authorised the expenditure for this extravaganza. We all stayed at the George V and vintage Dom Perignon flowed like there was no tomorrow. Someone was showing off big time.

My films were quite good! I don't recall who won the football match.

Chapter Nine

CYPRUS

I was moved to a new office in Jermyn Street and given very vague instructions about starting to prepare for the opening of the Pegasus. I
was not even aware if there was a General Manager. I had the feeling
that I had been parked.

As it turned out, this intended move did not proceed according to plan.
The new hotel in Jamaica was, it transpired, months behind schedule. I
was only made aware of this after my appointment. I was then asked to
go to the company's hotel in Cyprus: the Apollonia Beach in Limassol. As
this was to be for just a few weeks, it was mutually felt that I should go on
my own.

It is, I believe, fair to say that the international hotels were at this time
in a bit of a muddle. The merger between Forte and Trust Houses had just
taken place and the division of responsibilities between people from the
two sides had far from settled down. I left for Cyprus with enough packing
for a few weeks. Chris was busy with the two boys and was still preparing
to go to Jamaica.

I arrived in Limassol having been collected from Nicosia airport by
taxi. I felt that this was very impersonal and began to have doubts about

this set-up. However, since we were looking at a few weeks, it wasn't really much of a problem.

At the hotel's reception desk I gave my name and said that the General Manager was expecting me. The girl told me that the General Manager had finished for the day and slipped an envelope across the desk. I was given the key to a room. I carried my meagre luggage to my room, which was pleasant enough. The letter said: '*Cunliffe. I will meet you tomorrow. Do not discuss the purpose of your visit to the hotel with anyone.*' There was no signature. Nor any indication of welcome. I poured a duty free whisky and contemplated phoning Chris. Something told me not to. I went down to the restaurant and had a lonely and inferior dinner.

One of the truest clichés is that (normally) things seem better in the morning. They did. The sun was shining and the Mediterranean sparkled. The reason for the secrecy about my purpose in being in the hotel was a mystery and it puzzled me.

A different girl on reception passed me another envelope. It read: '*Cunliffe. I am busy this morning. I will see you this afternoon.*'

Again no signature or even a name. I could only assume that it was from the GM whose name of course I knew. Another Italian. How rude!

I walked around the gardens and the ground floor. The hotel had been open less than a year but little effort had been made to develop the gardens. The swimming pool area was a sea of concrete. A tide break made of large boulders stretching into the sea added to the stark appearance of the place. I was glad I was not paying to spend a holiday there. Inside, floral arrangements were few and far between. The lobby area was a landscape of marble, unadorned by plants, rugs or other ornaments.

Eventually I made myself comfortable on a sofa and read tourist literature. At about 2 p.m. a besuited man came over to where I was sitting. 'Cunliff-e?' he asked, pronouncing the "e" at the end of my name so that it sounded Italian. I decided not to correct him. No handshake.

'Yes,' I replied simply. He escorted me to his office behind reception and closed the door. The room was largely taken up by an ornate desk behind which he sat and extended a hand to invite me to sit in one of the two chairs on the opposite side of the desk. He was perhaps fifty-five, short with grey hair, a pepper and salt moustache, and glasses.

He made no attempt to introduce himself. He made no enquiries as to who I was. Had I had a good journey from the UK? Was my room alright? How was dinner the previous evening? Had I slept well? What had I been doing all morning? Was I concerned at the nature of his messages? Did I know what was going on at the hotel? To what extent had I been briefed? What impression did I have of the hotel so far? What did I know about him? His wife? What did he know about me? My wife and family? Where did we live? Where did he live? What did he think of the hotel? What did he think of Cyprus?

'We are having considerable problems with trade unions,' he said, without any preamble.

'They are very strong in the hotel business here in Cyprus.' He spoke good English with a defined Italian accent.

'They are particularly suspicious of expatriates. The union bosses feel that there are Cypriots able to do the jobs that foreigners do who would then supposedly earn the same money as we do. This will not happen for a long time. They have a great deal to learn about the expectations of our guests who are mostly English and Italian with a few French and Germans.

'We have a meeting with the trade union representative this afternoon to explain to him why you are here. That is why I did not want you to discuss your situation with anyone else before.'

While I had been mooching around during the morning, I had decided to avoid falling out with this man if possible, even though his behaviour was unacceptable. I reminded myself of this resolution.

'Mr Bonni,' (I will call him here), 'you mentioned just now about explaining to the trade union representative why I am here. I am not sure that I know myself why I am here except that I have been replaced in my job at the Café Royal and the opening of the Pegasus hotel in Jamaica has been delayed so the company needs to find something for me to do.'

Mr Bonni regarded me for some moments without saying anything.

'Are you telling me that those idiots in London did not explain the situation to you?'

He screwed up his face as he pronounced the word 'idiots'. Clearly he was not a fan of head office.

'All I was told was that I was to relieve the Food and Beverage Manager who was away on holiday,' I said, 'and that during his absence there was both a conference in the hotel, which would be full, and a large wedding. Some four hundred guests I believe. No-one seemed to know why the Food and Beverage Manager should be allowed to take holidays when such important events are taking place.'

The tone of Mr Bonni's reply indicated that he had detected the implied criticism of his management.

'Cunliffe,' he said, pronouncing the "e", 'I don't tell head office any more than I have to. They are not very bright. They do not really understand hotels like we Italians who have been brought up with hotelkeeping in our blood. Peter's holiday was arranged before this hotel even opened. An important family event I believe. Clearly we could not refuse the conference or the wedding. So I asked for help. That is why you are here.'

As if dismissing further conversation on these or related matters, and almost certainly wishing to avoid discussion about why he, as a hotelier with hotelkeeping in his blood was unable to manage these functions, he carried on, 'I am a very busy man. I will call Renos, the house manager, to join us before the meeting with the union. I only speak a few words of Greek and the union man speaks no English or Italian. Renos speaks very good English so he will do the translating.'

He picked up the phone on his desk and asked that Renos be found.

Renos entered a few minutes later. Mr Bonni introduced us. The plan for the meeting with the union man was discussed and Mr Bonni asked Renos to fetch another chair so that all four of us could sit down.

The union man arrived a few minutes later and was ushered in by a receptionist. He was apparently called Sterios. We all shook hands and sat down. Renos and Sterios started talking in Greek.

Then without warning they started shouting at each other. They both waved their arms around and at one point Sterios got up from the chair and banged his fist on the desk.

It was obvious that Sterios was not going to accept my presence and I envisaged myself as on the way back to London the next day. Thank God, I thought.

Sterios sat down again. The shouting continued. Clearly neither Mr Bonni nor I were able to contribute to the proceedings in any way. Then

Renos and Sterios both stood up, shook hands and smiled.

'That's OK then,' said Renos. He held the door open and the union man departed without any further contact with Mr Bonni or me.

'What was that all about then?' asked Mr Bonni. 'It didn't sound OK at all.'

'Oh just the usual stuff,' said Renos. 'Bitching about all the senior jobs being taken over by foreigners. He was particularly angry about you Mr Cunliffe (pronouncing the "e") being brought out from England to oversee a wedding between two Cypriots. He felt that a Cypriot like myself might actually be better qualified to manage such a function.'

'I think he might have a point,' I said.

'Well I don't,' said Mr Bonni. 'This hotel is run by a British company and managed by an Italian general manager. We will ensure that functions are done properly.'

Renos shrugged.

'Sorry,' I muttered.

'What are you sorry for? My honesty?' Mr Bonni almost shouted.

'Your rudeness I would call it,' I said. I could feel my resolution not to fall out with this man vanishing into the ether.

Mr Bonni opened his mouth to say something, his moustache twitching with emotion. Presumably he decided better of it and his mouth closed again. Then Mr Bonni asked Renos to show me round and introduce me to everyone. Clearly the meeting was over.

Before I left the office I explained to Mr Bonni that I must stay in touch with my wife back in England, who had two children to look after, one just a few weeks old. I asked, just out of politeness, if it would be in order to telephone home every other day.

'Of course,' he replied. 'But you have to pay.'

The important functions came and went. The wedding was particularly difficult for me personally, not just because of the language difficulty between myself and a crowd of very untrained casual Cypriot staff, but also because of the difference between my expectations and those of an almost entirely Cypriot guest list.

I felt that the food and service was dire. But no-one seemed to care.

There had to be a briefing to the waiting staff before each course was served. Renos had advised me not to hold a comprehensive briefing at the start of the function. He explained that many of the casual staff were peasants with little education and they would be unable to absorb and retain more than one instruction at a time. This spun things out more than I would have wished as Renos had to translate each instruction into Greek. But no-one seemed bothered, not even George the Head Chef, who was a very placid Cypriot who had trained in England.

Much of the hotel's stock of china was expended by being thrown on the ground and trampled under dancing feet. This seemed to make the guests happy. Of Mr Bonni there was no sight nor sound. Such hotel activities seemed to be outside his interest zone. He apparently worked (well that's one word for it) Monday to Friday from 8.30 a.m. to 5.30 p.m. with two hours off for a siesta. He never left his office. I doubt he would have known where the restaurant was.

The wedding was outside in the gardens in front of the hotel. The dancing went on till 4 a.m. to deafening local music. The mostly British residents started complaining at around 11 p.m. All the complaints came to me. I was powerless to stop the proceedings. Only Renos stayed around to support and help me. The two of us did our best to tidy up after the last of wedding guests had left. I got to bed at 6 a.m. At 8.05 exactly I got a phone call in my room from a British army general who was staying in the hotel, complaining that his room service breakfast ordered for 8 a.m. had not been served till 8.04. Strains of Lawrence of Arabia!

I was waiting for Mr Bonni outside his office at 8.30 on the Monday morning. 'Ah! Cunliffe,' was all he could come up with.

I told him of the events of the Saturday night and Sunday morning, about the complaints and the broken crockery. I told him I thought it was very poor that he had shown no interest in the function, not even to welcome the bride and groom.

He fiddled with his stubbly moustache but said nothing.

'I assume,' I concluded, 'that now that these important functions are over, Peter will be returning from his holiday and I can return to London.'

'Ah Cunliffe,' he said for the second time. 'I am afraid it is not as simple as that. The Regional Director for Europe and the Middle East is arriving here tomorrow. He will be speaking to you.'

'About what?' I asked.

'Staying here for longer. Peter is indeed returning, also tomorrow, but only to work his notice. He has resigned. By the way, so have I. I can't work with these Greek Cypriots anymore.'

'Who is this regional director?' I asked.

'He's called Nigel Smallbone. I have never met him. New to the position I believe. I hope he's clever. He needs to be. The unions are going to have great fun with this one.'

I met Nigel Smallbone by chance the next day. I was just chatting with Renos in the lobby when I saw a man in a suit and tie walking up the steps into the hotel carrying a small case. I excused myself from Renos and offered help with the suitcase.

'You must be John Cunliffe,' he said, putting down the case and extending a hand. 'I'm glad we bumped into each other before I see old Bonni, which out of courtesy I must do first. Not really looking forward to it to be honest. You and I have got a lot of talking to do I gather. How about dinner together? Meet in the bar at six?'

'Delighted,' I said. 'Let's get you to your room. I believe you haven't been here before.'

'No.'

I led him to the reception desk. Renos was hovering so I introduced them. I obtained Smallbone's room key and he seemed happy to see himself up.

'Shall I tell Mr Bonni you're here?'

'Yes please. Tell him I'll be down in five minutes.'

I thought he seemed genuine. I had not had much contact with honesty since Vincent left the Café Royal. I felt direly in need of some.

He was already in the bar, glass on the table when I got there. He stood and we shook hands again.

'Thought I'd try the local speciality. Brandy Sour I think they call it. Pretty horrid. Think I'll swap for a glass of Chardonnay. You?'

'Fine thanks.'

We sat. 'I've done the honourable thing with Bonni. He didn't want to talk much anyway.

'So...' He looked me straight in the eyes, which I felt was a good start. 'So let's talk about you John. Do you mind if I call you John?'

'Of course not.'

'Good. And you please call me Nigel. As you know, I'm new to this job although I have been with Trust Houses for about twenty years. So the whole Trust Houses Forte thing is new to me, never mind Cyprus and the other hotels I'm responsible for. This one seems to have become a mess which is why I'm here. I hope you'll help me sort it out. And in turn I will do my very best to help you and your family. I've done quite a bit of homework on what's gone on recently both here and with you and it seems to me that you have been messed about.'

An understatement, I thought.

'As far as I can see,' he continued, 'and this view is shared by many of my friends in the old Trust Houses company, this merger has gone far from smoothly and there have been quite a few casualties. I am sure too there will be others before we can put the whole issue to bed. I would prefer it if you kept that opinion to yourself. There are too many alliances at work, some for the good and some not, and my job is to help settle things down, not escalate them. I am told that you did an excellent job at Ring & Brymer, which is why you were offered the very important role at the Café Royal. From what I have heard, but you can tell me more if you wish, the handling of Ron Zanre's appointment was not done very well as far as you were concerned.'

'Yes, quite...'

'To be very honest, I don't think you were seriously in the running for GM at the Café Royal. It's a massive role with huge profit ramifications, even without the complication of being Charles Forte's big love. But someone should have realised that you might have expected to be considered and at least given you a hearing. Am I on the right lines so far John?'

'Absolutely.'

'Good. Carrying on then, I believe that Ron Zanre's brief is considerably different to Vincent Franzini's and given that you and Vincent were very much a team, it was felt that a clean sweep was best. I understand that. It was the handling of it that was poor, particularly when your wife had been a key figure in the International Division's personnel department.

I am sure that when you were offered the position in Jamaica it was done with the best of intentions and I have more to say about that in a minute. But equally, I am sure that there must have been doubts about whether the Pegasus would open on schedule. Again, I think the offer was made in good faith but perhaps a little more candour about the timetable would have been in order. So we wind up with a situation where the job you have been offered is not really available yet and where at the same time, the company has a problem here in Cyprus. And again, I don't believe you have been properly briefed about what has been going on here.'

I listened intently.

'No one seems to quite know what the deal was between Charles Forte and Archbishop Makarios, but clearly it involved a degree of control by a Cypriot board of directors. And such a board does exist. Strange to believe, Bonni does have a good track record and his behaviour here is out of character. He did apparently tell my predecessor even before the hotel opened that he had been told by the Chairman of the local board that he, the Chairman, and the board considered London an irrelevance and the Apollonia was to be run as Cyprus saw fit, and God help Bonni if he did not conform to that view. He was also told, so the story goes, that not all of the staff were exactly as they seemed and that he should be very careful in his dealings with certain individuals – who were not identified, thus leaving the threat floating – and in his dealings with the trade union.'

He continued: 'The local board is made up entirely of Greek Cypriots and I think it was also mooted that allegiances would be expected to align with Greek Cypriot thinking. Apparently too, and arguably this point should have been considered before Bonni's appointment, Bonni's family were ill-treated – whatever that means – by the Brits in the last war and consequently Bonni is not a great fan of English people. So the conclusion in London is that virtually ever since he took up this appointment he has been running scared of the local board and the Cyprus situation in general. To add to these difficulties, the project ran hugely over budget – London believes there was a bent Cypriot quantity surveyor – and a lot of the planned niceties like garden planting were just left undone. I have not had time since my arrival to form a real opinion on this, but my initial view is that the place has an unfinished feel to it.'

Another understatement, I thought.

'Now John, you will no doubt be thinking that much of what I have just said is hearsay. You are also a new boy here but does it seem to make sense? It is very important for me to have the right background because some decisions have to be made. Bonni, as I know you know, has resigned. Peter has resigned and while that is a pity, I am not surprised. The hotel is operating at a loss. And then there is the question of the Golden Sands Hotel in Farmagusta, which is supposed to open in eighteen months or so. Any views?'

'Several,' I replied. 'But first may I thank you for taking the trouble to fill me in. If I had known a half of what you have just told me, I would have been much wiser and happier about my own situation since leaving the Café Royal, and I think I would have been better equipped to deal with the situation which I found here and particularly as far as Mr Bonni was concerned. I can't really comment on what you have told me about what has gone on here and I probably know no more nor less that the next person about the situation in Cyprus. I can't believe that the United Nations would be here unless the island was regarded as somewhat of a crisis location.'

I continued: 'I think I understand something of Mr Bonni's fears. There is an uneasy feeling about the whole place. There's tension in the air. The hotel doesn't feel at home with itself. The staff don't seem happy. It's very difficult to judge when you don't speak the language and you don't understand the culture. All the Cypriots seem to do is shout at each other. It feels as if war is about to break out. Then they shake hands or throw their arms around each other and it appears as if they are the best of friends. It's very difficult to interpret.'

'I have heard it said,' Nigel replied, 'that that's a good measure of the Greek-Turkish problem. But don't let's go there.'

While Nigel had been talking, I had been weighing him up as best I could. Probably late forties; good education; decent; typical Trust Houses background; suspicious of the Forte side of things.

I liked him. The restaurant manager came over and offered us menus. I introduced Nigel.

'Well look', Nigel said. 'We probably don't need to solve all the world's problems tonight, but I thought it was as well to lay out the map. We're both new to this patch, and to be honest it seems to be down to you and me to decide what to do.'

'To you certainly. I'm not sure it's down to me.'

'Possibly true. But we're both here, unlike the boys and girls in London.'

'What notice does Mr Bonni have to serve?' I asked.

'Two months contractually, but he asked me this afternoon if he would be required to do that. He says he would prefer to leave as soon as possible. He sent his resignation in last week. We may have someone suitable to take over – chap running an old Trust House in the UK. But he'll need to be replaced there. And then there's you. And to further complicate matters, Andreas, the local Chairman wants to appoint a Cypriot.'

'You said "and then there's you". What about me?'

'Do you think the Pegasus will open soon?' asked Smallbone.

'Are you trying to tell me something?'

'I'm not trying anything. I promised to be honest. But the Caribbean does have a reputation. Alright. I'll stick my neck out. I think there will be further delays in Jamaica. They've only just appointed a GM. Guy called Herman Dorner. He's not even out there yet. So they're not going to send the F & B wallah immediately. The company isn't going to pay you to count paper clips. Trust Houses might have done. They had an administrative bias. But the Forte side of things doesn't think that way. I suppose some other temporary position might crop up but it will only be temporary by dint of Jamaica.'

'You seem, if you don't mind me appearing to creep – which I am not – to be very well appraised of what is going on', I said. 'Do you think Jamaica should remain on my radar?'

'Yes I do, and so does London. The Pegasus will open. It has to. And Forte wants it to. He has a soft spot for the Caribbean. He loves to stay with his family at the Sandy Lane in Barbados. Different culture I know, but the perception is that the Jamaican government is determined to clean-up crime and make tourism the country's economic driver. And the reason why everyone thinks Jamaica is right for you is that it is a big food and beverage operation. Banqueting for a thousand; three restaurants; four bars – well you know all that. Your experience particularly at Ring & Brymer and the Café Royal is spot on for that sort of gig.'

He concluded: 'Look. I'll come absolutely clean with you – not that I haven't to date. I think we should let Bonni go; you take over as acting GM while a new permanent man is appointed. It won't be a Cypriot and I will be telling Andreas that while I am here. As soon as the new GM arrives, you sort out the F & B department here; make the function operation efficient – look there's a ballroom which seats five hundred. I don't think the plastic has even been taken off the seats. Make the restaurant menus attractive. They're like a Trust House in Wigan! And then you move to Jamaica when the time is right. Unless...'

'Unless?'

'You open Farmagusta. But I didn't say that.'

'And meanwhile Christine and the boys?'

'They must join you here of course. ASAP.'

Chapter Ten

CYPRUS WITH CHRIS

I wasn't looking forward to phoning Chris. In our conversations to date I had not painted a very happy picture of the Apollonia Beach or of Cyprus. And now I was about to propose that she dropped the preparations for Jamaica and bring our two very young boys to an island policed by the United Nations and regarded as possibly on the brink of civil war.

As happened often (and still does) she surprised me. 'How exciting,' was the main conclusion. We had sold our share in the housing association property in Apex Close and bought a semi in Caterham to let while we were abroad. Our belongings destined for Jamaica would have to go into storage. A lot for her to do.

I took Nigel to the airport a couple of days later in the hotel's car. I thought he had been very fair and upfront. Bonni was to leave in a few days. Peter was back. I chose two adjoining rooms for Chris and I to make as much of a home as is possible in a hotel. I would have preferred to rent a house away from the hotel, but it was necessary to live in. I bought a small car. The paperwork was akin to buying a nuclear submarine but Renos helped me to do this after we had opened a bank account. The red tape for the latter was akin to taking over the Treasury. Chris was exhausted when she and the boys arrived at Nicosia airport, but we were delighted to be reunited.

Living without a kitchen was the biggest problem, particularly for Chris. We were entirely dependent on room service. Barney started at a local nursery. Time flew. We made friends with many of the British services personnel based at Akrotiri and Dhekelia. There were many inexpensive local restaurants for them to use, but the Apollonia Beach was the place for treats.

We were particularly befriended by an army colonel and his wife and family. Both their sons were in the same regiment as father. They were superlatively superior in a senior army officer tradition, and my first encounter with Andy was when he complained about being unable to book a room at the hotel for a visiting VIP officer from the UK. But after we had got over that we became good friends. There were thousands of services personnel on the sovereign bases, but very few civilian Brits. Andy told us, although he shouldn't have, that there was a top-secret plan in the event of serious trouble, which could be internal or could come from Greece or Turkey. Andy told us that we were included in the plan. This was a great comfort.

Peter went. The new GM arrived and I was able to turn my attention to the F & B department. There was much work to do. One of many concerns was the swimming pool. In those days, as probably now, sitting by the pool was resident guests' primary activity. Despite the name of the hotel, the beach was non-existent, and activities like golf and horse riding were not available. One problem, which we never solved, was the Germans and the loungers by the pool. There were nothing like enough loungers if the hotel was busy. The Germans, with nationalistic efficiency, bagged the chairs with their beach towels before the Brits were even up. The Brits, with nationalistic typicality, complained to the management. Me. The Germans could see nothing wrong with the procedure and asserted that it was a worldwide routine which neither I nor the hotel were about to change. What do you do? Nothing. Precisely.

The other pool problem was the condition of the area. The pool attendant was another Andreas and his brief was to look after the pool, the beach, the pool furniture and everything to do with that area except the catering. Andreas was frequently not to be found. I asked Renos if he knew what Andreas got up to. He gave me a shifty look (I had come to understand Renos's moods and gestures) and merely said that he had been appointed by the chairman and Bonni left him well alone.

One day, the complaints about loungers had been exacerbated by the fact that apparently the furniture had not been cleaned from the day before, thus rendering availability of suitable beds even more fraught than usual. I asked my secretary, a charming local girl called Vasso, to get someone to find Andreas and ask him to come to my office.

Five minutes after this request, Vasso stuck her neck into my office. 'Andreas has told reception that he is not going to come to your office. He says you must go to him at the pool.

'John,' she added in a serious tone, 'be very careful.'

'Why?' I asked.

'I can't tell you. But my advice to you is not to mess with Andreas.'

Vasso had become a real friend to Chris and I and she adored the boys. She quite often babysat. Rightly or wrongly, I did not think it was right to eat in the restaurant with such young children, so always eating in our room was tiresome, particularly for Chris, who apart from her excursions to the roof (out of bounds to guests) to see to the drying of clothes, was very confined. Our laundry situation was particularly trying as Chris had no access to a washing machine and terry towelling nappies washed in a bathroom sink were a challenge. Disposable nappies had not been invented. Chris would have loved a part-time job but the union would not agree – even though she had exactly the same qualifications as me. The only trouble with Vasso babysitting was that we had to have a chaperone to take her home. The traditional Greek Orthodox families were very bound by convention.

My instinct was that I could not allow Andreas, whatever his secret power was, to decline to meet me in my office. By now the whole hotel, possibly most of the town, would know that Andreas had declined to come to my office. Vasso retreated like a scared rabbit. I went down to the pool. Andreas, as if making a point, was vigorously wiping down loungers. He saw me and came over.

'You come with me,' he said, scowling.

I followed him to the store under the pool where the chemicals were kept and the filtration machinery was housed. He had installed a small desk and two chairs there and liked to call it his office.

'You do not send for me,' he said. 'You fucking English bastards are so stupid. You know nothing about Cyprus, Greece, Turkey, EOKA [the Greek Cypriot guerrilla organisation that fought to end British rule in Cyprus], Makarios or me. You think I am just a pool attendant to look after you fucking English, Germans, Italians and United Nations arseholes.'

I determined to stay calm. I was not sure if I was more angry or scared. I was not happy being alone with this man in his subterranean lair.

'Andreas,' I said placatingly, 'I don't know if you understand the meaning of the words you are using, but you can't talk to your boss like that.'

'I understand very well,' he said. 'Unlike you British fuckers who cannot be bothered to learn a single word of Greek except ouzo and moussaka, I speak very good English. And you had better understand that you are not my boss.'

'Who is?' I asked him.

'General Grivas,' he said.

And as if to emphasise the point he was making, he opened the drawer of his small desk and pulled out a pistol which he turned on me. I had no idea what sort of pistol it was, but I suspected that even though he was the pool attendant, it was not a water pistol.

I wondered if a shot would be heard at the poolside. Or might I just disappear off the face of the earth, my body carted away in some clandestine nocturnal operation. Or dissolved in chlorine. How would Chris fare, I mused?

My thoughts were terminated by Andreas shouting 'now you fuck off English'.

I did.

I hadn't really got to know Hugh, the new GM. He seemed to be content to get on with his side of things and to let me get on with mine. But I felt that he should know about my spat with Andreas. He was obviously concerned and said he would pass on the details to Nigel.

Thereafter I avoided contact with Andreas. To this day, I am not entirely sure if this was wisdom or cowardice. I took to straightening the pool furniture myself and wiping the tables.

I came to understand Bonni's anxiety about dealing with the Chairman. Like all Cypriots I came across, he seemed to shout the whole time. Whether this was anger, or forcefulness or just Greek-ness I don't know. But it led one to believe that every conversation was a confrontation.

There was a strong Cypriot partisanship in the way the local Cypriots behaved, particularly the members of the local board. Whenever they used the restaurant, the music for the whole night became Cypriot, even if all the other guests were mainstream European. This also led to complaints, particularly from Brits.

One night chairman Andreas sent for me, even though it was my evening off, and demanded in front of a large table of locals why we did not have Johnny Walker whisky available. It was obvious that he was drunk. I told him that I had no input into what brands we bought and that this was laid down by London.

'But I am the chairman of this hotel,' he shouted, 'and my company owns the franchise for Johnny Walker. See that it becomes our pouring brand in future.' He waved his hand in dismissal.

Hugh at least shared evening management shifts with Renos and me. This made for a far more acceptable regime than under Bonni, and I saw more of Chris and the boys.

One evening Chris got a phone call from her dad to say that his mother had died. Chris had been very fond of her Gran even though she had been (by Chris's admission) extraordinarily careful with money and had even short-changed her as a child on her pocket money for doing cleaning. Chris also tells, with heartfelt pathos, of her great disappointment when she was given, at age thirteen as a present from her grandparents, her first bicycle. She had been told it was in the pipeline and had dreamed of a shiny new bike with a silver-coloured bell, and Sturmey Archer gears. The reality had been a second-hand and somewhat rusty contraption with no frills. Chris observed, after telling this story, that her grandparents were not mean, just careful in the aftermath of two wars which made working class people feel insecure. Typical Chris loyalty. They were plain mean!

We had been planning on going to Gordon Blue (not a typo – that's what the restaurant was called) in Limassol, and Vasso was looking after the boys. Instead, we sat on the steps going down to the little beach and she cried and cried. This loss made her very homesick and we decided to ask Reg and Audrey if they wanted to come out and stay in the Apollonia for a week. Hugh said they could have a complimentary room if we paid for their meals and extras.

I took a week off and we did the sights, although it was a tight squeeze in our little Fiat. Audrey did not like Cyprus and said she felt uneasy. She was that sort of Yorkshire person. But she adored her grandchildren and played endlessly with them both. This gave Chris a bit of a break.

The evening before they were to go home, we were sitting in the bar having a drink before dinner. We had decided that if we were in the hotel, it was alright to leave the boys with a baby listening device in reception. An English couple who were staying came into the bar, sat and ordered two large brandies. They looked very upset and I felt I should enquire why.

They told me that they had been in a UN convoy en route to Kyrenia in the northern part of the island and had decided that as the convoy was so slow they would overtake. The rear UN lorry had simply pulled over and forced their hired car into the ditch where it turned onto its roof. Because the speed had been so slow, no-one had been hurt. The convoy had halted and they were given a lift back to Limassol. But the captain in charge of the convoy had told them that the same procedure would have been adopted had there been a precipice not a ditch. A sobering thought.

Shortly after Reg and Audrey's return I started to have bouts of nausea and generally feeling unwell. I attended a doctor in Limassol. Although the area was crawling with RAF and army doctors, one of the protocols of the sovereign bases was that civilians must only deal with civilian doctors. This man, who spoke very good English, prescribed castor oil, which only had the obvious result. I made appointments with several other doctors but none seemed to know what was really the matter. I tried to keep from Chris how ill I really felt. But she knew.

There was an RAF surgery, obviously for RAF personnel, on the outskirts of Limassol, not on the base. I went there and explained the circumstances. The corporal on the reception desk would have none of it and asked me to leave. I explained that I was a British citizen and taxpayer who needed medical help. And I sat down in the waiting area which gradually emptied as closing time approached.

When there were no other patients in the waiting room, the corporal again asked me to leave. I told him that I would only leave after I had seen a British doctor.

The corporal retired behind the scenes. After a wait of ten minutes or so, a Wing Commander came into the now empty room and approached me. He asked me what the problem was. He was very compassionate and took me into an examination room. I was admitted the same evening to the RAF hospital and had an operation the next day. The Surgeon Wing Commander became a close friend of Chris's and mine.

Whether related to this or not, Hugh asked to see me a few days after my return to work. He had been asked by Nigel to tell me that Jamaica now seemed imminent and he had been instructed to consider a replacement for me as Food and Beverage Manager. He wanted to know if I thought Renos was up to the job. I told him that I thought he was. He agreed and we decided to see Renos together the next day. Renos was delighted and accepted.

I contacted the Fiat dealer to sell the car and Chris and I started making arrangements to fly back to London, where it was felt she should stay for a few weeks while I sorted out accommodation in Kingston.

By the time we returned to England three weeks later, we would have been in Cyprus for just over a year. It was a good thing that Farmagusta had never been mentioned again. Less than six months after we flew out of Nicosia, the Turkish invasion began and the Golden Sands Hotel became the headquarters of the Turkish forces in Cyprus.

Chapter Eleven

JAMAICA

Fortunately, our house in Caterham was not let so we were able to stay there. Chris hated the house and area but it didn't matter for a few weeks. I had to spend some time in head office on various matters, and a number of meetings were held with Herman Dorner and other people who would be involved in opening the Pegasus. Chris and I decided that it would be a good idea to have an evening party to meet some of these colleagues as well as to say goodbye to friends and relatives. I wanted Chris and I to be free from serving drinks and food, so I asked Peter Crook (who with his wife Jane were among the guests) if the Café Royal might lend us a couple of staff if we bought all the food and drink.

It was a lovely summer evening and the party went on far into the night. We offered the guests champagne cocktails on arrival, although I suspect they were made from prosecco or some such. There were to be many people who did not know each other, and I wanted the party to get off to a lively start, so I told the barman to be generous with the brandy (which was duty free Cypriot) in the cocktails until I told him to ease off. This I forgot to do. Herman repeatedly called Jane Crook "hotpants", the skimpiest of which she was indeed wearing. It took two days to clear up.

I flew out to Kingston with Ian Baxter, who was the project manager for the Pegasus. He was nervous, having just been to a meeting in head office with all the top brass, as well as medium-sized brass (like Herman), and small brass (like me) present, at which it had been made very clear that not a penny of overspend on the budget would be tolerated. I felt sorry for Ian. While he did not have operational responsibility, the control of a multi-million-dollar project was a massive obligation, with many factors partially or completely outside his control.

As we made our final approach into Norman Manley Airport, Ian pointed out the Pegasus – an impressive structure, with the Blue Mountains in the background. I wished Chris and the boys had been there. It was a poignant moment soon pulled back into reality by the rough welcome at the hands of the immigration officials, and aggressive attitude of the porters. Nor was the journey to New Kingston a preview of heaven.

Since the hotel was still a building site, Herman and I had temporary offices in the building of the Jamaica Tourism Association, where I met Herman the next morning. I had spent a comfortable night in a charming guest house which had once been a sugar plantation. Herman was very welcoming and the surroundings were idyllic. Unlike the slums through which we had passed on the way from the airport, our office building was surrounded by manicured gardens, hibiscus, bougainvillea and jasmine. The Blue Mountains, as ever, shimmered behind us, partly sheathed in an azure veil. Clearly no expense had been spared on the air-conditioned offices of the bosses of Jamaica's primary industry. Nothing had been provided for me and my work area was to be in a corridor. It didn't matter.

It never ceased to amaze me in those days, and indeed subsequently, the extent to which bosses just let you get on with things, assuming I suppose that you know what you're required to do. Herman told me that the proposed date of opening was in just over four months' time and more or less said 'be ready!' His secretary, who was a well-educated Jamaican lady, gave me the details of an estate agent whom she thought would be most suitable for finding us accommodation.

I had use of a hotel vehicle 'for a week only', Ian had told me very firmly the day before. Ian had given me the address of a car dealer who seemed to be the favoured choice of expats in Kingston. I suggested to Herman that sorting out arrangements for living and getting to and from work was probably my most important mission. He agreed and put in a call to Mr Jones at Barclays Bank to introduce me. I met Mr Jones an hour later and I left the branch with a temporary cheque book. Mr Jones and I were subsequently not to see eye to eye.

That same afternoon I had a telephone call from the estate agent whom I had briefed earlier. A town house in Norbrook Mews, a highly desirable area (of course), had just become available for a minimum one-year let. The rent was about right. The lady said it would be snapped up but she would like me to have first option as there would be other expats from the Pegasus wanting to rent accommodation. She could meet me there at six. She gave me directions. She told me that her name was Stephanie.

As I drove into the estate I knew this was it. The other side of me (the bit I had inherited from my father and the one that Chris would have subscribed to) said out loud 'but you can't just take the first place you see' and 'you have to negotiate on the rent – you can't just accept the asking price'.

Then the original bit of me said, 'Look. You haven't even seen the house yet'. True. There were about twenty-five town houses in a rough rectangle. They all faced an enormous lawn with many mature trees dotted around. A swimming pool with a fence around it was visible at the far end. Safe for the boys. The house in question was second from the end near the pool. I met Stephanie on time and she escorted me inside. A large sitting room was separated from a walled private garden by just grills. No windows. The garden had wrought iron gates giving onto the communal lawn. The kitchen was OK and led into maids' quarters – I had not even considered maids! Upstairs were three bedrooms – plainly furnished but with air-conditioning units.

I loved it – particularly not having windows downstairs. But I thought that would be what worried Chris.

The front door had been left open and a voice called 'cooee! Anyone in?' And in stepped a girl of about my age. She said to the world at large, a tinge of northern England apparent in her voice, 'Hello. I'm Iris. I live next door. Just come to vet the new tenants. See if they're going to be fun.' I laughed and introduced myself and Stephanie.

'Actually,' I said, 'it's the first place I've seen and I haven't made up my mind to take it. I've never picked a place to live before without my wife being involved.'

'John,' Iris said bossily. 'I'm married to a Jamaican and we've lived here for years. Take it from me, there's nowhere better in Kingston. And you'll never find a better crowd of neighbours. It's like a club. Your wife will love it. And it's very safe – as far as Jamaica goes,' she added.

I took it. Chris and the boys arrived a week later. After the paperwork for the house had been signed and sealed I bought a car, and felt that I had done well as I drove to the airport to meet my family. Chris adored the house. Iris and Lloyd were to become lifelong friends. He was a clever and far-seeing man who recognised that the Caribbean's lifeblood – tourism – was going to need materials that were hard to come by, if available at all. He travelled the world, including its newest producer – China – buying anything available and selling it to the Caribbean islands. He was often away from home and Iris frequently popped in for a chat or a G&T if it were that sort of time of day.

My joy (or was it relief?) at the success of the house and the beauty of our surroundings soon gave way to some realities which were quickly to become important in our lives. The first of these was that my salary was totally inadequate. The expat community, particularly within the New Kingston hotel brotherhood, was small and intimate, and we quickly got to know our colleagues at the Sheraton, the Skyline and other foreign owned and managed hotels. The Americans laughed at my salary and proclaimed (which was true) that the people in London had not done their homework.

I discussed my anxieties with Herman. He didn't admit to a problem but it was quite obvious that he knew he had one. He and his wife Mavis lived in the hotel – or would when it was tenable – so he would to a large extent be protected from the cost of living. I am not suggesting that he didn't care. I suspected that his particularly hard-nosed bosses had their heads deep in the sand. This was later to be proved to be exactly the case. Our discussion was left without any conclusion.

The second problem, which was related to the first, was that there was no suitable public transport for white people. This had and has nothing to do with race or colour. There was huge resentment of white people by many Jamaicans, and when you considered the difference in living standards, this was hardly surprising. But the self-evidence of this did not solve the problem. A second car was out of the question. Thus when I left home in the morning, Chris was cut off – completely.

The Pegasus's sales manager, the head chef, the sous chef, the pastry chef, the chief accountant, the front office manager, the chief engineer, the house manager, the head housekeeper and others were arriving from Europe at this time. Some of them were couples, but Chris and I were the only expats with children and the need to get them to and from school. Even before the hotel opened, there was a damaging lack of cohesion within the senior team. Unlike the question of salaries and indeed the larger issue of remuneration packages, which arguably (and indeed head office did argue) had an element of subjectivity to it, the family transport issue was elemental.

Once my voice, which was purely realistic, not rebellious nor greedy, came to be backed up by that of others, it must have been clear that some action was needed. It was quickly agreed that the expat staff could be collected from home by taxis and returned home after work by the same method. In my case, unlike most of the other expats who largely worked office hours, apart from the senior chefs, this could be midnight or not infrequently four in the morning. Nonetheless, this decision meant that Chris had the car for the school runs, shopping and other necessities of life.

She rarely sought me out at work due to the third major problem. There were no telephones. Mobile phones had not been invented and the telephone system in Jamaica was such that waiting lists for private phones ran into years. There was one public phone box for the whole of Norbrook Mews and it was usually out or order. So once I had left home in the morning I had no way of communicating with Chris about anything, including when I would return. She had no way of communicating with me if there was any sort of domestic, school or health issue. A very worrying, indeed rather desperate state of affairs. While the prompt solution to the transport issue had been welcome, the other complications remained and I began to feel a festering resentment at the way we were being treated. This was not what I expected from a company for which I had worked and to which I had given my all for many years.

The general financial position was worsened by the immediate obviousness of the need for some domestic help. Keeping house in that climate with two small children was out of the question without assistance. We were very naive in the process of recruiting and operating with a maid. Iris was enormously helpful.

The build-up to the opening of the Jamaica Pegasus was gruelling but very rewarding in terms of personal satisfaction. The food and beverage outlets were manifold and the local managers and supervisors had little concept of responsibility as we knew it. Training for operative staff often started with what a shoe was for. Trade unions, supported by the Labour Government of the time, attempted and succeeded in making enforcement of standards almost impossible.

The senior food and beverage team were a joy to work with and very unified and focused. We moved mountains. I was proud. The chief difficulty in restaurants and banqueting was that we had to appeal to Jamaicans (a political necessity), English guests, Americans and Canadians, visitors from other Caribbean and South American countries, as well as Europeans. Locals were from all strains. And throughout everything ran race and politics. Basically we were not welcome.

Our bosses were from London, British Airways, which had a stake in the hotel, and a local Board of Directors. All the local suppliers and American ones wanted our business. The issue of import licences and work permits was corrupt.

A visiting executive from Head Office agreed to a meeting with me about conditions. I would like to think that I was honest in what I said. He offered no word of gratitude or praise for the success of the opening, and suggested that Chris was spoilt. He was disinterested in the salary levels of peers in American-run hotels on the same street. We both knew that his attitude lacked sincerity and we parted in a way which no senior manager should have allowed to happen. I was bitterly disappointed. Chris was fed up with deprivation. All our neighbours were so much more affluent.

Chris and I talked far into that night. She was very loving because she knew how much I personally had put into the opening and first few months of operation of the hotel. Relations with Herman, his successor, and everyone else from London cooled overnight. I stopped working such ridiculous hours and tried to be a bit more of a husband and father. I would like to believe that this was partially successful. I took to taking two days off a week and we went on expeditions to the beaches and other parts of the island. We discovered a touch of paradise in Port Antonio on the north coast. We went for weekends to a small apartment hotel called Goblin Hill which offered affordable rates to locals – as we were counted. San San beach offered magical snorkelling and both boys became good swimmers and very much at home in the water.

The social life at Norbrook Mews was considerable, and if you wanted to participate there was generally a party on somewhere. The residents were a mixture of affluent Jamaicans, expatriates from the UK, the USA and Canada, accountants, lawyers, embassy employees, business people and minor government officials. Some seemed to be always around and we got to know them; others came and went.

Chris recalls an occasion when she had been sitting at the pool with a girlfriend, talking innocently, or so she thought, about the comings and goings of neighbours. They had been commenting on the fact that the so and so's from number twenty-nine seemed to be going to the States a lot. Were they about to leave? A handsome young man in swimming trunks who had been sitting in the next lounger to Chris had come over, knelt down and whispered in an American accent: 'I know who you two are. It's my job to do so. You don't know who or what I am. But do yourselves a favour and don't talk about people in the way you have been doing or you might find yourself at the bottom of the deep end of the pool with a weight round your ankles.' He said no more. They discovered no more. Iris had commented to Chris that evening that in Jamaica you never knew who was what. Probably CIA, Iris ventured.

One day a hurricane hit Kingston. With my usual stupidity, I felt it essential to go to the hotel. In fact, it was far more important to look after my family. As soon as I had driven out of Norbrook Mews, it became apparent that the road was impassable. Storm drains were disgorging torrents of water, debris, wheelbarrows, bicycles, drowned dogs, even cars onto the road. It was clearly very dangerous. Herman would have to cope. The spirit of Dunkirk set in at Norbrook Mews.

*

The hotel had not been open for sufficiently long to have established a regular clientele. However, a man called Francis Mortimer starting coming quite often for several nights at a time. He was obviously a Brit but gave an address in the USA. He was inquisitive and friendly and soon came to know all the management. He was a small man who always dressed impeccably in a dark suit and one of a handful of brightly coloured ties. He reminded me in appearance a little of Vincent Franzini at the Café Royal.

He didn't seem to have anything to do other than to wander around the hotel talking to management and staff. When he checked out his phone bill was invariably a couple of hundred US dollars. He ate and drank well in the hotel's bars and restaurants, sometimes alone, sometimes with one of our secretaries.

He seemed to have taken a particular shine to my secretary, Sonia. I didn't mind. I wished her well. Whether because of this liaison or because he wanted to chat to me, he not infrequently stuck his head round the door of my office and asked if I could spare him a mo, which invariably became half an hour.

Although this was somewhat annoying, I found him interesting and he had become an important guest for the hotel. One evening when I was just considering packing up, he asked for his usual mo, and before I could answer he had plonked himself into one of the chairs by my desk. 'John. May I ask your advice about something please?'

He had previously asked me to address him as Francis. This was unusual in those days in a hotel. But he had dismissed my reluctance and insisted.

'Francis. On what can I advise you?' I asked. 'You are undoubtedly older and wiser than me.'

'Thank you,' he laughed. 'Am I a bit of a nuisance in the hotel? Always talking and chatting up the secretaries. Does Herman wish I would just bugger off? Stay at the Sheraton or the Skyline? Do you?'

'I can assure you that none of those things apply,' I said. 'We all think that you are a charming person to have around and you are a very important guest in the hotel. As you know, the Pegasus has not been open long and we value enormously a person who stays with us as often as you do and who spends in our restaurants and who indeed befriends us all. I suppose you are a bit of a mystery because you don't ever seem to be busy. But that's your business, not ours.'

'Thank you John. "Business" is the significant word. I do business in many parts of the world. I travel a lot. I make a lot of money. I enjoy company. I love women but never want to marry one. I study the world, make judgements and am normally right. That's why I make a lot of money. Sound judgement.'

He tapped the side of his nose. 'There's a lot of money to be made in the Caribbean at the moment. As well as a lot to be lost. You're right. I don't have a lot to do. I get other people to do it for me while I enjoy myself. I have a talent for spotting the right people. You're not happy here for one. Right?'

I said nothing.

'Herman's going back to Europe soon and the hotel is rudderless. Your people in London don't have a clue what's going on in Jamaica. They don't know that had it not been for you in particular, and a few of your colleagues – and you know who I mean – this hotel would never have opened as smoothly as it did. Anyway, enough of me. You have all made me welcome and I wondered if you felt that it would be appropriate to host a little private lunch for maybe eight or nine people at the Pegasus just by way of a thank you.'

He reeled off a list of names including Sonia and some other pretty women – but notably excluding Herman.

'Why not Herman?' I asked.

'I wondered about him. He's the boss. Might spoil the fun a bit. What do you think?'

'I think Francis that if you don't ask him, he will be very suspicious and wonder what the hell all his people are doing having a nice lunch while he's left to run the hotel. Whereas if you do ask him, and he will probably accept, he will give the event his blessing.'

'Done,' he declared.

Twenty-four hours later Sonia handed me an envelope, beautifully calligraphed in heavy black ink.

Inside was a gold-edged printed invitation:

Mr Francis Mortimer
Chairman
Requests the pleasure of the company of
Mr John Cunliffe
For luncheon
At 12.30 p.m. on 23rd March
In the New Kingston Suite of the Jamaica Pegasus Hotel
Kingston, Jamaica.
RSVP

I read the invitation twice. Chairman? Of what? Very unusual.

Francis had declined my offer to arrange the luncheon. He said I was to be a guest. He would deal with a member of the banqueting team.

The Pegasus had opened just before austerity in Jamaica seriously set in and we had been able to stock quite a fine wine cellar, including bottles from around the world. Francis had evidently decided to push the boat way out on the day of his luncheon, whether for his own delectation or just to show off. The banqueting head waiter who normally ran larger functions was presiding and the head chef personally carved the roast fillets of beef. Crystal champagne in cut glass glasses (where the hell had they come from?) graced the reception, A Dog Point Sauvignon Blanc from New Zealand accompanied the scallops; a 1960 Saint Joseph was served with the beef, a delicious Californian Gewürztraminer catapulted the crème brûlée to stardom, and a Taylor's vintage port slid down delightfully with the international cheese board. Someone in my department had worked very hard and Francis had parted with a lot of pourboires!

At around 5 p.m. Herman somewhat incomprehensibly announced that he needed to sign the mail – an unlikely errand since his secretary was by now sitting on Francis's knee. He left, and several others took the cue. Francis then called for Remy Martin to accompany the coffee. By 6 p.m. only Francis, myself and two others were left. I had started drinking water after the dessert wine had been served, so was fully in charge of myself. Francis too seemed in control – surprisingly.

He swished the brandy around the balloon glass and took a sip. Then he pushed his chair back, stood and walked over to the window. He glanced at the amazing view for a minute and turned around.

'I'm flying to the Turks and Caicos Islands tomorrow,' he announced out of the blue.

'Next big tourist destination in this neck of the woods. I'm in the final stages of buying an island. Then building a hotel. Anyone interested? Must pack now. Thanks for your company. See you soon.'

He walked to the door and waved as he left the room.

Chris's parents came to stay for a couple of weeks and it was not a happy time. Audrey was clearly not well. Even I could see that. She had no energy and had an unhealthy grey hue. Chris and Audrey had a complicated relationship. It was obviously based on deep love and included some telepathy. Yet they weren't comfortable with each other. I thought at the time that it was a parental respect thing from Chris's point of view, mixed up with Chris's greater experience of life – even at Chris's much younger age. Audrey had lived a fairly simple life very much dictated by Yorkshire traditions.

Chris knew her mother was ill, whereas I could only suspect it and listen to what Chris told me. I trusted Chris's interpretation of events. Reg said there was nothing wrong with her. Audrey didn't seem to have an opinion about it. She did not complain. However, Audrey pronounced within minutes of arriving at our home, that Jamaica was evil and she hated it. She implored us to come home and bring her only grandchildren to safety. This sent Chris into a freefall of anxiety, uncertainty and lack of confidence, fuelled no doubt by her awareness (not shared with Reg or Audrey) of our financial position and my disillusionment with my employers. With the house full, privacy for Chris and I to talk was difficult.

As if to prove Audrey's point, a frightening occurrence took place just a couple of days after Reg and Audrey's return home. Both Chris's and my bedroom, and the boys', had windows and a glazed door facing onto the mews. There were no curtains – just shutters, which didn't close very well. Outside the windows of both bedrooms was a narrow balcony. On the side of the mews right outside our bedroom was a streetlamp.

Something woke me. I looked at the alarm clock on my bedside table. It was just after 2 a.m. I sat up in bed. Then the light from the streetlamp was briefly extinguished. Something or someone had walked past our window on the balcony and cast a shadow.

Now I was fully awake. Had we locked the upstairs windows thoroughly? Had we locked downstairs properly? Gun crime was rife in Jamaica and we all lived with a degree of fear – particularly those living in supposedly prosperous homes. There was no telephone with which to call the police. Should I wake Chris? To go the boys' bedroom would involve walking across a landing with windows also facing onto the balcony – but with no shutters. I would be a sitting duck. Should I open our shutters to see what was going on? But that might alert the intruder and possibly initiate an attack.

The balcony was only accessed from the bedrooms. So either a ladder had been used – unlikely – or someone lithe had scaled a drainpipe. The shadow eclipsed the light again. I heard the handle of the door onto the balcony rasp. A few moments later, the front door rattled. Either the man had descended from the balcony very quickly or there were two of them. Or more. A gang perhaps.

To go downstairs would be folly. I crawled across the landing almost flat on my tummy. I stopped to look up at the landing window. Nothing. The boys were fine and sleeping. But were the windows and door properly locked? I could not check this without opening the shutters. I had nothing with which to defend myself. Who keeps knives in a bedroom? Not that a kitchen knife would be much use against a gun or a machete.

Then I noticed Barney's toy gun leaning against the wardrobe. It might fool someone in the darkness broken only by the light from the streetlamp. I hurried back to our bedroom carrying the toy gun. Chris was still asleep. I lay on my side of the bed, toy gun in hand, facing the window.

And that's how she found me in the morning.

Francis collared me a few weeks after his lunch party. He told me that he was proceeding with Turks and Caicos and suggested there would be no harm in us finding out more. He wanted collaborators, was how he put it.

I discussed the rather strange events with Chris. Like me, until a few weeks before, she had never heard of the Turks and Caicos Islands, and like me she did not know what this rather strange man was suggesting or offering. We both felt that there was little to be lost by having a look. Something was going to have to be done to change our lives.

The cost divided by three people of chartering a small plane for a couple of days to fly to Providenciales was surprisingly modest. We had hoped that Francis might volunteer to pay for this. But he didn't and it was unclear what he wanted from us. What is a collaborator anyway?

Our pilot was a charming Jamaican called Carl. As we took a north-easterly course from Kingston, he chatted amiably about his quite exotic life, usually flying Americans around the Caribbean.

As we were about halfway, with Guantanamo Cuba on our left and Haiti on our right, a stern American voice came onto the radio: 'JK6924 you are entering an area designated for USAF exercises. You must turn left or right immediately. Over.'

Carl replied: 'We are headed for Provo. What's the problem? Over.'

'JK6924 you are heading directly into a USAF exercise. Turn left or right immediately. Suggest you turn right and fly over Haiti then north to the Turks and Caicos Islands. Please confirm. Over.'

'JK6924 to control. I don't have enough fuel to comply. The best I can do is to turn right onto 55 degrees then head north to Grand Turk rather than Provo. Otherwise we will be in the drink. Please confirm. Over.'

There was a long silence.

'Control to JK6924. Proceed to 55 degrees immediately and then as suggested. Over and out.'

'Shit,' said Carl. 'That was not funny.'

He fiddled with some dials.

'We'll just make it. I need to call Grand Turk. Grand Turk this is JK6924. ETA Grand Turk 1830 hours. OK? Over.'

'Grand Turk to JK6924. Grand Turk airport closes 1800 hours. Can you divert to Provo? Over.'

'JK6294 to Grand Turk. Permission to proceed to Provo denied by USAF. Have to land Grand Turk due insufficient fuel to go anywhere else. Please confirm OK. Over.'

There was another long silence.

'Grand Turk to JK6924. We'll leave the runway lights on. Switch off behind control tower door on arrival. Happy landings. Over and out.'

Due to the absence of a toilet, we had all been avoiding attacking the duty free bottles. But the Captain Morgan came out at this point and all but Carl participated. He made up for it as we sat in the bar of the small inn at the end of the runway.

He admitted that there was barely a teaspoonful of fuel left.

We did the best we could to explore the islands over the next two days. On the much less eventful return journey to Kingston we made extensive notes which we expanded into a rudimentary plan for a tourism business. This was discussed in detail at our house at Norbrook Mews over the following few days and the polished version was typed by a secretarial agency to keep it away from anyone else at the Pegasus. I handed this to Francis in his room on the occasion of his next visit. He gave me a business card: Francis Mortimer. Chairman. No company name; no address; no telephone number.

I smelt a rat. We never saw him again. Turks and Caicos is now a thriving tourist destination.

I did not resign my position at the Pegasus. I had no other job to go to. But I let it be known around the island that I was not happy. I did not neglect my duties. I just stopped working with the passion that had been my norm at Ring & Brymer, the Café Royal, the Apollonia Beach and the Pegasus to date. The banqueting department in particular was very busy, and word had it that the other Kingston hotels were suffering as a result of the Pegasus's success. Herman left to go elsewhere and his deputy took over as GM. I did not regard this as encouraging.

It did not take long before I received a phone call, at work of course, from the Managing Director of another hotel on the island. This, had I but known it, was the inauguration of a nasty leap from the frying pan into the fire. I have over subsequent years mused not a little as to whether I could have anticipated the consequences of accepting the offer made to me and thereby prevented some of the heartache that was to follow.

Perhaps a partial answer to this introspection lies in another phone call received not long before we moved to the north coast. It was from the British chief engineer of the property. George (I will call him) and his wife Pat were in Kingston that night on the way back to the UK – for good. Could they come and see Chris and I that evening?

He sounded serious and I felt sure that the proposed visit was not just social. I invited them home and (unusually) sent a note to Chris by taxi to advise her of the visit and to ask her to make sure we had some nibbles. They arrived only five minutes after I got home and I had only just changed out of my suit – yes we wore them all the time. And a tie!

George wasted no time in coming to the point: 'John and Chris. Thank you for seeing Pat and I. We have heard that you are going to the hotel which we are just leaving and feel a responsibility to offer you as fellow Brits, some advice which you will not welcome.

'I have been at this hotel for just under a year – long enough to find out what is going on, particularly if, like us, you have been around the Caribbean for some years and got to know how to read the vibes. I do not believe that the hotel will succeed in getting a work permit for a Brit GM, when there is already a Brit MD. It is not a large or complicated property – nothing like the Pegasus.

'Your appointment is highly suspect. There are several reasonably competent Jamaican assistant managers who have worked there for some time. They are already rattling sabres at the news of your appointment, as is the Spanish head chef who has been there for so long that he is untouchable, as are the unions.

'Your success at the Pegasus has not gone unnoticed on the island and Jamaicans, as you will know, don't like having their cages rattled. Pat and I are leaving after some very alarming events which have scared us to death. I'm a tough old Scottish ex-Navy bird and I don't take fright easily. But that place is another matter. And I believe you have two little boys to worry about and take care of. So sorry.'

There was silence.

Finally Pat added, 'He's right you know and I don't know the half of it. Only went through the front door once, or any other door for that matter. That was enough.'

Try as we might, we were unable to extract from George the nature of the 'alarming events' to which he had alluded. They didn't stay long. They were embarrassed.

Chris and I were deeply shocked. We needed security; continuity;

peace; belonging; respect. Not conflict and more worry. Chris and I again talked about our circumstances for the rest of the evening. We had both liked George and Pat but their views seemed to be too vague. But why had they been so insistent about visiting us and telling us only half a story? Why not the whole story if it were true? Their perception of the property seemed to fly in the face of the hotel's reputation.

I checked and was categorically assured that a valid work permit had been issued for me.

We decided to stick to our plan. What a mistake that turned out to be.

The Pegasus gave me a rather half-hearted send-off party. We had good friends there, including eight Brits who had shared the birth pains of a new hotel as only people who have done that can know. But they had their own careers to look after.

On arrival at our promised house, it was not as agreed. The first floor had been divided into two parts via a crude plasterboard partition which had not even been painted. Loud reggae music was audible from the other side. No attempt had been made to clean or make the place welcoming. Had Chris and I been in charge we would have arranged a vase of flowers and put in the fridge as a minimum a bottle of wine and some milk. Chris cried her eyes out. I went in search of my new boss. He was apparently in the USA for a couple of weeks, his secretary told me. What was wrong with the partition on the first floor of the house? There was a need for accommodation for one of the assistant managers so a separate apartment had been created. It had its own door and staircase. We didn't mind did we? Who was I to report to work-wise? No-one really. Just spend time getting to know everyone and the place. Meet the guests.

I felt like crying my eyes out too.

The aura that George and Pat had described enveloped me as I went to work the next morning. I had no office and no one knew where it was to be. No one seemed to really know who I was or what I was doing there. I was expected to solve spurious problems with no background to work off and no one to provide it.

The chambermaids' rota had (apparently without consultation) been changed the day before the MD left the island. A strike was threatened. The head chef thought that the maître d' was useless and he couldn't work with him. What was I going to do about it? The import license for French wines had been turned down due to import restrictions. The affluent American clientele would not settle for plonk. The MD would know who to speak to. What was I going to do about it in the interim? The hotel was overbooked by thirteen rooms the next Friday. Where did I want to place the bounced guests? And presumably I would tell them. Oh yes! They were a group of lawyers and their spouses from New York. The deep fat fryer had been condemned as dangerous – it should have been replaced a year ago. As far as anyone knew, no import licence had been applied for to replace it. Yes the menu could be changed to obviate the need for fried food, but could I imagine serving burgers without chips to Americans – or anyone else for that matter? The concessionaire who ran the water sports had had a meeting with the MD some months ago about the delay in making payments. Nothing had been done and over $10,000 was outstanding. Would I authorise the payment?

Yes. I had been well and truly set up. But by whom? And why?

A couple of days later, my bleeper went off as I was checking the tables and chairs along the beach front. It was the devil of a job to see that the staff left these clean and tidy after the beach bar closed. The girl behind the reception desk was pallid, even though she was quite dark skinned.

'Come into the back,' she beckoned. 'I don't want anyone to hear this.' I followed her into the screened-off area where telephone reservations were taken. 'I have just had a telephone call from the couple in room 29. They told me there's a man on a deckchair outside their window who hasn't moved for hours. I went to take a look. I think he's dead.'

'Wait here and don't tell a soul,' I said.

I walked onto the beach and headed in the direction of room 29. The light was beginning to fail. Dusk comes early in the Caribbean. No-one was on the beach except the man outside room 29. The net curtains of the room rippled. I knelt beside the deckchair. The occupant, a large white man, was warm, but so had the sun been until half-an-hour before. But I could detect no pulse in his wrist or his neck. His sunglasses and book had fallen onto the sand. I had no idea what to do. Back at reception I asked the girl to summon a doctor.

'Do we know who the guest is?' I asked her.

'No,' she replied.

The bell on the reception desk pinged. Carrie, I thought the girl was called, was in no fit state to deal with anything so I went out to the front desk.

'Can I help you Madam?' I asked the anxious looking white woman on the other side of the desk.

'I've lost my husband. I walked into town to do some shopping and left him on the beach. He said he would meet me back in our room. That must have been several hours ago.'

I knew then what was coming. I now had a corpse and in a few minutes I would have a widow.

'What room are you in?' I asked.

'Twenty eight'. I knew it. I looked down at the card index. Mr and Mrs Ian Ingram from Halifax, England.

'Mrs Ingram?'

'Yes.'

Should I pretend there was nothing wrong? Should I show her the man on the beach and ask her if this was Mr Ingram? Mercifully, a man in a suit was approaching the reception desk. He carried a bulky bag.

He turned to Mrs Ingram and said in a strong Jamaican accent, 'Please excuse me for interrupting. I am a doctor and I believe there is an emergency.'

'Doctor please follow me,' I said. 'Mrs Ingram please have a seat. I will be right back.'

But she knew. Her upper lip quivered. 'It's Ian isn't it? He's the emergency isn't he?'

'We don't know yet,' I said gently. 'Please wait here.'

'No. I'm coming with you. Where's Ian? What's the matter with him?'

I couldn't see any way round it. 'Doctor. Mrs Ingram. Please follow me.' I led them to the deckchair outside room 29. The darkness was now broken only by the soft light of the electric lanterns on the hotel's walls and by the glow of a chalky moon. The crashing of the surf onto the beach seemed inappropriate. The net curtains in room 29 ruffled.

'It is Ian. He's dead isn't he?' Her voice was faltering. The doctor knelt in the sand and took a stethoscope from his bag. He touched the instrument to the man in various parts of his body.

'Yes. He's dead,' he confirmed in a matter of fact voice. 'I'm sorry.'

'Mrs Ingram,' I said. 'I'm so sorry. I just need to talk to the doctor. Can I take you back to reception?' I asked.

'Let's both take Mrs Ingram back,' the doctor suggested. 'I need a few details and Mrs Ingram may need some help.' In the end we both escorted the now-sobbing woman back to her room which I opened with my master key. The doctor gave Mrs Ingram a pill and asked me to fetch her a glass of water.

'His doctor back home said he shouldn't travel all this way,' Mrs Ingram volunteered. 'He hasn't been well. But he insisted. Said that all he needed was a break. What happens to Ian?' She looked from the doctor to me. 'I want to take him home.'

'We'll sort that out,' I said.

She seemed to be calming down. 'Please leave me now. I need to make some phone calls. I'll have to tell the children. We have two girls and a boy. They thought the world of their dad. Are you the manager?' She asked, looking at me.

'Yes. I'm the general manager. John.'

'Thank you for your help, John. And you doctor. John, could you please tell the girl on reception that I will be making some calls to England. It's only lunchtime there. And don't worry about the bill. I have plenty of money. Even more now. Ian was a very successful man.' She started to sob again.

'Just dial zero if you need anything.' I said. The doctor and I let ourselves out.

'What do I do now?' I asked the doctor.

'He'll have to be taken to the morgue.'

'Do we get an ambulance?'

'They won't attend once the patient is dead.'

'Then how do I get him to the morgue? Do they have a collection service?'

'Not after 6 p.m.'

'I can't leave him on the beach.'

'No indeed. Do you have a hotel van you could put him in?'

'Yes. But the body is halfway along the beach frontage. It's several hundred yards to the nearest road access. And he's a big man.'

'You'll need help. Your staff won't help you.'

'Why not?'

'Duppies. They're terrified of the dead. I'll have to help you. I'll come back in the morning and do the paperwork. Get the van as near to the body as you can please. I'll meet you at the beach.'

I collected the keys to the hotel van from reception and updated Carrie, then drove it to the nearest access point to room 29. The doctor and I more lugged than carried Mr Ingram to the van and lifted him in.

'The morgue is at the back of the hospital on Third Street,' he said. 'I'll see you in the morning.'

'Thank you,' I said.

Mr Ingram deceased and I were left together. Duppies! I found the morgue with difficulty. Many of the overhead lamps were not working. It was hard to make out the street names. The man in charge of the morgue wanted a lot of information which I did not have. I did not even know the name of the doctor. In desperation I slipped him fifty US dollars. I could not possibly be left to look after the dead man all night. He fetched a trolley and took the body away.

I returned to the hotel to check on Mrs Ingram. There was no reply to my gentle knock on the door of room 28. The doctor, true to his word, returned the next morning and we dealt with the business of exporting a corpse. Mrs Ingram was surprisingly put together.

Chris received a letter from her dad which had taken two weeks to come. Audrey was in hospital with flu. Chris smelt a huge rat – as did I – and she phoned Doncaster Royal Infirmary. So far the only benefit of our new position was having a phone in the house. Despite relentless questioning of anyone to whom she was allowed to speak, no-one was about to give Chris a reason why Audrey was in hospital. Influenza was a euphemism for 'don't know'. We booked a flight for her and the boys for the next day and I took them to Montego Bay airport.

I returned from Montego Bay to find all the guests on the road and the kitchen ablaze, firefighters manning hoses from every angle. The wretched deep fat fryer had finally taken its revenge. In my absence, other members of the management team had had to make decisions. Coaches had been hired to take all the guests to another hotel for dinner. No longer term decisions could be made until the extent of the damage could be assessed.

I was not involved in those decisions. Two days later I was arrested for being on the island illegally and for working without a valid permit. I was ignominiously handcuffed in the lobby of the hotel and taken to the police station, where I was interrogated by officers who clearly thought that the situation was white man's comeuppance.

I was escorted to a cell and locked up with much rattling of bars and clanking of keys. The condition of the cell made me appreciate that a custodial sentence would be a fate almost worse than death. No-one told me how long I was to be kept in the cell. There was no daylight from which to ascertain the time. Some muck was provided by way of dinner – I presumed. I was unable to sleep even though I was exhausted.

Eventually I was released and told not to return to work premises until my case had been tried. My observation that I lived at the hotel and therefore was obliged to return to it, caused disproportionate consternation and a more senior man was consulted. He told me that the only alternative was to be kept in prison. He suggested that I would not like this. Eventually it was agreed that I could return to my lodgings providing that I had no contact with the hotel's management, staff or guests. I readily agreed to this.

The Magistrates Court was an unimposing building. Proceedings faithfully followed the British system. We went through the 'all stand' bit as the magistrate entered. I was the only white person in attendance. The solicitor who was representing me had advised me in a very brief consultation that I should plead guilty as, it transpired, I did not have a work permit, nor a leg to stand on.

The sun was shining and it was a lovely Jamaican day. The palm trees outside the courthouse were swaying in the balmy breeze. I felt keenly aware of my own stupidity. Or was it naivety? But I was over thirty years old. It was time to stop making silly mistakes. I had a wife and family to look after. The solicitor told me that I would almost certainly be required to leave the island. And that's what happened.

Chapter Twelve

GROSVENOR HOUSE

D uring the flight back I was introspective. We were homeless, job-
less and Audrey was seriously ill. The children had no schools to
go to. My wife must be beginning to doubt my judgement.

We stayed at Reg and Audrey's house. The daily vigil at the hospital
was harrowing. No medical illumination was forthcoming. Audrey was
not only ill but understandably very depressed. This state of affairs went
on for many weeks. She was angry with Chris – and presumably with me
but she didn't say so to me – for going to live abroad and depriving her of
her grandsons. She was angry with Reg. She knew she was dying and was
angry with everyone and everything.

Looking back on that sad time I think we should have done more to
find out what was really wrong with her. We were told that she had an
infection which was damaging her vital organs, but the situation was left
with no further diagnosis due to a strike by laboratory technicians. This
led to septicaemia and her unnecessary death at the age of just fifty-four.
But in those days, particularly in South Yorkshire, doctors were gods and
nurses were their angels. You didn't challenge them. These days you would
raise merry hell. We should have done just that.

I had never in all my life witnessed anything approaching the extent of Chris's grief when Audrey died. The last time Chris saw her (I wasn't there – we kept the boys away: this scenario wasn't for impressionable children) Audrey had told Chris what she thought of her, me, Reg, Jamaica, God, life and just about every other imaginable entity. As a consequence they had not said goodbye in a manner that reflected their true love. This made the whole tragic business twice as bad as it would anyway have been.

I was offered the position of Apartments Manager at Grosvenor House Hotel in Park Lane. This was a Trust Houses Forte hotel. Past sins had come back to revisit me as the board of the new merged company (not yet renamed the smoother sounding Trusthouse Forte) had by then moved their offices to my patch, which was the whole of the south block of this enormous building.

I loathed the ethos of the place from day one. I was responsible for 155 flats of varying sizes let to tenants ranging from cast-off relations of royals from obscure ex-empire countries to multinational companies. The former wanted me to have gin and tonic with them before their lunch was served and the latter thought I was their resident PA. And then there were the playboys from the Middle East – and their playgirls!

I also had to look after the shops. I knew nothing about retail. And the health club and spa. I knew little more about that. I also had to do duty management, which mostly involved people claiming to be personal friends of Charles Forte who would ensure that I was fired if I did not get them a room. I wished!

The other aspect of duty management was dealing with the IRA bomb threats which occurred on an almost daily basis. Our bleepers had two pitches: normal for the "I want a room or I'll get you fired" type of situation, and one with a fast shrill tone for bomb threats. Quite why we should have been exposed to this level of danger was somewhat beyond me but "first on the scene" was the order of the day and a requirement to make a decision whether to evacuate the building or not. We never did. It would have involved some two thousand people flooding out onto Park Lane – three thousand or more if big banquets were taking place.

The pile of documents which were the tenancy agreements for the flats were years out of date or non-existent. It was an utter disgrace and the re-sultant workload which I decided to undertake as a matter of self-respect was as backbreaking as it was really outside my experience. And the result-ant battles with tenants over rents which were also obsolete were upset-ting, particularly since the situation was based on indefensible negligence. I did it and got no thanks.

I hated the General Manager, who treated me little better than the creep at Browns. The hotel swarmed with overpromoted sycophants seeking tips for services which should have been standard. London was in boomtime and decent rooms were at a premium due to demand from British busi-nessmen, Americans and Arabs. I was once offered £1,000 to get an Arab a room for the night. Had there been an empty room I might have been tempted. The standing order issued by the powers that existed then was to overbook the hotel rooms by fifteen percent every night to compensate for no-shows. The situation with credit card guarantees was much less clear than it subsequently became. Hotels, airlines, restaurants, clubs, railways, car hire firms all suffered. Thus the policy was not altogether unreason-able. But the furore which we duty managers had to stomach when the overbooking exceeded the no-shows and guests had to be bounced was very unpalatable, particularly when quality rooms could not be found in comparable hotels. The "I'll see that Charles Forte fires you" brigade were onto an almost daily winner.

My principal job was to maximise profits from the flats for which I was responsible. This objective was hindered by inability to get authorisa-tion for expenditure to refurbish flats when they became vacant at the end of tenancy agreements. People will, by and large, put up with an inferior hotel bedroom for a night or two. It depends of course on how much the guest is paying. But they will not take on the tenancy of a flat for months or even years unless it is in top condition.

I had one particular flat – a large one overlooking Park Lane – which became vacant. The previous tenant had died towards the end of a long lease. In its existing condition it was unlettable. I frequently had to give prospective tenants a tour of flats which were vacant or due to become so. This was a very boring chore at which I was however rather good. Some people made appointments, but mostly, particularly Arabs and Ameri-

My paternal grandfather Ernest Nicholson Cunliffe (Lt. Col.) showing King George V and Queen Mary around the Royal Army Medical Corps Facility at Manchester during World War One. He and his wife Harriet, my grandmother, moved to Gilpin Lodge at the end of the war, but grandfather died in March 1919, aged 41, from tuberculosis contracted in Flanders

Grandfather Cunliffe was a prominent officer, doctor and administrator in the Royal Army Medical Corps

Auntie Gertie on the porch of old Knipe Tarn

Knipe Tarn was the scene of family gatherings, picnics, walks, fishing and boating from when Auntie Gertie bought it. Elizabeth and I joined in these events in later years. Above and above right, in the middle of the photographs, is my father Tony, at Knipe in the 1930s. Also pictured above left, on the the left, and below, third from the left

A family gathering at Knipe. Auntie Adgie is on the left

A party at Gilpin Lodge, and more activities at Knipe Tarn

My parents, Tony and Mary Cunliffe, on their wedding day

The author learning to read

My older sister Elizabeth

Elizabeth

Dad in later life

Me (above, front right), taking notes in a Reception lecture at Battersea College (right) in the early 1960s Below, in my morning suit as a trainee restaurant manager at J Lyons and Co during my third year

Christine relaxing with friends after a long day on the *RMS Transvaal Castle*, one of her summer work experience postings

Our wedding day,
on 5 February
1966, at the
Catholic Church
in Bentley, near
Doncaster

Below left: A
telegram from me
me in New York
to Chris, hastily
arranging our
wedding so that
she could join me
to work in the US

The Knipe Tarn
visitors book,
6 February 1966.
Address: Waldorf
Astoria, New York

Chris on the old *Queen Mary* from Southampton, approaching Manhattan, in February 1966

Outside the apartment in Flushing

The 'bed alcove' in Flushing

Across Manhattan towards Central Park

A day off at Jones Beach, Long Island. The ban on socks with sandals had not yet been invented!

JOHN CUNLIFFE

The Waldorf-Astoria
A HILTON HOTEL
NEW YORK

ELDORADO 5-3000

Leaving work at the Waldorf.
Above, the hotel in the
1960s, and my business card

With Mary

So in love

Head waiter Walter Pattison in the restaurant of the new Beech Hill Hotel.

LUXURY IN LAKELAND

LUXURY accommodation coupled with superb French cuisine and unsurpassed Lakeland views from the restaurant lounge and from many of the bedrooms for good measure. This is the formula which 60-year-old Manchester accountant Mr. Bernard Myers believes will achieve success for the Beech Hill Hotel at Cartmell Fell on the banks of Lake Windermere.

Beech Hill will be one of the few residential hotels in the Lake District to remain open all year—the majority are seasonal and concentrate on good plain food and homely accommodation. "I believe that with accommodation of luxury standard and top flight service we can attract business, including small conferences and seminars, from all of the northern cities including Manchester, Liverpool, Leeds and Newcastle, all year," he said.

£100,000 Scheme

Mr. Myers acquired the 18-bedroom hotel 12 months ago from Lord Wakefield. In the past three months he has carried out a £100,000 modernisation scheme which has involved the replanning of the public rooms, provision of a split level restaurant with panoramic views of Windermere, and reconstruction of bedrooms with built-in furniture, the majority with private bathrooms.

His maxim has been simple—to rally round him consultants and specialists to advise and plan the perfect Lakeland hotel. Having established his requirements Mr. Myers leaves his advisers to get on with the job.

Manager of Beech Hill is Mr. John Cunliffe, a product of the University of Surrey Department of Hotel Management. After leaving college he worked at the Waldorf Astoria, New York, becoming banqueting manager. On returning to this country in 1967 he joined Browns Hotel, London as assistant manager.

At Beech Hill he has the opportunity to try out some of his own ideas. For example, guests staying three days or more are offered a 15 per cent discount on luncheon and dinner taken in the restaurant.

Explained Mr. Cunliffe: "While we want to encourage guests to dine in the restaurant we do not want to restrict their movements in a tourist area by en pension terms or create the feeling

Reception foyer and lounge of the Beech Hill Hotel, Windermere. In the picture, Mr. John Cunliffe, general manager.

they were paying for food not taken.

Normal bed and breakfast terms range from 55s to 75s per person (inclusive of morning tea and newspaper).

Already there are plans to increase bedroom accommodation. Six rooms on the second floor of this four-storey building, at present required for staff accommodation, will be released as soon as a new staff accommodation block has been built. There are also longer term plans for a further bedroom annexe.

A new extension has been built to accommodate the kitchen which has delighted the chef, Mr. Bernard Sigrist, who moved to Beech Hill from The Bridge, Prestbury. Main suppliers were E. W. Proctor Ltd., Huddersfield. The kitchen is not encumbered by vegetable preparation and storage sections, which have been located at service road level and connected to the kitchen by service lift.

Said Mr. Myers: "With a hotel of this type there is always a strong temptation

to exploit the delightful old world atmosphere. Many lakeland hotels fall into that category.

"But I believed we would only succeed as a thoroughly modern hotel and this has influenced all our thinking."

Mr. Cunliffe said H.C.S. Management Consultants had been called in to advise on accounting procedures. The hotel also had its own engineering and electrical consultants. "Management is an all embracing function and, I recognise that many aspects of hotel operation call for expert advice. In many hotels there is a failure to recognise that the manager cannot know everything about every aspect of hotel operation nor keep abreast of every new technique.

Other key members of Mr. Cunliffe's staff of 25 are Mr. John Maxwell, assistant general manager, who was formerly manager of the Swan Hotel, Newby Bridge; and Mr. Walter Pattison, formerly restaurant manager at the Alma Lodge, Stockport, who is head waiter.

A Ring & Brymer ('Caterers Since 1690') van in the City of London in the early 1970s

Chris with Barney at Apex Close (and a partial view of the multi-screw sideboard...) Below, a presentation at the Café Royal, with me back row, fourth from right

An article from Hotel and Caterer in 1968 on the Beech Hill Hotel. 'At Beech Hill Mr John Cunliffe has the opportunity to try out some of his own ideas.'

Cyprus: The Apollonia Beach Hotel, Limassol

Jamaica: A day out in the Blue Mountains

Bath time

Christine's dad, Reg, acting the goat on a visit to Jamaica. Christine's mum, Audrey, with the boys

My taxi to work from Norbrook Mews in Kingston

Looking on as visitors meet trainee chefs at the Jamaica Pegasus hotel

Pegasus opens from tomorrow

Jamaica's newest convention hotel, the 350-room Jamaica Pegasus, opens for business tomorrow and will be the venue that evening for the fourteenth annual Rotary Ball.

The hotel which is operated by Trust Houses Forte Hotels Limited (International Division) in association with British Airways, will be officially opened in September following the completion of the late night restaurant "The Talk of the Town" on the seventeenth floor.

Local as well as international groups and organisations have already been making use of the additional room accommodation

The Daily Gleaner on the opening of the Pegasus

Enjoying the sun and the lifestyle at a friend's rum palace!

Barney and the toy gun that saved the day...

A function
at Grosvenor
House

The State Dining Room,
10 Downing Street

From left, Abraham Bejerano, general
manager, the London Press Centre;
Ron Zanre, Managing Director of the
Restaurant and Banqueting Division;
John Coomb, Director, Ring & Brymer
City Catering

A City of London banquet

Receiving the Freedom of the City of London, with Chris, Barney, and Ring & Brymer Chairman and former Lord Mayor of London Sir Lindsay Ring (second from right)

His Holiness Pope John Paul II arriving at Coventry on his 1982 visit to the United Kingdom. Three hundred thousand people turned out for the first mass, at Coventry. But we had catered for an expected 700,000...

cans, just turned up and demanded to be attended to immediately.

On the day in question a resplendent Arab, who claimed to be a Royal, arrived with two assistants and stated that they wanted to rent a flat immediately for a period of five years. This was big money. He loved the now-vacant flat overlooking Park Lane and said he would put down a deposit of one year's rent providing that he could have access in four weeks' time. He demanded an answer there and then. It was a Saturday. No top brass around. No-one to consult. I calculated what the rent would be for five years and decided that no sane person in senior management could turn this down. I accepted the deposit and agreed a date.

On the Monday, at the daily managers' meeting known as "Morning Prayers", I explained the circumstances. The House Manager, my immediate boss, agreed that I had taken the only sensible action. Together with Mary, the Executive Housekeeper, with whom I had a great relationship, we put together a decorating and furnishing plan and costed it. We included dates for the various activities. The appropriate form was typed up to get approval for the expenditure. The House Manager signed it and it was sent on its merry way – a route designed to be as complex as possible and to accommodate the potential for maximum indecisiveness.

Nothing happened. No assurances were given. The tenant-to-be turned up regularly to check on progress. My life became impossible. It turned out the tenant *was* a Royal, and eventually the foreign office became involved. But it was almost too late in the day. Mary and I had to spend the best part of a week finishing off the flat and buying soft furnishings at retail prices.

The benign attitude of the old Forte company directors had disappeared. The rule about management visibility was still in force. I particularly suffered as the day job generated massive amounts of paperwork. The temptation to slip off to the office was huge. Sometimes I did. Once in doing so I was absent from the lobby when a particularly repulsive director shareholder had come in and sought the duty manager. None of the idiots on duty thought to call my office. The shindig that took place the next morning was out of all proportion.

The director responsible for the hotel was the one I had clashed with in Jamaica. Fortunately I had very little to do with him, but I could feel the malignancy in the background. The only compensation was that there were some very charming people in the line management team. I think the general feeling about the operation and ethos of the place was universal. But it was not discussed. No-one knew for sure who was a spy!

The best times for me at Grosvenor House were when I came in on days off to do paperwork. I brought my own sandwiches and shut myself in my office. No visitors. No phone calls. No 'there's a man in reception who would like to see some flats'. No-one knew I was there.

Chris and I had rented a rather nasty little flat in Hampstead. How she managed juggling the boys and their schools and the job of Restaurant Manager at the Hampstead Post House I did not know then and I do not know now. Once again I was expected to sleep in several times a week. I never understood why when the place crawled with management of various sorts morning, noon and night. But the order of the day was to keep your head down and be in a position to pay the rent.

And then a knight in shining armour rode up. The GM moved on and was replaced by John Donnithorne. Into my office one day strode this tall, debonair, smart, sophisticated, intelligent, experienced man who introduced himself to my secretary, Helena, and then asked if he might sit down and have a cup of coffee with me. Gin would have been better – I was not accustomed to being treated like this.

In the space of maybe ten minutes he had appraised himself about me, Chris, the kids, my background and explained the same about himself. He said he had read the correspondence about the leases and apologised on behalf of the company. He said that he was restructuring the activities of the management and that it was clearly outrageous that I had had to do duty management along with all my other responsibilities, and that this would cease with immediate effect. This of course included being required to sleep in and responding to bomb scares, which became the role of specialist trained security officers. He was a Trust Houses legend of the old school and had managed prestigious properties in the UK and abroad. My life changed and my self-respect began to return.

I left Grosvenor House not long after this astounding metamorphosis, and parted company with John on the best of terms. I believe a legal man was appointed to look after the leases of the flats. What a pity I had not been paid a legal salary. John was later to play an important role in the direction of Gilpin Lodge.

The only other benefit to come out of this otherwise drab and unrewarding job was meeting Richard Marriott, who was the front office manager at Grosvenor House. We did not have a great deal to do with each other but our paths crossed then and were to continue to do so shortly thereafter.

Richard is still a part of the team at Gilpin having come there with Chris and me in 1987. So we have known each other for more than forty years.

Chapter Thirteen

RING & BRYMER: ROUND TWO

Ron Zanre phoned me not long after my chat with John and asked me in so many words what I was doing wasting my time when he had a serious job for me at Ring & Brymer. Ron had taken over as Managing Director of the Restaurant and Banqueting Division which embraced the Café Royal, Ring & Brymer, a score of fancy restaurants, and for some reason a raft of pubs up and down the country.

I did not take much persuading, even though life had become very different at Grosvenor House under John Donnithorne.

Not much had changed since I had last been at Sun Street, particularly in the way things were done. Interestingly for me, in terms of the direction of my career, my raison d'être was not unlike that at the Café Royal.

I could not begin here, never mind finish describing "the City", which to most people, myself included until my involvement, was just a part of London where the policemen wore different hats and where the Bank of England and St Paul's Cathedral were located. In fact, the administration of the City, the relationship between the Sheriffs and the Old Bailey, the role of the Lord Mayor and the activities of the City Livery Halls are worthy of a book in their own right, and indeed many have been written.

Catering and entertainment were behind every breath, whether it be a state banquet at the Guildhall for a visiting Royal or a dinner at the Mansion House as a platform for the Chancellor of the Exchequer. And the politics behind who got catering contracts was akin to the court of Joseph Stalin. The consequences of failure (either to get a contract or to deliver the goods satisfactorily) were not entirely different either. The eight grams!

But, the administration of Ring & Brymer needed focus, and the Deputy Director, the job to which I was appointed, was additionally responsible for the catering at the Farnborough Airshow, and for securing the contracts. These amounted to approximately 60,000 lunches in forty or so different locations over a ten-day period. The selling of these contracts and administration of the event was massive and the impact on the firm's profitability in the Farnborough years (bi-annual) was make or break, as I came to find out the hard way.

It was perhaps indicative of the way that Ring & Brymer was run, that very little assistance was afforded to the new man in charge, the previous incumbent having been promoted elsewhere. The methodology of costing out the contracts was based more on likelihood of acceptance of a price rather than a properly and scientifically calculated quotation. While this made a certain amount of sense (in that failure to win a contract rendered the price irrelevant), the resultant impact on the overall financial result of Farnborough as an event was unpredictable. This situation led Ron and I to implement a much more effective way of preparing quotations.

In a hotel or traditional in-house banqueting situation, certainly in any establishment where I had worked, including the Waldorf Astoria, the Café Royal and indeed Ring & Brymer, the selling price of a meal was calculated by taking the food cost and multiplying it by a (normally) fixed number according to the desired profitability. Thus, a food cost of £7 might be multiplied by three to give a selling price of £21, which covered all of the other direct costs (the largest of which was usually staff wages), and a contribution to indirect costs such as the upkeep of the building, housekeeping, insurance, flowers and a host of others, leaving an element of net profit.

Ron and I came to realise that although this methodology sort of worked, it was very crude. It also had the disadvantage (which applied even more to beverage sales) that an expensive bottle of wine, let's say costing £50, had to be sold (using the three times multiplier) for £150, rendering a gross profit of £100. Very nice too! But how many people are going to pay £150 for a bottle of wine, particularly in a banqueting situation where the host may be coughing up for several hundred guests? So the more likely outcome is that the guest settles for a bottle of wine costing £15, selling for £45 and giving a gross profit of £30. £70 less profit than the scenario with the more expensive bottle. And yet, the cost of serving the two bottles was the same, except (if you want to be really nerdy) for the cost of the money invested in the respective bottles. So we came up with a formula for pricing wine, where we added a cash mark up to the cost price of the bottle. Thus we added a £50 mark up to the £50 bottle of wine, giving a selling price of £100 – a third less selling price than under the multiplier method, much more palatable to the client and enabling the company to show a profit of £50: £20 more profit than had the client chosen the cheaper bottle of wine – and they had a better product. Win win. The moral is that you can only bank pounds – not percentages.

At the risk of boring you silly and suspecting that you did not buy this book in order to become hotel accountants, so much for the wines. But going back to food. In peripatetic catering situations the costs of transport, porterage, often staff transport, sometimes (like Farnborough and Paris airshows) staff accommodation and meals, staff entrance tickets (a very big overhead at airshows) and the like made a traditional multiplier quite useless and delivered a false selling price. Hence (I'm nearly finished!), we came up with a formula which took into account all of the anticipated costs (including food and liquor), to which was added a static cost per guest to cover central costs (like management and running the depot), which was finally topped up with a required element of profit. Voilà, the selling price.

In alternate years to Farnborough, Ring & Brymer undertook catering at the Paris Airshow. This was a smaller operation than Farnborough but the logistics were more complicated. The French caterers hated the involvement of British ones and having failed to get us banned, went out of their way to make life as difficult as possible – including (so we believed) looking after the French police and encouraging them to make it as hard as possible for us to get around the site. Then we had the language problem which complicated arranging supplies. We took all our own staff with us, as our clients at Paris tended to be British companies who had become used (at Farnborough) to Mary being behind the bar, Fred serving the drinks and Derrick and his team doing the cooking. The staff found being in Paris and away from home great fun, and we not infrequently had to deal with incidents, usually alcohol-fuelled. I won't pretend that the management didn't have some fun too, and dinners after an exhausting day could be amusing – also alcohol-fuelled!

I recall one year at Paris when, on the day of our arrival, the door of a refrigerated lorry came off its hinges and fell onto Ray Seaborne, Ring & Brymer's Senior Head Waiter. Ray was a loveable rogue and a great showman, but rather too close to many of the staff under his command – particularly the female ones. I wasn't too sure how badly hurt Ray was but he insisted it was just a bruise and that he did not need medical attention, never mind hospitalisation or to be returned to the UK. Either of the latter options would have been a disaster. Ray looked after our biggest client which relied on him totally.

Back at the hotel we were staying in, Ray said he didn't want dinner and would settle for a sandwich in bed, and probably about ten whiskies! Halfway through our own dinner in the Novotel restaurant I thought I had better check on him and took the lift to the floor on which I thought his room was. I forgot that in many French hotels the ground floor was Floor 1, and thus I arrived on the wrong floor. Nor did I check the room number – I just threw open the door of the room which I thought was Ray's (which as fate would have it had been left unlocked) and shouted into the darkness, 'How are you, you old bastard?' On switching on the light I realised that this was not Ray's room. Rather a startled couple were by now sitting up in bed. The male part of the couple bawled at me in a frightfully English accent to get out of his room. I fled. I found Ray's room on the floor above and relieved him of a large tot of whisky.

The selling of contracts to Farnborough and Paris clients varied from easy to very difficult. Some clients took the view that if we had done a good job the previous year then they were comfortable to appoint us again, and there was usually no dogfight over prices. At the other extreme were companies who had had other caterers in the previous years, but which we wanted to poach. Our success or failure in getting these contracts was partially due to how well the other caterers had done.

One Monday in November, the CEO of an important American corporation which made parts for aero engines turned up at Sun Street and demanded to see me. It was the day of the Lord Mayor's banquet – probably the most important and prestigious event in the calendar. I was at the Guildhall. Mr Graham (I shall call him), from Seattle, was not taking no for an answer and claimed to have come over personally from Seattle to see me. My secretary got hold of me and I talked to Mr Graham on the telephone. I explained that I had an appointment with the Lord Mayor in ten minutes and that it was, with great regret, impossible for me to come to Sun Street to meet him today. Would tomorrow do? Or any other day? Any time. Anywhere. No, it would not – he was flying back to the US that night. He hung up on me.

My secretary phoned back and told me that Mr Graham had flounced out saying that he did not want to see anyone else and that we had not heard the last of this. We hadn't indeed. Ron got hold of me the next morning. Mr Graham had caused a major stink with the Society of British Aerospace Companies (which organised the Farnborough Airshow), the secretary of which had got through to Ron's boss. I was to telephone Mr Graham immediately and arrange to see him in Seattle that week. The nuance was not that this was all rather silly and that we had to placate the man, particularly as we might get his contract, but rather that we were rude and inefficient. We did get Mr Graham's contract and I used the time in that part of the US to call on other existing and potential clients.

Events at Farnborough and Paris were very hard work, fraught with last-minute problems which could not have been anticipated (like the breakdown of a vehicle or the above incident with Ray) and offered almost irresistible temptations to ease the pain with a glass or two of vino. Our clients liked to look upon us as friends and were keen to ply us with the odd glass – from bottles chosen to persuade their clients to order the odd Airbus or a brace or two of Rolls Royce aero engines. A soupçon of Dom Perignon or vintage Condrieu can do wonders when an apparently insoluble problem raises its head. It is all too easy (at the time of making the decision to have this odd glass) to forget that the decision, once made, to accept the libation, makes the solution to the original problem even harder to solve.

I usually succeeded in resisting this temptation. But since I said right at the beginning of this book that truthfulness was the order of the day, I will not claim total blamelessness. But for some of my colleagues in other catering companies (of course) a good lunch had become an expected part of the daily routine. Ron arrived one afternoon at the Paris Airshow, and having satisfied himself that all was tickety-boo with the Ring & Brymer clients, he decided to check out the competition. We all knew each other and were friendly enemies. We entered the compound of "Diana Dors Caterers'" (yes – a fictitious firm) and asked for Henry Bossman.

Henry appeared and tottered over to where Ron and I were standing. 'Ah Ron. John. Lozely to see you. I was just passing the time of day with our many esselent clients. Come in and join us in a glass of fizz.' In those days, fizz meant the real thing. Not Prosecco. 'Ists very good'. At Churchill Caterers (another fictitious company) just down the road, Ferdinand Topman greeted us in much the same way. These gentlemen (and such they were) did in effect visit the airshows to show that their clients were so important that they had to be there. Ron was puzzled.

Chris and I had talked at length about the direction of her career. Rightly or wrongly, and it probably has to be admitted wrongly, what I did seemed to be regarded as the lead role, with Chris following on behind. It was almost certainly the way things were in those days, but that did not, with hindsight make this approach right. But there was no doubt that, under the circumstances, Chris had to be responsible for the boys and as such her job had to accommodate that. This effectively ruled out any jobs with other than standard hours. Chris has always been ambitious and keen to work. She never wanted to sit at home and just be mummy, although she was a great and loving mother. The boys were at school by now which clearly left the school holidays as a problem. We did not have grandparents to help out. I think we took the view that we would cross that bridge almost as we came to it.

She landed an enormous job which by and large met her requirements, and that was as the head of the school meals service for the Borough of Bromley, where she was responsible for 120 schools and over 600 staff. I took my hat off to her in the most heartfelt way for accepting such a position at the same time as looking after the boys. I would like to think that I helped as much as I could, but my hours were all over the place, with frequent absences away altogether for considerable periods. We spent many days off together working on new kitchen plans for her schools and preparing addresses to her staff. She was profoundly fulfilled in this important job, even though it did lack glamour as such.

She found the slightly civil service culture a strange contrast to the profit-led ethos of previous employers. She particularly disliked the fact that the kitchens in her schools, large buildings stuffed full of expensive commercial catering equipment, were only used for a few hours a day, Monday to Friday, in term times. She discussed with me using them for private functions or meals for old people. But whenever she broached this topic with her bosses their eyes dimmed. She was encouraged to research modern equipment and to buy it, even if such a purchase was not strictly necessary. On one occasion she mooted that she might not be able to spend all of her capital budget for the year. She was commanded to do so, lest the budget be cut for the following year.

We had bought a lovely townhouse overlooking Beckenham Place Park. Life was very busy and very good, and quite often I did get weekends off. The City and Government like to be home at weekends, and functions on Saturdays and Sundays were the exception. But, conversely, weddings, bar mitzvahs and outdoor catering activities such as Twickenham rugby matches were invariably at weekends. But it was probably, from an hours of work point of view, the best I had ever had it – or ever would again. For almost the first time, we started doing things as a family. Because we did the catering at the Chelsea Flower Show I was given honorary membership of the Royal Horticultural Society, and visits to Wisley garden near Guildford were a favourite. They did the best afternoon teas in the world.

Ron had in fact urged me to make obtaining weekend business a crusade. While most businesses within the group were busy at weekends, particularly the hotels, restaurants, airports, motorway service areas and pubs, noises had apparently been made on high about R&B's supposed slothful weekends. Little did they know.

The Chelsea Flower Show was a feather in my cap and a big activity in our annual calendar. It had taken much work, persuasion and hospitality to wrest it from a rival company who had done it for years. Probably the biggest and most prestigious horticultural show in the world, Chelsea was established in 1862 and in recent times catered for 157,000 visitors a year, limited only by the capacity of the eleven-acre site. Visitors pay as much as £65 for a full-day ticket. And we nearly lost the contract on day one of year one. The first bus bringing the staff to man the public snack bars had been involved in an accident and it took an hour to get another bus to bring them in. To compensate for the inevitably appalling service (delivered by management already on site), I made the decision not to charge for the relatively simple fare until it could be properly delivered without queuing for long periods. Others did not agree with this decision, which was perceived as uncommercial. I think it saved the otherwise jeopardised contract.

The only other crisis that year was that we forgot to provide toilet paper for the Queen's loo. This is never used, but the RHS (quite rightly) did not see it in that light. Convenience stores do not abound on Chelsea Bridge Road, not until you pass into Lower Sloane Street and then to Sloane Square. Seldom has a taxi fare been expended on such a critical issue.

The camaraderie at Sun Street had changed little since I was there before. This was in no small measure due to John Coomb's ridiculously low-key style of management. Most of the catering managers had to change from morning suits into dinner jackets in preparation for the evening functions. John, I think oblivious to the strangeness of his behaviour, wandered around the office floor in front of all the secretaries and other female staff, while tying his bow tie (made-up ones were strictly de trop) resplendent in multi-coloured boxers, before putting on his dinner jacket trousers with equally resplendent multi-coloured braces, occasionally taking a pull from a gin and tonic on his desk. No-one cared. This was Ring & Brymer.

And then John Coomb was poached by a rival company. Ron had the decency to discuss with me what we should do. He and I had a very open and honest relationship which served well. He was forthright to a fault and we did not always agree, but he never played politics with me and we both said it as it was. We also knew the score with regards to our lords and masters. Ron told me at this time that he thought the structure of Ring & Brymer, split as it was between City catering and racecourses, with Manchester and Newcastle floating as add-ons, was wasteful and unwieldy. He wanted to put the whole lot under one Director: me.

This was some proposition. There were many older, more seasoned and more experienced men and women than me in Ring & Brymer, including one man who had been a director of the company for years, and Ron's proposal would detonate an explosion within the company and in the City. I accepted. It did!

This was a very important time for Chris and me, for Ring & Brymer, for my many colleagues, and for Ron, and we were embarking on what, for me above all, was a very interesting but also a very turbulent period.

All this was interrupted by Margaret Thatcher succeeding James Callaghan as Prime Minister on 4th May 1979. The ramifications of this were of course far greater for the country – indeed the world – than for me. But I nearly died on the night of the General Election. Callaghan's sojourn as Prime Minister had been a grim time including the country having to take out a loan from the IMF, the "Winter of Discontent" and the constant baying of the trade unions at the heels of progress or recovery. All this following the previous Government headed by Harold Wilson, which had been much of the same poisonous medicine. Everyone was very fed up and business was not easy. Expenditure on luxury catering was not a priority either by Government or the City of London.

Towards midnight on this fateful day, it became likely that the Conservatives would get elected. Chris and I were avidly glued to the television, sitting up in bed. I proposed a toast to celebrate. I went downstairs to the kitchen and poured two whiskies and sodas. In my haste not to miss the action, I had only put on one light. Having made the drinks, I accidentally dropped one of the small glass soda bottles. I picked up the pieces of the broken bottle and put them in the bin.

Heading for the staircase to carry the drinks to our bedroom I was shocked to see that the kitchen floor was covered in blood. I reached for the light switches and put on all the lights. Blood from my right ankle was spurting about six feet across the kitchen floor. I felt no pain at all. I shouted Chris who ran downstairs. I don't think we knew how serious this was nor how much blood I had lost, hence (presumably) we thought an ambulance was not required. We messed around, necessarily no doubt, rousing a neighbour to look after the children. Then Chris took me to Beckenham hospital.

I remember nothing after I fainted in the car. Chris told me the next day when she visited me in hospital that she had been told that I was un-likely to survive the night. But thank God I did. Then, following such ex-cessive blood loss, I had a pulmonary embolism and Chris was again put on standby. I was in hospital for several weeks. It had been a harrowing time for Chris having to anticipate widowhood so young and with two children. I had not been too happy either!

On my first day back at work, Ron phoned me. He welcomed me back and asked after my health, Chris and the boys. Then he told me that there had been a major row over a function at Number Ten which had not gone well, and a very senior minister had contacted Charles Forte on behalf of the new Prime Minister. Although I was technically out of it at that time, it was my responsibility, and I accept my share of blame for not anticipat-ing a significant swing in expectations from those of the previous Labour Governments to those of Margaret Thatcher. Callaghan had been a beans on toast man. Wilson sandwiches and beer. As the country was to come to expect, Maggie was a perfectionist and the catering at 10 Downing Street was no exception. I was instructed to personally attend every Government function for the foreseeable future

This was compounded by the death of my mother at almost exactly the time that this was going on, and by the arrival with surprising speed of a stepmother. At least we thought she was – more of that later. To further complicate matters, Maggie Thatcher (who had been Secretary of State for Education) decided to scale down school meals, and while this had not inconsiderable ramifications for her personally and indeed for society, this process sent Chris and her department into a freefall of work and activity.

Reg had also remarried. His new wife Trudie had been the wife of Audrey's brother George, who had been killed in a motor accident. This made Trudie Chris's stepmother, aunt and Godmother. The whole package! Trudy and George's son Jim – Chris's cousin – now also became Chris's stepbrother. He and his wife Kelly remain close friends and family.

Chris and I had discussed moving to a house with a bit more garden. One day I came into Sun Street from an appointment and my secretary told me that Chris had phoned and she had bought a new house actually in Beckenham Place Park, which was being built and we would be able to move in in six months or so. Would I please arrange the mortgage? She had! I did! By now we were not exactly earning a fortune, but we were on a reasonable package.

I suspected that Ron's proposal for the restructuring of Ring & Brymer was not entirely supported by the parent company. Certainly it felt to me that there were forces working against me rather than with me. I had a lot of friends in the wider company by then, and this feeling was not mine alone. The company was a far cry from the old Forte & Co. The City too was suspicious of John Coomb's departure and I was given a hard time by some of the formidable committees which organised Corporation functions.

Our chairman Sir Lindsay Ring was supremely supportive and helped me a lot. I gradually became accepted and was even given the Freedom of the City. It was a moving ceremony and Sir Lindsay took Chris and me out to lunch afterwards. The lunch was of course out of my budget, and I got stick from Ron for ordering an expensive wine. He always reviewed our expenses, and as a matter of honour had to cross off at least one thing as unacceptable. Parking fines were a hot potato. Sometimes they were truly inevitable in our circumstances and I maintained that they must be regarded as an acceptable business expense. Company rules dictated otherwise. Ron, the only person outside Ring & Brymer that knew the true nature of the beast, supported me.

The reorganisation of Ring & Brymer taught me a lesson which possibly I should have learned before in life, and that is that people hate change. I knew of course that my appointment as Director of Ring & Brymer would cause some waves, but I was not fully prepared for the height of them.

Ron felt that it was essential that I should move out of Sun Street if I was to truly assume responsibility for the other areas of the business. I was uncomfortable with this because I thought that the City clients, the Corporation and the Mayoralty would consider this a second desertion in the wake of John Coomb's departure. Ron's counter-argument was that the reorganisation would be harder for Racecourses, Manchester and Newcastle to accept if Sun Street became a sort of mini head office. Both of these positions held water. In the end, an office was found for me in Saxone House adjoining the Café Royal, where Ron and other members of the Restaurant and Banqueting Division team had their offices.

On balance I think Ron was right, but I missed the fraternalism of Sun Street. As compensation, it was nice to be working in the environment of the Café Royal again. As it turned out, the whole situation was temporary. To this day I shall never quite know why the erstwhile little backwater of Ring & Brymer became of greater interest to the parent company and to Sir Charles, as Charles Forte had become. But there is no doubt that that was the case.

One Farnborough Airshow, at best a stressful and intensely hard working event, was particularly marred by the arrival of a new security manager seconded to Ring & Brymer. The presence of security people never worried me – indeed I regarded them as a part of the management team and as assistance to me. This man, let's call him "G", was another matter altogether who made it extremely clear that he was not working with us but was present to dig up any failures available to find and to report on them.

One day I came back from one of my daily rounds of our clients to find G going through my filing cabinet, which was kept in my Portakabin office. My secretary was in tears having been ignored in requiring G to desist. G and I had the most audible row and I insisted that he leave the compound. He replied that it was the company's filing cabinet – not mine, that the contents were company property – not mine, and that I was in no position to require him to do or not to do anything whatsoever since he reported to the company's chief security officer, who reported to Rocco Forte, Sir Charles's son. All this was technically true but the damage to morale which G was causing was out of all proportion to the potential benefits of his presence.

Ron used to visit most evenings (the team called him the pigeon: he used to fly in, shit all over the place and fly out again) and I protested strongly about G, who was still hanging around making notes. Ron, G and I had a stormy meeting in one of the Portakabin offices and Ron was supremely supportive. The words Hitler and Gestapo were included in the dialogue. Ron made no more progress than I had.

A few weeks later, G's report, submitted initially to the security chief, not to Ron or me, was published. It was a sickeningly one-sided document identifying many failings in the operation with little understanding of the difficulties under which such temporary catering events struggled, or of the many and varied demands of our clients. To add insult to injury, it was announced that G was to become Ring & Brymer's permanent security man based at Sun Street.

These events serve to demonstrate what the company had become. The ramifications of these decisions were truly devastating, and one particularly bright young manager who had been scathingly criticised in G's report on Farnborough left as a consequence.

I too considered my position. Not for the first or last time in my corporate career did I have to weigh up situations which I did not like with the existence of a family and a mortgage.

Not long after G's secondment to Sun Street, another report was filed, again to the then security chief. It pretty much suggested that our managers' relationships with Livery Hall bosses were improper and that the traditional feeding and watering (well, white and red wine and lashings of port actually) of Livery Hall personnel amounted to misappropriation of company property. The police were involved and an arguably less than perfect tradition (which I had for some time intended – at the right moment – to address) was escalated to a totally inappropriate level.

A massive brouhaha followed, and the head chef and cellar manager were fired. I had to do the firing. I was far from convinced that the matter had been handled wisely or fairly. My conscience over these dismissals was eased by the fact that there was a lot more to the problems generated by the unfortunates than was suggested in G's report, but it was a thoroughly unpleasant and badly conducted business. I think everyone came to realise that this state of affairs could not continue and G was moved on.

Another nail in my corporate coffin emanated from the election of a new Lord Mayor who was a director of a major beverage company. He asked that the brands of his company be used in the Mansion House during his year in office. This seemed to my colleagues and I to be so obviously sensible that we started to serve the requested gins, whiskies and brandies. This was picked up in one of the periodic company audits into use of authorised products and I was summoned to Ron's office to decide what to do. Ron thought like me: the guest/client/customer must, within reason, come first. We both knew that to renege on the agreement with the Lord Mayor would have the most damaging consequences, including the probable loss of the Mansion House contract the following year. Ron (who also had four children and a mortgage) told his boss, who reported to Sir Charles, that the arrangement could not be changed. That was the end of it as far as I was concerned, but not (as I was to find out later) as far as Ron was concerned.

The young manager who had resigned over G's report had been the Catering Manager at the Tallow Chandler's Hall – the job I had held when I first joined Ring & Brymer many years before. I interviewed and instantly took a liking to Tony Jupp, who took over as the manager at that livery hall and was to become my most stalwart ally in Ring & Brymer and in a subsequent job. He quickly moved into more senior positions. He and his family became close friends with Chris and me and our boys. They still are.

We had by now moved into the new house in Beckenham Place Park. The boys, whose early education had undoubtedly suffered while in Jamaica, were at St Dunstan's, a delightful day school in Catford, and were thriving. Barney started to discover girls rather early but that's also another story.

It was a profound privilege to be involved in the catering at 10 Downing Street and Ring & Brymer (one of several appointed caterers) undertook many functions there. I was particularly involved when Margaret Thatcher was PM, and I made it my business to be at Number Ten as often as I could be when Ring & Brymer was on duty. She was a charming "client" who showed personal interest in the arrangements, menus and staffing and knew all our senior people by name.

She approached me after one particularly busy cocktail party and said, 'Mr Cunliffe. I am worried about the carpet. There have been a lot of people smoking this evening. I know it's not my carpet,' she smiled, 'but I regard myself as the guardian of Number Ten while I am in office, which will I hope be for a very long time.' She laughed. So she and I crawled around together on the carpet looking for cigarette burns and butts. When she found a stub, she handed it to me. Quite right. Delegation!

The functions at Number Ten were interesting for many reasons. We arranged the menus with Government Hospitality, arguably a more important department of government than might be thought. They presided over (and as far as I know still do) wine cellars second almost to none. I doubt the French government would agree. Ring & Brymer provided the chefs and the food and the waiting staff. But the latter were managed by government butlers.

We R&B management were not allowed in the function rooms. It was a strange setup and one with which I personally was not happy. I never understood how we could excel if we were not managing the function. Even I, stubborn and tactless as I can be, realised that this was not negotiable. The Government Hospitality mandarins were mini-gods, backed up by Foreign Office mega-mandarins when VIPs from other countries were involved.

Additionally, the government butlers, employed only to undertake catering at the highest level, were the ultimate professionals. So we catering managers had to settle for dining in the "outmess" with the Government Hospitality bosses – usually retired brigadiers or admirals. They were normally amiable and interesting men (never women) unless something appeared to be going wrong. A word from one of the butlers to the affect that the PM, or the Secretary for Education or the Minister for Sport was less than enthusiastic and all hell would break loose.

Another interesting aspect of catering at Number Ten was the somewhat strange attitude to security. This was ensured (at face value anyway) by only using one door: the front door onto Downing Street. All other exits and entrances were locked. And of course it worked. Only one door had to be guarded. This was fine except for the poor caterers who had to manage the arrival of their staff, goods and equipment with precision. There were no rising bollards nor gates to the entrance of Downing Street, as there are now, and an arriving dignitary could be whisked up to the front door within seconds. One evening I was unloading from my car (permitted to stop outside Number Ten) when the President of France was delivered to the door. Who has priority? The President or the terrine of foie gras?

I mentioned earlier that in my first period at Ring & Brymer I had on a number of occasions driven the lorries. Although at the time this was merely a convenience for the company, it served two other purposes. One was that I became far more familiar than most of the managers with what went on behind the scenes, including late at night when the transport came back to Sun Street from evening functions. This was to serve me well when I became Director in terms of knowing where there were flaws in the operation. The other purpose was that I got to know in a rather unique way the operatives of the many venues at which we catered. At the livery halls, these men were called "Beadles" and they (and their wives even more so) exerted significant influence in terms of which catering firms catered at their halls. Similar pressures were exerted by officials with differing titles at such places as the Mansion House, the Guildhall and 10 Downing Street, to name but three.

The general feedback that I had received when I was driving was that it was a pleasant change to have a civil and helpful driver. I began to look into this and came to realise that while we concentrated on training our catering staff, we by and large neglected to do this for our drivers, whom we regarded as just that. We were of course missing a massive trick here in that our drivers were pre-eminent ambassadors for the company. By and large they were a fairly uncouth bunch who did not understand the niceties of the hospitality business. When I became Director we took particular pains to ensure that the drivers received proper training, and this went a long way towards improving relations with clients' staff.

One day I took a call from Ron saying that Mr Somigliare (as I will call him) wanted to see us both. He was Ron's boss, who reported to Lord Forte as he had become. As usual we were kept waiting for some time after the scheduled time of the appointment. The unwritten perception over this procedure was that since the company paid your salary, your time was theirs. Finally we were shown in.

'Please sit down Ron, Mr Cunliffe.'

There existed a fairly precise protocol over the use of Christian versus surnames. Ron got 'Ron' because he was only one level down. I got 'Mister' because I was further removed by one level. In turn, Ron referred to Mr Somigliare as such; I called him 'Sir'. Neither tea nor coffee were ever offered.

'Lord Forte attended a dinner at Number Ten last night,' said Mr Somigliare. 'A guest of the PM,' he added rather unnecessarily.

'Was it good, Sir?' I asked. I gave Ron a quizzical look as much as to ask if he knew where this was going. Ron shrugged very slightly.

'What did you think?'

'I wasn't there.'

'Why not?'

'We weren't there last night.'

'We?'

'Ring & Brymer, Sir.'

'Why not Mr Cunliffe?'

'I don't know. We never get invited to tender for functions at Number Ten. The caterer for a particular function just gets nominated by Government Hospitality.'

'Don't we do all the catering there Mr Cunliffe?'

'By no means Sir. Smaller events are sometimes done in-house and a panel of four caterers do the larger functions.'

'Why weren't we there last night then, particularly with the Executive Chairman in attendance?'

'I don't know Sir.'

'Can you find out? Lord Forte wants to know.'

I was silent for a minute. Not for the first time when catering for Government Hospitality Fund was discussed with main board members, I realised that there was little understanding in that corner of how sensitive the issues were. Being a nominated caterer, particularly for Number Ten, was regarded as an honour, which it was, and I dreaded to think how an enquiry into why a particular caterer had been chosen would be taken. Particularly if Lord Forte had been a guest.

'May I be honest Sir?'

He nodded.

'I don't think such a question from me would be appreciated by GHF.'

'What do you mean "from you"?'

Ron, to my relief, stepped in: 'I know what Mr Cunliffe means Mr Somigliare. I've met some of these people. They're nearly all ex-senior ranks in the forces or civil service and pretty precious about who caters for what function.'

'But I can't go back to the boss and tell him that I can't find the answer to his question,' replied Mr Somigliare. 'Besides, surely they choose the best caterer for the more important functions don't they?'

'I just don't know how it works Sir, or who judges which are more important functions,' I said. 'I don't even know who judges which is the best caterer.'

'But Mr Cunliffe, surely you can see that if Lord Forte was a guest it must have been a very important function. You would think that as a courtesy to him they would choose the best caterer.'

I knew we were straying into shark-filled waters.

Ron said, 'I am sure there is an element of sharing out the functions between the caterers. We were there last week doing the banquet for the French President. That's pretty prestigious.' Good work Ron, I thought.

'But Lord Forte wasn't there that night.' Now I knew we were in a vice. 'Find out will you and let me know by tomorrow.'

'It's Saturday tomorrow Sir,' I said.

'Well you work Saturdays don't you Mr Cunliffe?'

I studied my fingernails.

'Anyway,' continued Mr Somigliare, 'that wasn't the main reason for asking you gentlemen to come.'

The red phone on his desk rang. He stood up stiffly to attention and lifted the receiver to his ear. 'Good afternoon Lord Forte.' He listened. The buzz of an animated voice from the telephone was audible, but not the words.

'Ron Zanre and Mr Cunliffe are here now. We're just discussing it, Sir.' More buzz.

'Just as soon as I have an answer.'

Buzz.

'Goodbye Sir.' The phone went down and he sat.

'An answer by Monday. Now, where was I? Yes. The Executive Chairman thought that the staff on duty last night were rather scruffy. Frumpy was the word he used. He thought that the man in charge was overly stern. He lacked hospitality skills.'

I waited, wondering if I had missed or misunderstood something.

'Well?'

I looked at Ron.

'They weren't our staff Mr Somigliare,' Ron said. 'And the man in charge would have been a GHF butler. Our managers and head waiters don't control the functions at Number Ten.'

'But if we are the caterers, surely we must control the catering.'

'But we weren't the caterers last night,' said Ron. 'So I don't understand why you are asking us our opinion about the appearance of the staff.' A touch of impatience had crept into his voice.

Mr Somigliare sighed deeply and leaned back in his luxurious leather chair uncrossing and recrossing his legs under the desk.

'You know, Ron,' he said, 'I get the distinct feeling that you two are not taking me seriously enough. I am relaying the concerns and wishes of the Executive Chairman of this immense company, the largest hotel and catering enterprise in the country and one of the largest in the world and you think you can play with me just because I am not as familiar as you with the workings of one little catering contract. I won't stand for it, and if you can't get me the answers I need then I'll have to talk to someone who can.'

There was a blessed knock on the door and a smiling secretary put her head in.

Excuse me please for interrupting. Mr Somigliare, your next appointment is here. The lady – Miss James – seems very agitated.' The head disappeared and the door closed quietly.

'A la Madonna,' Mr Somigliare (another Italian) muttered. 'By Monday. A suggestion for a new uniform for Downing Street by Monday.'

'But Sir,' I almost stammered, 'we can't dictate how other caterers dress their staff.'

'We can if we buy them out,' he said with a victorious smile.

'By Monday?' I asked.

Ron mouthed 'idiot' at me.

*

The premises from which R&B operated in Manchester were very old, only marginally hygienic and inefficient. One day I was told that we were to take over the banqueting operations of the Grand Hotel in Manchester (a THF hotel obviously) and do the outdoor catering from there. Some genius had worked out that there would be a massive saving in costs to the hotel which could, under this scheme, get rid of all the hotel's banqueting staff and costs.

I was deeply suspicious. I often stayed at the Grand when I absolutely had to stay overnight in Manchester, and parking was a nightmare. Where would our lorries park? Needless to say, this small irrelevance had been overlooked. Arguments were not brooked. It was to happen in six weeks' time. The management of the Grand were furious. How could two different companies share responsibility for the activities of one hotel?

The result was a mess. My previously infrequent visits to Manchester turned into weekly events and since the concept was ill-conceived, there was little chance of a successful outcome, particularly when no-one directly involved believed in the scheme. The man who had been running R&B's activities in Manchester had been fired just as the move to The Grand was about to take place. Sometimes, when a proposed change in personnel is deemed advisable, a misdemeanour can be overlooked and the plan changed. But when a senior manager is caught red-handed undertaking functions in his own name and to his personal profit, using the company's equipment, vehicles and staff, there is not much room for manoeuvre. He had to go.

So who was to oversee the move? Me presumably. Ron knew this was out of the question and pulled out all the stops to recruit a new manager for Manchester. James (we will call him) came to an interview in London with Ron and me and made the great mistake of entering Ron's office, hand extended and saying 'good morning Ron'. This would probably be accepted now or possibly even twenty years later, but in that era it was unforgivable. Ron's reaction was predictable.

'My name is Zanre and that is what you will call me.'

For the second time in a couple of weeks, I saw myself moving indefinitely to Manchester. The interview had got off to a bad start and never really got onto the right track. But James seemed determined to have the job and Ron, who had not fallen in love with James from the start, did his best to scare him off. I did my best to persuade James that if he did succeed in this appallingly difficult appointment, he would find that the rewards and advantages for his career would be overwhelming. James was offered and accepted the position. I contemplated unpacking my suitcase again. James had the sheer determination to pull it off and the marriage between the Grand and R&B entered a purgatorial state. One up from hell!

The visit to The United Kingdom of Pope John Paul II in 1982 was a memorable experience and probably cemented Ron's and my fall from grace within THF. Being the largest event catering company in the country, we were asked to submit proposals for catering at the open air Masses in York, Coventry, Edinburgh, Glasgow and Cardiff. Being a notable Catholic as well as businessmen, this was important to Charles Forte and instructions came from on high (read into that what you will) that this was the ultimate event. We were to get the contract; it was to be conducted like there was no tomorrow (read into that etc.) and every stop (on the organ as well as on the ground) was to be pulled out. I cannot now swear whether the expression "money no object" or similar was used. Knowing the commercial nature of the company, I imagine it was not. But the message and its source was crystal clear.

Meetings which made conclaves of cardinals look like tea parties were hurriedly convened and Ron was obliged to ask me to hand over to him all my responsibilities so that I could concentrate solely on the Papal visit. So no pressure and little ambiguity about where the buck stopped. Thus sometime in late 1981 I explained to Chris and the boys that I would see them whenever.

The first job was to get the business. We felt that it was essential for the success of the endeavour for us to cater at all the venues except London, which was being handled by the Archbishopric of Westminster. We were confident in our extreme arrogance that no other firm could come near to organising such an event. As armoury for this stance we did have the massive in-house supply chain which provided all consumables to every unit the length and breadth of the country, including management, quality control and hygiene specialists, meat, fish and greengrocery buyers and a fleet of vehicles, drivers and logistics specialists. It was a difficult arsenal for any of our competitors to compete against.

I decided that the best way to sell the deal was to appoint at this early stage in the proceedings the supremo for each venue, and they (as a team) and I should be the salesmen to the committees appointed by the Church to co-ordinate the visit, as well as to the clerical committees appointed by the dioceses. Thus those involved on behalf of the Church could start to bond with the man who would deliver the event on the ground. Our team of six set up the appointments and made the travel arrangements.

If suitable audio-visual equipment existed, we did not know about it. Our presentations, probably appropriate given the nature of the beast, were divided between the six of us, with the man for the venue in question giving the main thrust. We were to be on the road for a fortnight. We flew between presentations and stayed at THF hotels. We rehearsed our pitches in the evenings before the presentations. And in-between meetings we discussed logistics.

The Pope's visit had special significance to me too, as a Catholic. There were some personal dilemmas for me over the whole set-up of the Papal visit which became (I suppose of necessity in that only big business could handle such an event) intensely commercial, and as I travelled between the various Mass venues to meet the committees, largely composed of devout priests themselves in awe of what was happening, I, as I felt sure they did, wondered if this was really what it should be about.

And so the behemoth gained momentum and even the war with Argentina over the Falkland Islands could not stop it. Pope John Paul II arrived at Gatwick Airport on Friday 28th May, 1982. I was already in Coventry masterminding, or as it turned out undermining, the catering at the first Mass, to be held on Sunday 30th May.

I made my headquarters at the Coventry Posthouse. I had one room as a bedroom and the one next door for meetings.

Three hundred thousand people attended the Mass in Coventry, mostly arriving in the early morning and leaving after the event. We had prepared for 700,000, arriving in phases from the previous afternoon in order to bag good places, and needing some sustenance throughout the afternoon, evening, night and following morning. Every police bulletin on the media pleaded with the public not to clog the country's roads by attending the Masses but to watch on television instead. The public complied. Our business plan was shot to pieces.

At 7 a.m. on the Monday morning I went to my hotel room in the Coventry Posthouse. I phoned Ron and told him what had happened. It was the only time I knew this tough man to cry. So did I. I went to bed for a few hours after three days without sleep and awoke late in the day to join preparations for the biggest mass burger freeze in catering history. The shortfall was mirrored at the other Masses, to which I shuffled exhausted and with a heavy heart. Neither Ron nor I were really forgiven, and all talk, actual or implied, of no expense spared disappeared from the boardroom dictionary. Somigliari convened an inquiry to ascertain what had gone wrong and to ensure that no blame fell on him or the main board. The conclusion (obviously) was that everyone associated with the project was a cretin. It would have been so easy (and under the circumstances so Christian) to have taken a big sigh and said, 'OK. Thanks for trying boys and girls. You did your best. Financial success was not to be ours on this occasion. Maybe your reward will be in heaven!' But no.

Some time after this, Ron and I were again summoned to Somigliare's office. The property department had revealed that the lease on Sun Street was due to expire in about a year's time and it was not available for renewal due to redevelopment proposals. What did we propose to do? Again I found myself flummoxed by this man's extraordinary attitude. Ron was as surprised as I was. He stated very seriously that the answer to this question would involve an in-depth review of Ring & Brymer's activities and how they were undertaken. I agreed with this and pointed out that if Ring & Brymer had to physically leave the city, the kernel business could be seriously affected both in practical terms and psychologically.

Ron and I repaired to the bar in Grosvenor House. We talked far into the evening and parted for the night having drawn two main conclusions, both of which were probably fairly obvious. The first was that, without either of us being property experts, it was very unlikely that an affordable replacement property for Sun Street would be available within the Square Mile or proximity. The second was that if our principal activity was far removed, the additional operating costs might prove unaffordable. Both of these considerations were highly negative. Indeed they actually brought into question the very viability of Ring & Brymer. When we felt that we had really talked it through as much as we could that evening, I had a thought. A big one. A stupid one? An absurd one? I had to share it. 'Do you think our bosses want Ring & Brymer to succeed?' I asked Ron.

'It's not the first time I've considered that,' he replied. 'Even before this business with Sun Street. The company just does not seem to have settled down since the merger. It's been quite a few years now. The understandable turmoil should have subsided. I don't mind fighting purposeful battles but I seem to spend my life fighting purposeless ones. I know you see some of it John as far as Ring & Brymer is concerned, but it's much the same with the Café Royal and the other areas of the business. I feel that my boss and I should be on the same side; aiming in the same direction. I don't.'

'It's not very difficult to see why,' I said. 'However the question I posed, which you have partially answered, has potentially serious consequences for you, me and a whole heap of other good people. If the company really doesn't want Ring & Brymer, and I'm sure you and I would both agree that Somigliare doesn't, then losing Sun Street as a base would be one hell of a good excuse to get rid. When Forte bought it, it had a real value I should think to a much smaller company. But does THF really need it? I can't imagine we are a major profit contributor compared with the hotels and other major sectors.'

'I don't know John. But I feel the wind of change in the air.'

This dilemma was resolved shortly afterwards by a decision being made at main board level that Ring & Brymer was to move to a vacant building already owned by the company, near Colnbrook, just off the M4 and around the corner from Heathrow Airport. It would be extremely convenient, I was told. It's at the juncture of the M4, the M40, the M25 and the M3. Transport into the City wouldn't be bad. The building existed, albeit it would need adapting. There were no planning issues.

It was probably more obvious to me than to Ron that this decision was wrong in every sense. We had once worked out that a banquet for 100 people involved approximately 3,000 items of equipment, napery, glassware, food and drink. The possibility or rather likelihood of overlooking a few items was high. With functions within the City representing the majority of our business, an oversight or mistake could inexpensively be addressed with relative speed and ease. However, a round trip from Colnbrook might take an hour or even two hours in bad traffic.

But above all was the question of image. Despite Racecourse Catering, Manchester and Newcastle, Ring & Brymer was *the City*. Take Ring & Brymer out of the City and you might as well close it down. I believe Ron understood this. I believe a lot of people in Ring & Brymer knew this. I don't think any other soul did. And they were not about to listen to us.

Then there was the question of the Parlour. This was the small dining room next to the main kitchen at Sun Street to which the hosts of forthcoming functions were invited to sample the suggested menu and wines. This had become a major City tradition and was undoubtedly great fun for our guests. In all probability, an individual or individuals (in the case of City Livery Companies, probably the Master, the Clerk and two Wardens) would only be invited to the Parlour once a year. But for the management of Ring & Brymer, this constant lunchtime entertaining was a time-consuming burden, with the added disadvantage that it was almost impossible to avoid joining one's guests in trying the selected wines and probably a port and brandy. It was easy for good intentions to be worn down by convivial or indeed difficult company. I found it relatively easy to apply solid willpower on these occasions, but some of my colleagues did not, and the management of evening functions after a lunch in the Parlour could be, shall we say challenging?

I was concerned, as Director, with the difficulties that these lunches caused us but could find no way out, particularly as lunch in the Parlour had become the absolutely expected entitlement for the organisers of future functions. I was in no doubt that curtailment or scaling down of these activities would seriously affect business. Several other caterers would have loved to inherit the fallout from any such decision. But while a man or woman working in the City could be at Sun Street in ten minutes, would they take the time (and pay the taxi fare) to Colnbrook? Could the Parlour work effectively out of say The London Press Centre? I doubted it. It was the image. Sun Street was an institution.

These and other lesser considerations taxed Ron and I profoundly. But the decision had been made and no questioning was permitted. Conversion of the Colnbrook premises commenced. The entire structure of Ring & Brymer was put into a massive melting pot. Ron and I agreed that it was essential that I make my office at Colnbrook, particularly since Racecourse Catering would now also be based there.

The move eventually took place. The consequences were catastrophic. That's another story. For me personally, in the relatively short term as it turned out, my journey to work had to start at 5 a.m. if I was to have any chance of beating the traffic and being into work at a reasonable time. Likewise, leaving to come home before 6 p.m. was pointless. Thirty hours a week travelling. I was tired and frustrated. Chris was furious.

A few months later I took a phone call at home from Ron. It was a Sunday. 'Giovanni. Bon giorno.'

'You're in a good mood if you're spouting Italian,' I said. 'What's the cause?'

'La causa, my friend, is that I have another job.'

'Well you're obviously pleased so good luck. May I ask doing what?'

'You may ask, but I can't give you an answer. Sorry. You're the first to know. I haven't even told the boss yet.'

'I'm touched. Sincerely. So you're leaving me with all the shit?'

'Depends who takes over.'

'Any ideas?'

'I think they'll break up the division and split out the various parts.'

'Would make sense. It's not very tidy.'

'Tell me about it. Virtually unmanageable.'

'You should know. Any particular reason why now?'

'You know me better than to need to ask that.'

'Yep.'

'I've had feelers out for a while. You need more than an Italian connection to survive this lot.'

'Yep.'

'When are you off to the Paris Airshow?' Ron asked.

'I'm planning on Friday. Give it a week before the doors open to deal with the usual crap.'

'Well I might try to get out. It depends as much as anything else on whether I'm required to work my notice or get booted out.'

'I bet the latter.'

'So do I. I'll keep you posted. Seeing Somigliare tomorrow morning.'

'Good luck.'

'Ciao.'

Ron left quite quickly so did not come out to the Paris Airshow. The show went on for two weeks so it meant an absence of about three. I hated this.

A few weeks after my return from Paris, I received a call from my new boss. His secretary put him through.

'John, Morning. I've got a tricky one so I'll come straight to the point. Why was your wife, Christine is it, at the Paris Airshow?'

'She wasn't.' I was shocked and felt an earthquake on the way. I didn't know the man very well, but he sure as hell should have been certain of my wife's name.

'I'm advised that she was.'

'By whom?' I was angry now and wanted to show it.

'I am not at liberty to tell you, but the Executive Chairman has been told by a reliable source that your wife was there. You know how much he hates management mixing their families with business.'

'So you don't believe me when I tell you that Christine was not there?'

'If the Executive Chairman says that she was there and that his source is accurate then she was there.'

'I will let you have a written reply to that observation by five o'clock this evening. Goodbye.' I slammed the phone down.

I asked my secretary to come in to my office, to drop everything else and to type a memo which I would deliver personally when ready. It read:

I found our telephone conversation of earlier today deeply insulting and the implication that I might lie to you, and therefore by implication to Lord Forte, flies humiliatingly in the face of my long and loyal service to this company and Forte & Co before that. To what extent you personally are aware of my record with the company I do not know. The fact that you are not sure of my wife's name, suggests to me that you have not done the homework that a person in your position should have done. I think however that the record would show that my attributes include (I hope amongst others), meticulous honesty and truthfulness.

This morning you did not just suggest that I was lying about Christine's presence in Paris – you stated it – categorically. I am aware that the accusation levelled against Christine and me must have caused you a dilemma. I am aware of the dangers of disagreeing with the Executive Chairman (and indeed others in this company). If my wife had been with me for a visit to the Paris Airshow, I can assure you that I would not bother to lie about it for the very simple reason that I would see nothing wrong with that.

While I am indeed aware of the company's attitude to entertainment of spouses, I feel obliged to bring to your attention that Ring & Brymer's activities are quite different to the mainstream business of the company, and if a senior manager (in this case me) is obliged in the best interests of the company to be away from home and family for a period of nearly three weeks, this to facilitate the ability to work without domestic distractions for up to fifteen hours a day consecutively, then in my judgement, a brief visit from my wife would be well-earned by her as well as me.

This not to mention that several of our Farnborough and Paris clients have, in the interests of securing their contracts for the airshows, been entertained at our home, and that Christine is well-known to their decision makers and incidentally to their wives or colleagues. The Americans in particular take a very different view to us of the involvement of spouses. If we are to court the contracts of American corporations, we have to bow to their customs. Apart from all this, my wife has her own important full-time job working for the London Borough of Bromley and would most certainly not be taking precious holiday entitlement to go to the Paris Airshow, which is by any interpretation a chore.

Whether or not she would be prepared to seek a statement from her employers to the effect that she was working throughout the duration of the Paris Airshow must be her decision.

It is clear to me in the light of what you said to me this morning that I no longer have the confidence of you or your superiors. I tender my resignation with immediate effect.

John Cunliffe

To this day, I believe that this decision was the right one. It was not impetuous. Had Paris been the only issue then the situation would have been different. But this was the last in a string of contretemps which convinced me that I should not waste any more of my life in this company. In those days, employment rights were sparse, bordering on non-existent. The fact that today such behaviour would have been deemed as constructive dismissal is irrelevant to my situation then. I had been around the company quite long enough to understand how it ticked and that this was not a game that I could win. Simple failure could be forgiven up to a point. But implied criticism of the supreme leader was high treason and that carried only one penalty.

I rang Ron immediately and told him what had happened. He agreed that any attempt to salvage the situation would be a waste of time.

'Giovanni', he said, 'ring the lovely Chris and why don't you come round to dinner this evening? We'll have a glass or two of vino, something simple to eat and talk.' I felt better.

My boss called in at Colnbrook the next day. He did not seem particularly worried about my resignation, nor did he show any regrets. There was no attempt to get me to change my mind. I would have loved to know the real truth behind it all. Was the "Christine in Paris" thing a put up job? A ruse to get me out? But why? Was it a punishment for the Papal visit? Did it come from Somigliari? I think he knew that both Ron and I thought he was not the brightest button in the box and he had told us over the 10 Downing Street uniforms business that he thought we did not take him seriously. Were they clearing the decks in preparation for closing down or selling off Ring & Brymer? Was there someone else in the wings whom they wanted to put in my job? Was I assumed to be so closely associated with Ron that I was a liability now that he had gone? Who knows?

I was promptly put on "gardening leave" and as Chris had a bit of holiday due and the boys were also on holiday, we headed for the Lake District and stayed at Knipe Tarn. We ascertained from the *Westmorland Gazette* that Gilpin Lodge had opened as a restaurant with a few rooms and I was very curious to see inside again and to let Chris see where I had spent much of my childhood.

We phoned and made a reservation. The name didn't seem to mean anything. Why should it have? The building was of course very small compared with the present day. The Drawing Room didn't exist, nor the Conservatory, nor the cocktail bar nor any of the nineteen bedrooms which we have subsequently added since we took over Gilpin.

On arrival, the lounge where we had an aperitif was where the main restaurant is now and the dining tables were in what we still call the Small Lounge. We had a good nosey around as best we could. The decor was unimpressive and the furnishings based on blue velvet. The service was pleasant. The food acceptable by the standards of the day. The worst part of the experience was that it was all too small. You felt you needed to whisper. We wondered what the future of Gilpin Lodge would be. We asked if we could see a bedroom but were told they were all full. Barney seemed particularly interested. Was this premonition?

Ron, bless him, offered me a job in the company he had joined. It transpired fairly soon thereafter that a significant restructuring was under way in this enterprise and we were both made redundant. I got a generous payoff which gave Chris and I time to explore other avenues.

Possibly too late in corporate life, I learned yet another lesson from this scenario. Ron took me on to join him in this company and I then went about recruiting several others from Ring & Brymer, including Tony Jupp. Our brief was to expand the catering activities, and as such, experienced managers were needed. These appointments were not made to spite the bosses at Trusthouse Forte, although in the short term we certainly stole some of their thunder, including capturing the highly prestigious Mansion House contract.

Without doubt, Ron and I brought ourselves comfort from surrounding ourselves with people we knew and trusted in an otherwise alien environment. What I did not appreciate at the time was the effect that this would have on old timers in the company, including Ron's peers and superiors. I suspect that this unwise strategy contributed to our early demise.

While understanding the rationale of people who recruit old colleagues when they come to a new job, I have since been cautious. They can seriously destabilise the original team.

Chapter Fourteen

THE HOLE IN THE WALL

To say that I was fed up with corporate life would be an understatement. I desperately wanted to buy a business. The value of our house in Beckenham Place Park had soared and we worked out that with a substantial loan we could afford to do so. Chris was very reluctant. She loved our house and her job. The boys were doing well in school and were happy. I was unemployed – again.

I don't think I have ever allowed male dominance to influence our marriage. As far as I can recall, Chris and I have made every decision by mutual agreement. But I don't think I listened to Chris at this time. It was obvious that we could not survive on her salary alone for long. With hindsight, she was terrified. To debate here and more than thirty years later what might have become of us had I just sought another job would be a pointless exercise into dream world.

I suspect that I would have got another job without too much difficulty. I surmise that my principal skills would have slowly faded from usefulness as computers took over so much of the hotel and catering world? I speculate that my refusal to be a yes man would have got me into conflict again with bosses and peers. It is unlikely that we would have gone into our own business. That game, as we were about to find out, was for people with boundless youthful energy. We were soon to discover that the skills we had honed in big companies were very different from those required in a small business. That delegation is not feasible if there is no one to delegate to. We were about to learn that cash flow (what the hell's that?) is god.

I worked out just what we could afford, and it was obvious that we were going to have to start small. I buzzed around the country looking at small hotels, pubs and restaurants. Chris carried on earning the corn and looking after the boys. Ron was also in the process of setting up his own business, and Tony Jupp too. Often I would return from these forays after driving several hundred miles, depressed and frightened. Sometimes I was hopeful.

We bought The Hole in the Wall in Bath, a famous restaurant within tolerable distance of London, and a well-established port of call on the dollar route. There were nine quite pleasant guest bedrooms. Of course there were refurbishments to be done, but nothing that prevented immediate trading. Everyone went to Bath didn't they?

One of the big issues was the boys. We were well aware that if we went into our own business we would have to give it our all. So we decided to send them to boarding school. We sought an appointment with the headmaster of Ampleforth, Father Dominic, and without sharing our intentions with the boys, we went to see him. Yes they always gave preference to sons of old Amplefordians. Yes they would take them. Yes Ben would be fine. At his age this should work very well. But Barney was another matter – at sixteen he would be joining the school at an age when his colleagues would have already formed peer groups. Yes they would take him too. But beware!

We told them just two weeks before they went for the Easter term. We thought Barney would be thrilled. He was not. And Ben was anxious. They went. The journey north was upsetting, the parting worse. Chris blamed me.

The vendors of The Hole in the Wall were helpful in our attempt to bring about a smooth transition of ownership, and I went several times to meet individual members of staff and to assure them that we were decent people who wanted to carry on the traditions of The Hole.

The accounts were encouraging, leaving scope for improvements which we felt sure we could bring about.

Packing up Beckenham Place Park was heartwrenching, and extremely difficult as we had far too much furniture to put into the small flat on the top floor of The Hole. A priority on arrival was to find storage, which we did in a garage not too far away.

We said farewells to our friends and neighbours in Beckenham and consoled ourselves that Bath was not so far away.

Bath was a horrible mistake. Entirely mine, assisted however by destiny. On 5th April 1986, on the day we completed the purchase and moved into the cramped, noisy little flat at the top of the building, the Americans bombed Libya. The hotel and restaurant's core business was Americans staying for a couple of nights on the circuit from London to Bath, to Oxford, to the Cotswolds, to Edinburgh, to York and then back to London. The cancellations poured in, and what had been expected to be an excellent summer suddenly looked dire. This situation was to us a mystery. Libya is hardly down the road from Bath.

On the first really wet day, the roof over two guest bedrooms on the third floor leaked, and buckets were needed to catch the ingress. A new roof was needed. Cost estimate £40,000. Our solicitors advised that legal action against the surveyors was unlikely to succeed.

Slowly the business started to come in again. Then the Chernobyl disaster struck. The whole of Europe was supposed to be engulfed in a radioactive blanket spawned in Ukraine, in the then Soviet Union. The business disappeared again. Chris and I were at loggerheads. Not a good background to building up an ailing business. When the boys came home for the school holidays we had neither time nor money for them. The flat was claustrophobic. Threatening letters from the bank were a weekly event.

George Street, where the Hole was located, was the main street in Bath and near to all the principal shops and sights. As summer progressed, the streets became increasingly packed with tourists and locals. Why did they not pour into our lovely restaurant but rather favoured burger and pizza restaurants? Was it cost? Was it a question of having enough time? Or had tastes changed so much? We didn't know the answers to these questions.

We weren't really restaurateurs. One thing was obvious: the business lunch was, certainly around here, a thing of the past. And while we had believed that proximity to London was a benefit, in fact the opposite was true. Bath could be done, particularly by rail, as a day trip.

Occasionally, the longstanding renown of The Hole in the Wall as a restaurant brought us famous guests, more often than not appearing at Bath's Theatre Royal just down the road. Cary Grant surprised us one evening having booked a room under a different name. He chatted amiably as if we were old friends. Chris recounts an afternoon when she was manning the reception desk and comic actor Griff Rhys Jones arrived to check in. She thought he looked familiar but being unsure, asked him his name. He replied in that unmistakable Welsh voice 'you must be joking'.

The business as a hotel was seriously flawed. There was no car parking, indeed just stopping a car to unload luggage was hazardous. And the bedrooms were noisy. There was no solution to the first of these problems and we had no money to address the second, which demanded double glazing and air conditioning.

Tiredness soon engulfed us and caused friction, poor morale and bad decision-making. The locals seemed unfriendly and unwelcoming, and indeed one day, after I had written what I thought was a charming note to an accountancy practice which owned the lawn onto which the restaurant looked at the back, asking if I could climb out of the restaurant window and collect the unsightly litter, I found the letter later that day pinned onto the small noticeboard in our entrance hall, suggesting in red marker pen that we piss off back to London. I never understood what we had done to deserve such crude animosity.

Friction with some of the staff started on the very first evening when one of the senior girls in the restaurant asked when she could take holiday due to her. I was very surprised as the agreement with the vendors had been that all holiday entitlement or money in lieu would be paid to staff before the sale. We went to court over this – a distraction we could have done without – and won, but we never got the money, which was about £6,000.

At Ring & Brymer and the Café Royal, and indeed in Cyprus and Jamaica, I had obviously been very involved with profit and loss accounts and budgets for the operations for which I was responsible. I had no involvement whatsoever with cash flow projections. At Beckenham Place Park, our next-door neighbour was an accountant as well as a friend. It was a bit of a love-hate relationship in that our agenda when we had free time as a family was to be together doing things, either chores like cleaning or gardening, or going out to Royal Horticultural Society gardens or trips to the seaside.

Chris and I were also quite keen tennis players in those days. However our accountant neighbour and his wife, who seemed to have plenty of money, wanted to drink champagne all day and all night, preferably with us. Chris and I have always hated drinking alcohol in the daytime. The initial buzz is wonderful but then the day dissipates and the evening is a non-event. Weddings, high days and holidays are exceptions to the rule, which otherwise is strictly six o'clock!

But we were quite close to this couple and when The Hole in the Wall came onto the radar, an offer was generously made to help prepare the proposal for the bank. At that time we banked with Clydesdale, which had been Forte's bankers. They were in principle supportive of the idea. The business plan was done as a favour. But when we had started trading in Bath, it was obvious that we had to start to pay for accountancy services. The fees of a qualified accountancy practice were more than a small business could afford and we advertised for a local bookkeeper to process invoices and do the payroll.

The response was surprisingly good and we selected and took on a rather aristocratic middle-aged lady who seemed to fit the bill. All went well until one Friday when she did not appear with the staff payslips, which was the basis of the cheques which I wrote every week. There was no reply to several phone calls. I knew where she lived as I frequently delivered paperwork to her home for processing. She preferred to work at home and this suited us as we were short of office space. In fact we had no offices except the area behind the reception desk which offered no privacy and was the scene of all check-ins, departures and other reception activities.

I walked to our car which sometimes had to be parked some way off – anywhere where a free parking space could be found – and then drove to the bookkeeper's flat, which was in a charming Georgian building to the south of the city centre. The problem was immediately apparent as I pulled up. The dustbin on the pavement was overflowing with empty Gordon's gin bottles. I spent half-an-hour ringing the doorbell and even throwing pebbles at the window, but there was no response.

Of course our bookkeeping was entirely manual. I had never run a payroll. Staff, when I got back, were beginning to ask for their pay cheques. I decided that there was no option but to tell them the truth. I promised to work on it all weekend and to see that they got a cheque by first thing Monday morning. I pored over incomprehensible tax and National Insurance tables and eventually completed the task, which I think contained a fair bit of estimation.

We advertised for bookkeepers and took on a small practice run by two girls. You surely can't be unfortunate enough to employ two alcoholics!

One morning we came down into the restaurant and found it flooded – literally under water. Investigations revealed that the plug had been put into the sink in one of the guest toilets on the floor above the restaurant and both taps had been left running. Negligence? Unlikely. Intentional? Possibly. But why? And what could be proved? Absolutely nothing, as the police helpfully pointed out. The feeling of persecution in the wake of this was overpowering. We had to shut for a couple of weeks to let the restaurant dry out and fit new carpets.

As with any catering business, the approach to Christmas brings good money and a lot of stupidity. The restaurant at The Hole was an interesting configuration, with lots of small private areas, each with an appropriate name. No table numbers here.

One Saturday night a section of the restaurant had been booked by a party of twenty. They seemed very pleasant when they made the reservation and had taken several bedrooms as well. But they arrived late and drunk and rowdy. I sensed trouble. They ordered Dom Perignon champagne and seemed reluctant to look at the menu or contemplate ordering food.

As the evening progressed, they became loud, rude and inconsiderate. The food was barely touched. Enquiries as to its quality were dismissed. A man and a woman left the table. After some time, another man asked the assembled company where Daphne was.

'Oh. She went off with Des some time ago,' someone volunteered. 'Mumbled something about going to check out the bedroom.'

The man jumped up, kicking the chair over in the process and raced up the stairs to the bedroom floors. By this stage I was more or less glued to this party. I thought it best to keep out of a local squabble. Soon however, the noise of a door being banged and kicked was audible in the restaurant.

I went to investigate. The door of bedroom two had indeed taken some punishment, but there was no-one there to be seen. I could hear sobbing inside. I knocked on the door but no-one came to answer. As I was walking back down the stairs, the man from the party passed me walking up. He was carrying an axe. This was not the time for James Bond stuff and I have never prided myself on being of that ilk. As I raced to reception to call the police, an earsplitting crash was audible from the floor above. Indecision as to my next move set in. Was this just a drunken display of jealousy? Or was The Hole about to become the scene of a bloody murder? Or two?

Fortunately, before I had time to answer these questions, the police arrived and asked me to take them to the scene. Our axeman was in the advanced stages of hacking down the door to bedroom two, and male and female screams were very audible from within. Two officers disarmed the man and led him away in handcuffs.

What was left of the door to bedroom two had by then been opened and I enquired of the partially clad man and woman what was going on. They had stopped screaming and now felt that the situation was quite amusing. They asked for another bedroom, proclaiming that a room with the door largely axed out lacked privacy.

I told them to leave and forced them to pay for the room, adding £500 for the damage. The threat of bringing the police back rather doused the party spirit. It was quite some time before diners, residents and staff returned to normal.

I had been approached by the headmaster of Ampleforth to see if we would host a parents' Mass, meeting and lunch for the south-west. Although to be able to send boys to Ampleforth you had to have a bob or two, the price suggested was paltry. But we could hardly refuse. We had

Barney and Ben's reputations to consider. Having generous parents with a nice hotel in Bath would be cool. To decline or haggle over the price would be decidedly un-Amplefordian. There were to be seventy people including Father Dominic, the headmaster, and several other monks.

We desperately wanted to show off, and despite the mean price, we spared no expense to set out our stall, including extravagant garnishes to the agreed menu – which made the deal even less profitable. The number of guests meant that the function room on the first floor would be packed. The guests would have to sit at their places at table while Mass was celebrated. Chris and I decided that despite being parents we would not join the other guests but would help. This number stretched our staffing level and expertise to the full. In his speech, Father Dominic thanked us generously and we received a round of applause. I had known Father Dominic for a long time. He had been a priest when I was at Ampleforth and I recalled the humbling ceremony of his ordination. I mentioned to him, just in conversation, that we had not been very lucky, happy or successful in Bath. He wandered around the public rooms and the kitchen and blessed the building.

In the light of the poor trading and limited profitability, a half reasonable sale seemed unlikely.

Then, just as fate had abandoned us over the past months, she showed her fairer side. One of the country's largest estate agents wanted substantial office space in Bath and offered to buy the premises, subject to planning permission for change of use. This they obtained on the grounds that due to traffic noise the premises were unsuitable for dormitory use.

The day on which Gilpin again came on the radar was extraordinary by any standards. Chris and I were having a coffee sat at one of the restaurant tables just before opening for lunch service and Chris was reading our principal industry magazine, *Caterer and Hotelkeeper*. She has always maintained that keeping abreast of what is going on in the industry is vital. Maybe circumstances guided her fingers to the "Businesses for Sale" section, or maybe it was fate. Or maybe it was Father Dominic's prayers. I was doing the seating plan for lunch. Not very difficult – there weren't many reservations.

'John. Gilpin Lodge is for sale. We need to get out of this place. Every-thing's wrong. It has been since day one. It's not right for us. It never will be.'

I looked up and saw tears welling in her eyes.

'I'll ring the agent next week,' I said. 'Don't cry. I think it'll go through with Savills.'

'Fuck next week,' she said, banging her fist on the table and causing coffee to spill on the cloth. 'Get up to Windermere today and see Gilpin again. Find out why they're selling. Get the accounts. See the bedrooms. You've always wanted to own a hotel in the Lake District. They don't grow on trees. You know the Lake District. It's in your blood. You know fuck all about this Godforsaken, snob-ridden tip.'

She's not prone to that sort of language or violence. I was shocked.

'It's Saturday,' I replied, trying to sound reasonable. 'We've got for-ty-eight booked for dinner, the chef's unstable and we're short of staff in the restaurant.'

'Just go. Grow some balls and get us out of this mess. I'll look after the restaurant and if the numbers go to seventy I'll cope.'

Vintage Chris.

It's impossible to do nothing when Chris is really fired up. I debated with myself what was for the best.

'Go,' she continued. 'If you go today, you can snoop around tomorrow and ring the agent first thing Monday morning. Maybe you don't have an appointment, maybe it's a bit unusual, but they're not going to tell you to go away. They want to sell otherwise they wouldn't go to the expense of putting an ad in the paper.'

I went, arriving late and stayed in a bed and breakfast in Windermere. After fish and chips and a few glasses of wine in a pub I phoned Chris. It obviously had been the right thing to do. She was positively cheerful, and pleased that the evening at The Hole had gone well.

As I walked around Gilpin the next day, Sunday, escorted by a rath-er surprised young manager with whom I had spoken on the phone that morning, three thoughts struck me in almost equal measures. One was that this was close to heaven. It was where I belonged. It was where I had spent so much of my childhood. Second, was that there was so much opportunity; so many areas for potential development. And third, was that there was a massive amount to be done before Gilpin could really be anything approaching the sort of place we wanted to run. But it was do-able. I felt it deep down.

I phoned Chris that evening. I was elated. After so many months of worry about what to do, I felt that we had a plan. We didn't have to think about buying Gilpin. It was the right thing to do. I made an offer to the agent on the Monday morning and met with the manager of the bank in Windermere on the Tuesday, having spent Monday studying the accounts. They weren't worth the paper they were written on. This was bad from the viewpoint of dealing with the bank, but good in that it was obvious that the immediate potential was much greater than the accounts suggested.

The purchase of The Hole in the Wall by Savills was confirmed. My offer on Gilpin was accepted. The bank in Windermere agreed to the loan we needed. There is a God!

Under the terms of the lease for The Hole in the Wall, we were not allowed to sell on the lease for twelve months. So we had to run Gilpin and Bath together for the better part of this time. We knew this was going to be tough in terms of work and being apart. Completion at Gilpin was set for 11th January 1988, so we decided to have a family Christmas at Knipe Tarn. It was to be the last for many years.

So just before Christmas in 1987 we locked up The Hole in the Wall and headed for Windermere via Yorkshire to pick up the boys from Ampleforth. Money was very tight and we had an overworked Ford estate car which I had bought second-hand when we moved to Bath. Gone the days of smart company cars. For good or for bad, there were very few bookings at Gilpin in January, so we had decided not to recruit staff nor take on payroll expenses until we were up and running.

Our journey north was filled with a mixture of hope, determination and not a little anxiety.

Chapter Fifteen

CHRIS AS HEAD CHEF AT GILPIN

We were driving north. 'John.' Chris cut across my reverie. 'When we open Gilpin, I'm going to be Head Chef. I can do it. I'm not going to be messed around anymore by arsey chefs who think they know it all and can't even boil an egg. I will do it.'

'You haven't seriously cooked since college more than twenty years ago.'

'Thanks. I thought we ate quite nicely.'

'You know what I meant. Commercially.'

'It's only five rooms for God's sake and I'm talking about mostly breakfasts. It's just like a family party. We had agreed we weren't going to do dinner – at least initially.'

'But the work Chris. It's going to be seven days a week. I know it's only ten guests but there'll be demand for omelettes and waffles and scrambled eggs with smoked salmon and boiled eggs and baked beans and eggs Florentine and kippers and smoked haddock and...'

'Sounds fun. I can do it.'

'I know you can.' Secretly, while I was worried, I was also delighted. The intransigence and inefficiency of the chefs in Bath was what had taken us to the brink.

'John. Let's be very clear about something. We fucked up in Bath. We're not going to again. And if that means working our arses off for the next umpteen years, so be it. Agreed?'

'Agreed. Also agreed is that your language is deteriorating.'

As we left the A1, it began to snow. While Chris was organising the luggage and doing the polite thing with the housemaster, I crept into the Abbey church and knelt down at a pew.

'Dear God,' I muttered. 'Sorry. I haven't got much time and forgive me for swearing. Not what you're supposed to do when praying. But we just seem to have crawled out from under the most enormous pile of shit and I know you helped. Thank you and please help us with Gilpin. We won't have another chance. Help us to do what needs to be done. Guide our decisions and give us the strength to work just as hard as we need to. Look after Chris and our boys. Amen.'

The boys were full of end-of-term excitement, exacerbated by the prospect of Christmas alone at Knipe Tarn and a new home. They had hated Bath too. They had tolerated it because they had had no choice. The roads had turned icy and the car was rubbish in snow. But as we drove past Gilpin Lodge to reach Knipe, I knew we had made the right decision. This was where we belonged.

That Christmas was a happy time. We did normal family things and enjoyed being together. Chris spent hours, happily – indeed excitedly she assured me – with her nose in cookery books, sticking Post-it notes in recipes and compiling menus. I had my fair share of work to do in anticipation of Gilpin's workload and the ongoing demands of The Hole in the Wall.

On Christmas Eve, we went to Midnight Mass in Kendal.

Christmas Day we had turkey and all the trimmings, and Christmas pudding. The boys were of course brimming with testosterone, and in the evening some girls – friends from previous visits to Knipe – turned up. It's amazing how this happens even in a place where you don't know anyone. Hormones must have a scent!

The Hole was fully booked for New Year's Eve so I had to return to Bath soon after Christmas. It was a nostalgic parting from Chris and the boys. We all knew that an epiphany was in the air, as well as in the ecclesiastical calendar, but would it be a good one or a bad one? By definition, can an epiphany be bad?

Chris and I had, over the past few weeks, debated at length how best to operate The Hole. Clearly Gilpin was our future. This was where our efforts must focus. We knew of course that a five-bedroom hotel could not be profitable. Actually Gilpin had six bedrooms but we had to live somewhere. So did Richard. We knew that we had to perform in a manner which would enable us to undertake much needed refurbishment and to add some more bedrooms. Much of the furniture in the existing rooms was cheap pine and many of the carpets were variants of nylon.

Richard was no more in love with Bath than Chris and I. He was a funny old stick (middle-aged stick?), then as he is now, but had become an adopted member of the family. He did not try to pull age-related rank on the boys and his single status, whether permanent or otherwise, was uncomplicated. He was excited about Gilpin and ever since it became a probability, had made several sorties from Bath with his camera. The temptation to leave him in charge of The Hole was very real but Richard, while a loner in personality, does not function well on his own in business. So it was decided that he would move with us to Gilpin after New Year at The Hole.

We appointed what we called a Chef Patron to run The Hole. The term was not quite accurate as he was not the "patron". But the budgets we had prepared after hiving off the bedrooms (now offices) did not provide for a manager as well as a Head Chef. This model assumed that I would spend some of each week in Bath and certainly take care of all the administration and accounting, as well satisfying the landlords that we were fulfilling the terms of the lease in personally running the restaurant. Richard had kept on a small flat in Bath, so I had somewhere to stay when I was there. In effect it was one room with a kitchenette and a bathroom. It sufficed.

Thus I was not at Gilpin when the purchase was completed. This was a great disappointment to me. I really wanted to be there on such a momentous day. And by any standards, this put a mighty strain on Chris, who of course rose to the occasion with grit and determination. But it did more than this. Although neither she nor I knew it at the time (well I didn't anyway – goodness knows what she knew) it gave her a very personal sense of ownership from day one. Owner indeed she was. But I mean much more than just in a legal sense – almost in a feral way, but excluding the implied brutality. But there was actually an element of brutality in that she was so determined to make Gilpin work that she would (and often did) fight for it.

This feeling of ownership was even to the point of putting me in second place. I was to become very aware of this soon after completion. I know it now. I have known it throughout the intervening period. What's more, I don't mind. I admire her greatly for the gumption which pulled it off. This is not to say that we don't share big decisions. Now decision-making is even more complex with Barney and Zoë and Ben involved. But much more of that later. Suffice to say that Chris put her stamp on Gilpin from the off. A real Penny Black. She and Richard formed a great bond and he came into his element at Gilpin. He was able to apply his hospitality skills without some precious idiot saying 'oh we don't do it that way here'.

I think it is important at this early stage to identify what the Five Commandments, as they became known, were. They were not etched in stone. They were just in the ether which surrounds and is Gilpin. They came from Chris – from day one.

1) The guest rules. Within reason, he or she gets what he or she wants. The team at Gilpin *will* get to know the guests and their requirements and their foibles and their peculiarities and who their children are and what makes them sad and happy. *All* guests *will* want to return – time and again.

2) Wastage of materials or time is not allowed.

3) All staff from owners downwards will do everything that needs doing. There are no lines of demarcation.

4) All staff will be treated with kindness, respect and if possible affection. In return they will be expected to follow these commandments and to act with loyalty.

5) There are at least two ways of doing everything. One is the easy way and the other is the harder way. By and large the harder way will be better and more thorough.

The manager of Gilpin prior to our purchase had let it be believed locally that he was the owner. In fact this was not the case – the owners had another business near Manchester. Rumours were rife locally and from

Jenny – the only employee whom we retained – of how Gilpin had been run. It appeared to be unsurprising that the business had not succeeded and had needed to be sold. This concept was reinforced one evening when I was home and Chris, Richard and I were sitting in the still room having a cup of tea discussing the purchase of a fax machine. The back door burst open (without a knock) and two burly, besuited men charged through the door. We were very taken aback and I don't think I was welcoming. It transpired they were from HMRC (or whatever it was called then) and had come to collect the unpaid VAT. They were disappointed when we were able to produce the necessary paperwork to establish that we were not the defaulters.

Gilpin, according to Chris, who is a housekeeper par excellence, needed spring cleaning from top to bottom, and Chris and Richard tackled this need in the first few weeks of our ownership. Thus I was quite pleased to be in Bath! Jenny worked part-time in the kitchen and elsewhere as needed. Chris also brought in another Chris (Chris B), whose family had been involved with Gilpin for literally generations. Her father had been the gardener there when I stayed with my grandmother as a youngster.

Life on the M6, M5 and M4 as I came to regard it, was not much fun. But Chris and I fed on adrenalin and determination. The Hole did not work very well and the Chef Patron concept was somewhat of a debacle. I had to frequently remind myself that we just had to get through the period until we could sell the lease. I had to accept more compromises than I would have liked.

We established a sort of pattern where I would return to Gilpin for the weekends, which quite quickly became busy, and then give Richard a day off or if possible two, before returning to Bath.

We were not at that stage doing dinners at Gilpin, never mind anything else. Chris's breakfasts were to-die-for, and all the guests so commented. Every element was cooked to order. Then she would do her "mine host" bit at the front of the house in her whites. She liked the Head Chef image. When all the guests had left or gone out, the tiny team, including me when I was there, would sit in what then was the still room and have a breakfast just as good as that provided for the guests, while the day ahead was planned. Everyone had their say. Some of the suggestions were useful and some were not. Everyone felt involved and motivated. Easy enough with such a small team.

My weekly returns from Bath were a great joy, even though they heralded more hard work. But it was work with a long-term purpose. It can't have been much fun for the boys either when they were home from school. I think Chris and I just assumed that they knew that they had got to do their bit. I don't recall any profound conversations about sharing responsibilities. And all credit to them for not protesting and going off carousing, as they might have done.

It became obvious very quickly that we were going to have to do dinners. It started on an ad hoc basis. Chris, the boys and I always ate together, whatever time we finished – even if it was just beans on toast and no doubt a few glasses of wine. This had been the "rule" even before Gilpin, and continued to be whenever possible. I think it has stood us in good stead as far as togetherness is concerned.

The only exception was if it looked like being a really late night. We never sent guests to bed or closed the bar until the last person had retired of their own accord. This perhaps ridiculous practice was often abused by guests who got less and less responsible as they became more and more inebriated. Bedtime for Richard or me was often in the small hours of the morning. I did once tell some guests at 4 a.m. that I was closing up. They subsequently wrote and complained. If possible, Chris and I would take Sunday afternoon and evening off. We had lunch out – often at the Lyth Valley Hotel, where we made friends with the owners. This was accompanied by a few glasses of wine. Then a siesta – the sleep of the innocent!

After only a few months, the accommodation side of things was becoming ridiculous for us all, including Richard. Our reputation was spreading – I suspect that we were doing things much better than they had been under the previous management – and many nights we could have filled all the rooms and generated much-needed revenue had it not been necessary for Chris, Richard and I to sleep somewhere. We used whatever bedrooms were vacant, but the inescapable fact was that one third of the hotel's accommodation was not lettable. We were effectively a four-bedroom hotel.

We had inherited, with the purchase of Gilpin, a very dilapidated caravan and, in an effort to ease this problem, Chris and I scrubbed this disgusting thing inside and out and had the cushions re-upholstered and some curtains made. We made the best of trying to make this work that first summer, but stuck in the field behind the outhouses it was not really a goer.

I think we only tried this for a couple of nights. The lack of a loo was impossible. The absence of anywhere to prepare food was not much better. I said to Chris as we neared completion of duties one night that I would make some sandwiches. We had got into the habit, more from practical necessity than preference, of only having two meals a day, and basically we still do that. So we had a big breakfast in the late morning and then a one-course dinner when we finished work. I know plenty of hoteliers who have a meal before evening service. That does not work for us, particularly as a glass or two of wine is an essential accompaniment to dinner – but not before service.

Chris headed for our caravan, torch in hand, and I said I would follow with the sandwiches. Chris likes things to be done right, even if we are roughing it! Her sandwiches have to have the crusts cut off and be quartered from the corners. We could have fed Africa by now with the wasted crusts! I set off – also torch in hand. As I extended one hand to open the caravan door, the tray of beautiful sandwiches slipped out of my other hand and fell into the mud. It was too late to start again. We went to bed hungry but probably not thirsty.

It looked like Barney would be leaving school sometime that year. This would bring a welcome relief from two school fees. How we did it I don't know. I used to kiss the envelope containing the cheque made out to Ampleforth College before I put it in the small letterbox opposite Windermere Golf Course in the hope that this would help it to clear. Only once did I have a phone call from a kindly monk telling me that the cheque had bounced and suggesting that they re-presented it in a few days' time. I rushed to the bank with every penny I could find. To hell with the pennies and pounds debate!

My Dad, Tony, came and stayed at Knipe Tarn with my stepmother Dorothy quite often. They had obtained planning permission to knock down the old Norwegian-style bungalow by the tarn and replace it with a substantial house back from the tarn by a hundred yards or so. The ground floor consisted of an L-shaped lounge and dining room, a kitchen, an entrance hall, a master bedroom with an en-suite bathroom, a study for my dad, who still worked as Director of Training for the Royal College of Pathologists, a cloakroom and a garage. Upstairs were two bedrooms, another sitting room and a kitchenette. The idea was that this would be for visitors and ultimately, when they needed live-in care, for staff. On the lower ground floor, facing onto the tarn, was an indoor swimming pool.

Old Knipe had been Cunliffe territory. New Knipe was Dorothy country and the rules and regulations were very different and very strict. We were not allowed to use it. Full stop. In those days, at least within my family, you did what your parents said. Frequently my father came to stay on his own. On such occasions he would invite us to Knipe for a meal but the question of staying was never mentioned. Then one evening he told Chris and me that Dorothy had decided that she did not really like the Lake District, which she felt was only suitable for sheep. This observation was a bit personal! He had undoubtedly had a few glasses of wine. So she would not be coming that often and preferred her flat in Ebury Street in London. Prior to this announcement he had been very subdued. We had concluded that they had had a row. Such events were not unusual. Dorothy was a domineering woman used to having her own way.

Dad was very supportive of us at Gilpin and of course he adored Chris. He would come down most days to collect his newspaper and stick around making suggestions, which were by and large not very useful. He particularly liked to be around Chris as she worked in the kitchen.

He must have been aware that we had an accommodation problem, but there was no mention of staying at Knipe.

As the summer holidays approached this had to be resolved and we bought a new static caravan, and had it put at the top of the kitchen garden, tucked away behind a wall. It was not like a house but it was streets better than being itinerant. It was home and had two bedrooms, so the boys had one and Chris and I the other. We had a kitchen to cook in. A fridge. A shower and loo. Privacy. To me it was pretty near to heaven. To Chris it was pretty near to hell.

A white cat had emerged one day from what is now the Executive Chef's office. Despite attempts to persuade it to go, it stuck around and adopted us, but particularly Richard. It was not allowed to sleep in the house so it became known as Outhouse. He was to be a part of Gilpin for some years and many guests in those early days came to know him. The only downside was that he had a very variable temper. He could be lying on his back being stroked, purring away merrily, and then, if he had had enough, instead of just getting up, saying 'thank you' and going about his business, he would sink his claws and teeth into you and scurry off.

By now we had five bedrooms to let. A twenty percent improvement! We never double-booked rooms but one day that summer, someone made a mistake and we had taken bookings for six rooms. This was before mobile phones and we were unable to contact the couple who had to be relocated. Although I had become used to abuse from "booted" guests at Grosvenor House, this was a different matter. This was Gilpin. Chris and I were quite nervous as arrival time drew nigh. The couple came in through the front door and I explained the situation with abject apologies. Chris joined me. It was a special anniversary and the lady became hysterical and started shouting. Her husband asked her to calm down. Then Outhouse came in through the door and sunk his teeth into her ankle. There was no winning after that. A brilliant way to handle a serious and genuine problem!

The expiration of the first year of the lease in Bath came surprisingly quickly, and we found tenants who took over without undue problems. I took my leave of Bath with a sigh of relief and headed north for the final time with a feeling of great jubilation. Richard and Chris had planned a little party, and we sat on a bench outside the kitchen in the sunshine and ate cake and drank wine. It was a happy occasion. We were not at that stage to know that this was not the end of our involvement with The Hole in the Wall.

The paperwork involved with the sale of the lease of The Hole at last got me my fax copier. Email had not been invented then, so there was no alternative to mail and telephone calls. The former was slow and the latter both expensive and left no paper trail. I can't survive without paper copies and lists. This habit (annoying eccentricity Chris calls it) started when I was only about eight years old and I discovered that, even at that age, life was a busy business with lots of things to do, and having a list to follow was helpful. I have done so ever since in various formats including, years later, on a mobile phone the size of a brick. This did not work for me and I reverted to my lists backed up by a manual organiser. The chief problem with this system is that there is no back-up if said lists or organiser gets lost or damaged.

I suffered the consequences of this disadvantage recently when Chris washed a pair of trousers with my lists still in the pocket. The resultant altercation included a suggestion that I wash my own bloody trousers in future. I refer here more to occasions in business rather than childhood, but I proved time and again that following lists leads to greater efficiency than reliance on mere memory.

To this day, without mentioning names, I find our managers who write things down immediately are streets ahead in efficiency compared with those who do not, yet claim that they will do so later or simply remember. I have received a lot of stick, some serious and some jocular over this, from family and colleagues but I care not a jot. Lists are good! And copies of correspondence. So the much fought-over fax copier greatly improved my personal as well as Gilpin's efficiency, particularly in the areas of bedroom and dining confirmations.

My dad and Dorothy came up to Windermere together soon after the sale of Bath. They had arranged to meet a couple for coffee at Gilpin and they invited Chris and me to join them. We sat in what then was the only lounge. My father was very fretful. Dorothy introduced the couple and announced that they were buying Knipe Tarn. Strangely, I cannot remember what anyone said thereafter. Nor can I remember leaving the room, nor the couple doing so, nor my dad and Dorothy. I do remember going to the caravan with Chris and indulging in a fair degree of angst.

We went up to Knipe Tarn the next day. Dorothy had returned to London by train. This was the only occasion in my life when I let rip at my father with no holds barred. Chris and I told him exactly what we thought of their intentions, the secretive way in which it had been handled – and we told him what we thought of Dorothy.

He called me a failure who could only run a five-bedroom bed and breakfast and was unable to provide a home for my family. He was right of course. I parried that Knipe Tarn was not his to sell, never mind Dorothy's. He had inherited it from Auntie Gertie and it was the family silver. We parted sourly and without conclusion.

A few weeks later, I received a long and very strange letter from Dorothy. The gist of it was that my attitude to Knipe Tarn was ruining both her and my dad's lives. She did not want to live in the Lake District and nor (she claimed) did he. They wanted to buy a house in the Home Counties and the only way to be able to do so was to sell Knipe Tarn. She claimed that my unyieldingness was making my dad ill. Chris and I had a long discussion about how to react to this. I could have written pages to her about what Knipe meant to us as a family (all of us), and had done since we were children. In the end I did not reply.

Freed of the need to commute to Bath, we felt able to well and truly start to make plans for Gilpin, and between Richard, Chris and I we worked out a rota that usually gave Richard two days off. Chris and I made do with Sunday afternoon when possible. Barney had taken his A-levels and left Ampleforth and he helped a lot doing, as we all did, a bit of everything. Ben too helped during the school holidays. Their efforts were always appreciated and I would like to think that rewards were adequate.

The absurd belief that this would be semi-retirement had long since been dispelled. Who needed retirement anyway? More importantly, who could afford it? I had been very distracted for a year with The Hole and Chris had been up to her eyes trying to get Gilpin off the ground. Business was better than at the beginning of the year but that wasn't difficult as we had started with nothing. Nothing plus a bit equals 100% improvement!

The word "marketing" was not in common parlance in those days although it existed. We certainly had no sophisticated agenda in this respect nor any fancy tools, bar entries in the most common guides such as the AA and RAC, and a certain amount of advertising in the local paper. Our feeling was (and to an extent still is) that just doing our very best by every guest and ensuring repeat bookings and recommendations was the best source of business. But it wasn't enough. As 1988 headed to a close, it was apparent that we would not make our budgeted sales which, ridiculous though it seems now, were £84,000. Bookings for Christmas were not good either and we invited Chris's dad and his new wife Ada to come for Christmas, just to make the place look busier than it would have done otherwise – a freebie of course.

I was not in Reg or Ada's good books. They had married a few months before and Reg had asked me to be his best man. Ada was his third wife and in Chris's and my opinion the marriage was all-too-soon after the death of Trudy. The thrust of my speech at the wedding was about his stinginess, and although I thought it was good-natured fun, I had misjudged (because I did not know) the sense of humour (or lack of it) of the guests. I recall one quip being an explanation of why Reg always had scrambled eggs for breakfast. Answer: it's the only egg preparation you can easily divide into two. Anyway, it did not go down well and I was roundly reprimanded by all and sundry. So I did not particularly relish them being at Gilpin for our first Christmas, particularly if it was to be so sparsely attended by others.

Just before Christmas, we took an afternoon off to attempt to do a bit of Christmas shopping. We did not expect to have much of a Christmas ourselves but wanted to do our best. Ben was back from school and the four of us were together. This was unusual and it felt just a little festive. We drove up the M6 to Carlisle and parked in the city centre. News broke as we entered the House of Fraser store of the crash at Lockerbie of Pan Am Flight 103, killing 270 people, including eleven on the ground where the plane had come down. Lockerbie was just up the road from Carlisle, so it was a very local tragedy. Carlisle was in shock. The feeling of festivity evaporated. As usual when such disasters occur, one privately wonders why.

Barney and Ben were both showing interest in Gilpin, which was encouraging for Chris and me. It was of course far too early to have any idea where this interest would lead, but their contributions to debates about the business were intelligent. Even then, we tended to share problems and debate potential solutions. One thing that was very obvious was that we had to grow the business. But in the short term we did not have the money to add more bedrooms, and based on the first year's trading we were reluctant to rely on the bank.

As I mentioned before, Chris made it her business, and indeed so had I when not in Bath, to listen to our guests. The overwhelming demand was for dinner. It is a disruption to go the two-and-a-half miles to Bowness or Windermere, never mind further. And drink-drive laws existed by then. We understood this. But the prospect of becoming a restaurant was daunting. We knew we had to do it. Although the "estate" was some 20 acres including the fields to the north, west and east, the only car parking as such was right in front of the hotel: quite inadequate.

The old walled kitchen garden behind the hotel was the obvious site for more parking. But access to this was blocked by two LPG tanks which had been cleverly positioned to be in the way of almost any alteration to this area. A new company was appointed to supply our LPG, and the tanks were to be changed over after breakfast on the day in question. The newly located concrete pads had been prepared according to the specification provided.

That evening was quiet. The Christmas guests were not due to arrive till Christmas Eve. But there were two rooms in and we had agreed to provide a fixed menu dinner for them. Chris's pragmatic view was that if we were going to do dinners, we might as well get on with it. We had been told by the new LPG supplier to let the old tanks fall to nearly empty. We did. The new gas company turned up at 4 p.m. and disconnected the old tanks. We had earlier made the assumption that they would not now be coming till the next day. Chris was furious. How could she cook without gas? A reasonable question. I pleaded with the contractors to return the next day. They said that if they did not do the job then and there and fill the new tanks, it would be into the New Year. The existing gas supplier could not offer a delivery until after Christmas, particularly as we were leaving them. There would not be enough gas.

It started to rain as only in Cumbria it can. It became dark and the tank changeover was being done by torchlight. Richard was off and I was the only person on duty at the front of the house. There was a problem, it transpired, with the legality of a valve which would have to be changed. This would take time and delay the switch-on. Chris was in a foul mood and as usual it was all my fault. I could not see why. The guests arrived and thanked us profoundly for providing dinner. The day was saved by the guests begging not to have dinner until 8.30 p.m. They had had a Christmas lunch with relatives on the way and would not be hungry till then. The gas came on again at 7 p.m. I changed out of my dripping clothes and gumboots and tried to restore calm. Barney, bless him, took the brunt of it in the kitchen.

New Year brought an abundance of resolutions. My elation at being freed from responsibility from The Hole had by then given way to a quiet foreboding about Gilpin. We had been operating for just under a year, and realistically had achieved very little. The Lake District had a plentiful supply of good hotels, some famous and long established such as Sharrow Bay on Ullswater and Miller Howe on Windermere, both with magnificent lake views and renowned proprietors. The Wild Boar, The Lakeside, The Old England and others were household names. Holbeck Ghyll near Ambleside had been bought by David and Patricia Nicholson, who were talented hoteliers who would put their all into pursuing exactly the same market as we were after.

The same applied to Mike and Jean Bevans at Linthwaite House, just down the road on the way to Bowness. Both hotels had lake views and skilled energetic proprietors. Why should anyone want to stay at Gilpin Lodge, even if they had heard of it? How would anyone get to hear of it unless they drove past or bumped into someone who had stayed? Even if they did drive past, what was special? It was an ordinary enough Edwardian house in an ordinary enough garden.

These depressing thoughts ran through my mind as I relaid the tables after the New Year guests had checked out. Richard always seemed to be off. I knew that this was not true, but it was how it felt. How could I make any improvements to Gilpin if I was always a waiter, or a host or a meeter and greeter or even a bedmaker? The girls who had prepared the accounts in Bath had agreed to do the same for Gilpin but now it all had to be done by post and was slow and inefficient. At least when I had been travelling to Bath I could exchange the invoices and sign the cheques.

Chris was overwhelmed with work and fractious. I think we were both wondering if we had made yet another terrible mistake. It started to snow heavily: great big white flakes which settled on the ground immediately. The picture postcard appearance did nothing to lift my mood.

Barney was going off to the University of Surrey in a week's time. This at least was a positive for him and gave Chris and I a bit more space in the caravan. I did not at that stage share my fears with Chris.

Then I had a phone call from my dad. Apart from a brief exchange of Happy Christmas on the telephone, we had not really spoken since the row over the proposed sale of Knipe Tarn. He told me that he and Dorothy were driving up at the weekend and would like to see Chris and me. I wondered what now? Discussions with dad were always elongated. He found decision-making very difficult and went round the houses for as long as he possibly could. The proposed meeting added to my sense of foreboding.

I went into the kitchen and told Chris that Pa and Dorothy were coming up. She wanted to know why. I couldn't tell her.

'I bet they've found another buyer for Knipe,' she suggested.

'I expect so,' I replied. I was not in the mood for ill-founded optimism.

'I'm glad Barney and Ben are both going away soon,' Chris said. 'It's miserable here. You can feel our failure. They can too. We're in the shit again aren't we?' I didn't answer her.

Chris and I have quite different ways of tackling adversity. I'm the lucky one because I always know that however bad things seem, I will bounce back. I think there are two reasons for this. One must be my faith. I believe that there is a rose garden of some sort at the end of life. So I believe that there must be mini-rose gardens along the way. This is of course not a very traditional way of thinking – in fact it's heretical, but if it works, so be it! I think it does work because so often when times seemed bad, there was a corner to turn with a brighter horizon as you came out of the bend.

I think I also have considerable trust in my own resilience. I know that once I have thought it through, I can deal with it. This tends to apply more to practical matters than emotional ones. Ever since Chris and I have been together, if we are at odds, then I'm a mess and this supersedes all practical considerations.

The problem with the rose garden theory is that while I may believe that it works for me, it quickly comes unstuck when you look at the wider world: people involved in wars, or sleeping on the streets or with terminal illnesses. They have no prospect of rose gardens. In this world anyway.

Chris is not so lucky. When she's in a black hole, she believes it's permanent. And she usually believes it's of my doing. This is very hard to deal with. I know beyond doubt that while we can do things with the best of intentions, so many of our successes are achieved through, shall we call it good fortune? And so many of our failures are due to bad luck, or at least due to forces beyond our control.

And when Chris is depressed, nothing can bring her out of it. Well, maybe a whisky or two. Not to suggest that we drink our way out of our troubles. But a glass or two sure helps when the tail is not wagging. Even this is hard in the hotel business as we have never mixed drink and work. Well very rarely! Churchill apparently had "black dog" moments and he had more to worry about than we did. I think Chris is a bit like him – not to look at I hasten to add!

Then there is the question of happiness. So many people now seem to believe that this should be a permanent state of affairs and that if it is not there, fate has deserted them. This is of course rubbish. There is only so much happiness that one may reasonably expect. More than that is greedy and unrealistic.

We found Pa and Dorothy drinking champagne. A sale had obviously gone through. Pa seemed relaxed and Dorothy was smiling. Suspicious. Dorothy was not a person to make one feel at ease and her invitation to sit was more like a headmaster's summons to do so.

'We're celebrating,' she said. I sensed a con.

'What are you celebrating?' I asked, determined to keep my options open as to how the conversation might proceed.

'We have made a big decision, and it's a huge relief for your father. I am renouncing my involvement with Knipe Tarn. I shall no longer regard myself as its chatelaine.' Her first husband had been French. She loved to drop French words into conversations.

I gulped some champagne from the glass that Pa had given me. 'I'm not sure that I know what you mean,' I said.

'Your father has decided that he doesn't want to sell Knipe. I don't like the Lake District and I don't intend to come any more. I'm going to stay in my flat in Ebury Street. I may travel. I have to have space you see. Tony will divide his time between Knipe and my flat. We haven't worked out the proportions. That'll have to evolve.'

'So Knipe will just sit empty for half the year will it?' I asked.

'We need to talk about that,' Pa stammered anxiously. 'And I need to discuss it with Elizabeth.'

I looked at Chris, hoping for encouragement to proceed. She knew what I wanted, looked at her hands and shrugged. I decided that this was not an issue to be deferred. Under the circumstances, whatever they were exactly, the opportunity to progress this might not arise again for a long time. Whatever Dorothy claimed, Pa would not be given autonomy to deal with Knipe.

'Well,' I said. 'I am very pleased that Knipe is not being sold, and I know I speak for Chris and our boys and probably for Elizabeth as well. But I do feel that the usage of Knipe is to at least some extent our business. The old bungalow, which we all enjoyed, has gone and for this house to remain empty while we live in a caravan, seems a bit rum.'

'That's up to you and your father,' Dorothy said.

'You can live here. Upstairs,' he said. Then added 'some of the time.'

'What do you mean by some of the time?' I asked.

Dorothy, becoming impatient, said, 'Tony means you can live upstairs but downstairs is his. And Elizabeth will have to visit whenever she wants.'

'Thank you,' Chris said simply. Then she added, 'and I hope that you two find happiness in your arrangements.'

They both returned to London the following day. Our move into the upstairs of Knipe Tarn was not complicated. We had jettisoned a ton of stuff before leaving Beckenham. The boys were able to get settled before they went their separate ways. Was this really home? For how long?

Richard moved into the caravan and made that his haunt. He is still there.

Chapter Sixteen

EARLY DAYS

Somehow, having all six bedrooms in the hotel to let was a psycholog-
ical turning point. Neither Richard, the boys nor Chris and I were
camping. We were not sharing a bed and breakfast with the guests.
We had homes to go to and the guests had a hotel to be in.

Richard's holidays were times that I dreaded. They inevitably brought
periods of very hard work, usually from early morning until the last guest
had gone to bed at night. The area which is now the Conservatory Restaurant was in those days a small lounge containing just one sofa and two
armchairs – the original blue velvet ones which had come with the place.
When I had to do really long days I tried to have a rest on this sofa, but the
success or failure of these attempts depended on telephone calls and arrivals or other interruptions. But the worst part of Richard's holidays was the
need to sleep on the premises. I did not want to return to the gypsy-style
sleeping-around days and nor did I want to occupy a lettable bedroom.
So I used Richard's caravan, which had the advantage of a small kitchen,
a fridge and the comforts of home. But it wasn't my home any more. I felt
dislocated and lonely. Chris preferred her new home to the caravan.

The transition to doing dinners was astonishing in several ways. The guests loved it and occupancy soared, both at weekends and midweek. Chris and her small team worked their socks off in the kitchen, and Richard and I did at the front of the house. We advertised that we were doing dinners. Non-resident business built slowly, mainly local residents and guests, and executives of Kendal-based companies.

We speak now of the strangeness of people's behaviour and extravagance of their expectations. I think it has got worse, fuelled by a general decline in manners. But odd things happened even then. One lunchtime a well-dressed man came into Gilpin and ordered a pot of coffee. I was on duty on my own. He seated himself in the lounge and pulled a newspaper from a carrier bag. When I returned with the coffee he was eating supermarket sandwiches with the packets spread out on the coffee table. 'Just pop the tray down on the table,' he commanded.

'Sir,' I said. 'This is a hotel. You can't bring your own sandwiches.'

'Why not?' He asked with apparent innocence. I admit to having been a little flummoxed as to how to reply.

'Because we're a hotel. We sell food, drink and accommodation. That's our business. You can't bring your own bed so why should you bring your own food?'

'I've bought your coffee,' he replied nastily. 'So I am bringing you business.'

'Just leave please,' I said. So I never even got the money for the coffee. Well handled John!

Paula joined us and took over responsibility for the bedrooms. Over time, Gill, Pat and Thelma joined the restaurant team and Harry joined Chris and the kitchen ladies. Harry was a large, somewhat clumsy man but a solid chef with a personality compatible with Chris. She pushed him to his limits and brooked no shortcuts nor second bests. Harry responded. The menu quickly moved from fixed to having limited choice: three first courses; soup; sorbet; a choice from three mains; various puddings and finally cheese or a savoury. The formula worked. It was what our guests wanted. The dishes were classical with an innovative twist. The food was hot and beautifully presented without any pretension.

Harry enabled Chris to spread her wings to other areas. Most of the bedrooms were very simply furnished. While we could not afford fancy refurbishments, we got rid of the nylon carpets and much of the pine. We had already introduced a lot of new furniture which we had brought from Bath, some of which had in turn come from my parents' house in Hampstead. Richard was also now much better supported in the front of the house and Chris and I were able to get out a bit. We started exploring the locality and in particular the furniture and antique shops for bargains with which to enhance Gilpin. We upgraded the televisions in the rooms and provided tea trays and minibars. Some nice pictures were added. Each room was examined to establish what we could do to make it better without spending a lot of money. Chris started taking an interest in decor. We engaged a part-time gardener to improve the outside.

All these measures increased costs of course. But business was building steadily and the model seemed to be working. We increased the tariff to reflect the additional costs and quality and introduced a weekend rate and a midweek rate with substantial discounts for staying for three nights or more on a dinner, bed and breakfast rate. Almost all bookings included dinner. I am sure we did not invent breaks, nor the term, but we certainly saw this business as becoming more our market than the traditional week's holiday. We split the year into four seasons: summer, winter and two "shoulder" periods.

After years of creating menus, in New York, at Ring & Brymer and in Bath, I fancied myself as a bit of a dab hand at it. But Chris demonstrated a natural talent and the menus constantly changed with interesting new dishes. She frequently went shopping rather than just ordering food to be delivered, and forged good relationships with the principal local suppliers. She encouraged them to stock products which were rarely seen outside London or major cities. In fact, while it would perhaps be disingenuous to compare her impact on the Lake District's reputation for food with the boys from Sharrow Bay or Miller Howe, I think it was significant. Another seed in a flourishing process.

The other communication tool which we missed was any form of computing or to be more accurate – word processing. The menu operated on a three-night cycle, which worked extremely well as the average stay for our leisure guests was three nights. Thus in principal no guest had the same menu twice. But consumption from the previous night, availability of produce and even the mood of the chef led to variations and alterations. Sometimes these occurred more than once a day. Sometimes more than once an hour! This led to huge stress with handwritten menus. Dorothy's son Bertie, whom we had known for a long time, sold us a used computer which he brought up to Gilpin, installed and showed Richard and I how to use. It was a cumbersome device with limited applications, but it sure made changing the menu easier. Later of course – much later – Gilpin came to rely heavily on computing and now? Well, that's another matter altogether. We're almost in Silicon Valley!

We were still only in our second year of operation and business remained variable, particularly midweek. We made a decision, for obvious practical reasons, not to take dinner bookings after 6 p.m. for that evening if we had no other bookings nor resident guests. This resulted in some cosy evenings sitting by the fire in the lounge and having dinner on trays in front of the small television borrowed from the kitchen. I don't think we would have permitted another chef to have a TV in the kitchen, but Chris wanted this and thus enough said.

I left the wine list almost entirely to Richard, who had a good knowledge. There were several excellent local suppliers and we developed a good list. We calculated the selling prices based on a mark-up rather than a percentage multiplier, thus avoiding silly prices for champagne and better wines. This was a highly successful tactic which resulted in sales of better wines and a real perception of good value for money.

The very first couple who had stayed with us at Gilpin returned time and again. They were always pleasant and friendly and were obviously well off, sophisticated and successful. One day when they were about to check out, they asked me if Chris and I could join them for a chat. We did.

We both thought that something or someone had upset them. The husband quickly dispelled this notion. He hoped we did not mind if they offered us an 'opinion,' was how he put it – as opposed to advice. We said we would welcome it. He did most of the talking and explained that they had a business, which like us they had started from scratch. They worked very hard and liked to relax very hard. They had to travel a lot and stayed in all sorts of hotels, mostly but not exclusively in the UK. They hated corporate, branded hotels although they sometimes had to make do with them if there were no alternatives. They found many smaller privately run hotels amateur and lacking in professionalism. They liked good food but were not "foodies" and avoided Michelin-starred establishments.

'Now,' he said, 'after all that preamble, let me come to the point. My wife and I like Gilpin Lodge the best of all the hotels we stay at. You have got the formula just right. You are obviously hard-working professional people with ambition to grow your business and we wish you every success. You will make it. But you must set your sights higher and rise above the norm, which you are already doing.

'Specifically,' he hurried on before we could interrupt, 'you need to do the following and we have taken the liberty of making a list,' which he produced from his pocket and from which he read.

'One: Evening room turn down.

'Two: Breakfast is wonderful – worth waking up for. But needs more choice.

'Three: Serve dinner until 9 o'clock at night.

'Four: Oblige Richard not to take himself so seriously. He's a lovely chap but needs to lighten up.

'Five: And you John. Try not to show it when you're panicking. No comparisons with Basil Fawlty, but...

'Six: You Chris. Just carry on doing what you're doing.'

We thanked them. They left. It was to be a defining moment.

Our policies on children and dogs evolved from bad happenings. Initially we welcomed both. Two experiences about each issue affected the decisions to change. To deal with the question of dogs first. Obviously and not surprisingly, everyone who brings a dog to a hotel makes out that their pooch is friendly, house trained and totally suitable to keep the company of other people and even other dogs. While we did not, initially, have any particular problems, Chris and I always had a slight worry that dogs' habits and practices are (one assumes) not quite as clean as those of humans.

We discussed with Paula extra cleaning routines for rooms which had accommodated dogs. As a part of our enhancement programme we had bought a rather beautiful antique half tester bed for the room called Cleabarrow, and a super comfortable mattress. We had, on taking over Gilpin, renamed all the rooms after local places. In addition to Cleabarrow there was Lyth, Winster, Crosthwaite, Crook and Wetherlam. We continued this practice into later builds and strayed into naming rooms after lakes, mountains and even local Roman forts.

I am only digressing slightly from the issue of dogs... A guest had given us the name of this antique emporium somewhere in Wales. Chris and I went. It was a real find and had three floors of all sorts. From the start, I have never had very much say in the selection of furnishings. I know what I like, but admit that decor is not really my thing. And when it comes to colours, I am pretty idiotic. But nonetheless, I think this detriment should be handled with consideration. A rather dour lady was in attendance. Chris had circumnavigated this particular bed several times and was plainly in favour. It was a large mahogany affair with a high foot board and a canopy, also in solid wood that extended from the top of the wooden headboard to about halfway down the bed. 'John, do you see that in Cleabarrow?' She asked me.

'I see it there,' I replied truthfully, 'but I don't like it. I think it's too solid...bulky. It'll be overbearing. I can get four posters,' I went on, 'they have a sense of privacy; hiding away; naughtiness even. But I don't see what this does for you.' Chris raised her eyebrows to heaven and looked at the assistant who choked on a smile but said nothing.

'We'll have it,' Chris said to the assistant. 'You should stick to the driving,' she said to me with a cheeky grin. The assistant doubled up.

So returning to dogs. The half tester in question was delivered and while it remained not my favourite piece of furniture for the duration of its life in Cleabarrow, Chris spruced it up with fabrics and cushions and bells and whistles and it was quite a statement.

Not long after the bed's installation, a couple who had not stayed at Gilpin before checked in with a Jack Russell whom they introduced as Robert. He wagged his tail on hearing his name and appeared docile and contented. There was no further trouble, at least until Paula entered the room the next morning after the guests and Robert had checked out. They had paid the bill in cash.

Paula came to fetch me and we went up to Cleabarrow. The mattress had been shredded. Tufts of whatever it had been made of were scattered on the floor. One of the sheets had been shredded too. The telephone number that the guests had left turned out to be non-existent. A letter sent to the address given was returned 'no such address'. This expensive saga led to inevitable deliberations about not only the question of dogs, but also of deposits, credit cards as security, procedures on checkout and related matters. We decided there and then not to take dogs any more.

The use of credit cards was far less commonplace then than now, and banks and credit card companies actively discouraged cardholders from giving details of their cards as security for, for example, reservations in hotels. The web had not been invented and therefore online shopping and the resultant widespread use of cards for telephonic transactions was not in place. Many guests making reservations used the card companies' stance on this as an excuse to avoid giving card details and thereby to avoid liability. In many instances I think that this was genuine. If a card issuer tells you that you should not give details of your cards over the telephone, the temptation must be to comply. But this situation left hotels much more exposed than now to no-shows, cancellations and situations such as that with Robert and his owners.

One day I took a call from someone seeking to make a reservation. 'Do you accept dogs?' The lady asked. I embarked on my usual apologia for why we didn't. The caller stopped me short.

'Please,' she said. 'I wanted to ascertain that you did not take dogs. They are alright in people's homes but I don't think they belong in hotel bedrooms. I would like to book the room please.' I was quite surprised as I had not previously considered this take.

A few years ago, as I write, we designated a few rooms, with direct access to private gardens, for dog use. The fee we charge for a dog is used for special cleaning and maintenance of the gardens.

Children are altogether a much more sensitive issue. It is relatively easy to lay down rules for animals, but children are a literal extension of their parents and any challenge to the behaviour pattern is regarded as a criticism of the parenting. Any grandparent can confirm this!

The couple in question were not to be challenged. That was obvious from before they reached Reception. He was someone fairly senior in the US embassy which had made the booking. Their name was Spicer. No: Hank was not going to be having high tea at six. Nor room service. A babysitter would not be required. Hank had dinner every night with his parents at the table. If the hotel's rules prescribed differently then this should have been explained when the reservation was made. No it was not the role of the embassy's travel service to ask this question. No they were not going to go elsewhere. The table in the corner by the grandfather clock would do very nicely. No the table on the opposite wall would not be acceptable. Who sat at the table by the grandfather clock last night was not their concern.

The bags were to be carried to the room immediately and no further discussion on this matter would be tolerated. It really made no difference if I was the owner or just an employee.

Hank and his precious parents came down to dinner at seven sharp. They did not want a drink in the lounge. This explained quite a lot. He wore a blazer and was trying to look frightfully British. They stood behind their chairs and even though there were already other guests in the room, he said Grace in an audible voice. Quite a long Grace. 'Almighty God. We thank thee for bringing us safely to this place of repose. May you bless this house and all who dine here tonight. We give you thanks for our food and ask for compassion towards those who find it necessary to drink alcohol. Amen.' They all repeated 'amen'. Then they sat. The man at the next table winked at me and took a deep draft of wine with an intentional slurp. I wanted to run away but didn't.

Hank was one of those kids whose age was difficult to tell. Somewhere between three and five I thought. His mother read the entire menu aloud to him and he told her what he wanted to eat. She then told him that he could leave the table, which he did. From her handbag she produced a range of toy cars which she handed to him. Hank started pushing these around the floor including under the other occupied tables. I mouthed 'sorry' at the other diners. I took the order from the Americans in the vein hope they might want to eat quickly and put Hank to bed. As I was about to go, the father added 'we're in no hurry. Hank likes to have a play before he eats.' As the restaurant filled, the nightmare intensified. None of the other guests really knew what to do about it all. I think they were sorry for me and I was sorely sorry for myself. I felt that I could hardly ignore the situation for long. Hank was by now accentuating his play with loud cries of roaring engines and screeching brakes.

I had a hasty discussion with Gill and Thelma. Of course they didn't know what to do for the best any more than I did. I decided that I must ask the Spicers as politely as possible to leave the room. But just as I was approaching their table, the gentleman who had witnessed the saying of Grace got up from his table, went over to the Americans, tapped the man on the shoulder and said loudly: 'Your child is very annoying. He should be in bed or in the care of a babysitter. This playing all over the restaurant is utterly unacceptable. What are you going to do about it?'

Mr Spicer looked up, smiled and replied 'nothing.'

The man turned to me and said, 'In that case, Mr Cunliffe, what are you going to do about it? You surely can't reply "nothing"?'

'No Sir, I can't,' I replied. I turned to the Spicers. 'I'm sorry but you are going to have to take your child and leave the public areas of the hotel. I cannot comment on what you do at home or elsewhere, but this is indeed a restaurant and not a playroom and what you are allowing here is un-acceptable to other guests. If you wish your dinner to be served in your bedroom I will arrange this.'

'We will do no such thing,' Mr Spicer said. 'We will have our dinner here.' I lifted two corners of the table cloth into the centre of the table and then the other two corners. Then holding all four corners of the cloth I lifted the entire cloth clear of the table with all the cutlery and crockery contained inside it. Some water from the posey of flowers dripped onto Mrs Spicer's skirt. She scowled. I handed the cloth to Gill who convenient-ly was just passing empty-handed. The Spicers looked on in amazement.

Then I put my hand under the table, released the bolt which held the table top in place, folded the table top on its hinge and lifted the whole table away from the Spicers. This was a trick I had learned at the Lyons Corner Houses. It came in handy for extreme situations including hanky panky under the table! The Spicers were thus left ridiculously sitting on their chairs with no table. The room was of course completely silent by now. Even Hank had ceased revving and braking. Then he burst into tears. Great haunting wails and sobs.

Mrs Spicer stood up and said, presumably to me, 'We are leaving now. You may fetch our bags from the bedroom in ten minutes precisely. Mr Spicer added 'you will be hearing from our embassy.' They stomped off. There was a round of relieved applause from the other guests. I fetched their bags as instructed and saw them to their car. We never did hear from the embassy nor was the bill paid. I seemed to be rather good at that!

I have never done this since, nor had occasion to.

The other incident over children was very different and quite alarming. Fortunately there were no other guests involved. It was a Sunday morning and a caller wanted to know if we had two rooms available for that night for two couples and three children. We had no other bookings for that night and a party of seven could not be turned away. Could they arrive fairly early as it was raining and the children were bored? I agreed. They arrived. The four adults were scruffy and badly dressed. I knew there would be trouble as soon as I saw the children – three loud, boisterous boys.

The children started to play up even before their parents had finished checking in. One of the mothers asked if the children could stay in the lounge while the adults saw the rooms. I wasn't happy about this lot being left without parental control, but I wanted to avoid trouble. I took the parents to the rooms, carrying some of the bags as I did so. The parents remained upstairs to start unpacking. When I got back to the lounge, cushions from the chairs and sofas were flying and an ornament was lying broken in the fireplace. It wasn't valuable – a plaster bust of Beethoven which had come with the hotel.

'What on earth's going on?' I asked firmly.

'You shut up mister,' one of the children shouted at me.

'You can't talk to me like that,' I said.

Then I felt and saw the hand on my shoulder. 'You 'avin a go at my boys?' the man shouted, his mouth almost in my ear.

'John. Go into the kitchen.' It was Chris. 'I'll handle this.' I felt it was probably wise to comply and did. Nonetheless I felt it was a cowardly action.

I could just hear from the kitchen. 'So what is going on?' Chris demanded.

'E was freatenin my boys,' said the man. 'I'm goin to ave im.'

'You're going to leave, that's what you're going to do,' said Chris frostily.

'We've just arrived,' said the man, heading for the corridor to the kitchen to find me.

I had quickly briefed Harry in the kitchen about what was going on. I don't think Harry was a natural fighter, any more than I was for that matter. But Harry filled the corridor and made it obvious that getting past him to get at me was not going to be plain sailing. The man gave up and went into the hall. He bellowed 'Elsie, Sal, George. Bring vem bags dahn. We're gettin aht of vis fuckin dump.'

No children under the age of seven, we decided. Why not six or eight? No idea! Very scientific and analytical!

One day I was in charge of breakfast and a lady who was staying with a younger girl, who turned out to be her daughter, called me over to their table. 'You have a very happy place here – spiritually' she said.

'What do you mean by spiritually?' I asked

'I'm a professional medium,' she said. 'The aura is good. You have two particularly active spirits in the house who visited me last night. They are both happy in heaven. I am a Christian. There is not necessarily a conflict between spiritualism and religion. One is a young girl who was killed on the road outside the hotel. And the other is an oldish lady with her grey hair in a bun. She used to smoke a lot. I think she might have been a relative of yours.'

A girl had indeed been killed on the road. The description of the oldish lady was my grandmother to a tee. I told the guest this. She was not surprised. The daughter was not surprised. I was – and a little spooked. When I told Chris and the others about this over staff breakfast, their reactions varied from sceptical to amazed. But "Mary" (as she came from then on to be known) had been born and thereafter anything which went wrong without an immediately identifiable culprit was blamed on Mary.

As far as I was concerned, and I believe Chris too to an obviously lesser extent, my childhood days at Gilpin and the presence – in whatever sense you choose to read that – of my grandmother had a significant impact on how I viewed Gilpin as an entity.

Of course I knew it was a business and must be treated as such. But it was more than that. It was part of another part of my life. It was benign. It was on our first side. This may sound daft but it influenced my tolerance of adversity and hard work. And so many of my family – living and dead – had stayed or lived there, including most particularly my father and sister.

I had confused recollections of my grandmother, and of course had never known my grandfather. For whatever reason I never knew, my mother always brought me and Elizabeth up to dislike all of the Cunliffe family. As I grew older, I came to realise that this was wrong and unworthy. My recollections of my grandmother were exactly as the medium lady had described her. Like so many of that wartorn generation, she was less than extravagant with emotion, but I recall no conflict and much kindness. There is no doubt that she was also somewhat eccentric and a titanic chatterbox.

I recall one big birthday – I think it might have been her fiftieth, when we were all taken to the Wild Boar hotel for dinner. This was a big treat. The Cunliffes did not waste money eating out. In those days The Wild Boar was a small, charming hotel which belonged to Malcolm and Joan Urquart who were friends of the family. It influenced my decision to go into the hotel business – but that's another story.

Food varied of course, but was inevitably, at least in my limited experience, along the meat and two veg lines. Mrs Hogarth, the cook at the Wild Boar, was a Lakeland institution for roast duck. None of your pink magrets. Just roast duck with stuffing and gravy, apple sauce, roast and new potatoes and peas fresh from the garden. Serendipity!

I think we all ordered the duck. There must have been six of us and we were seated at a round table. The service was simple and efficient. The vegetables would be placed on the table in serving dishes and the meat was placed plated in front of you. Several of us received our duck. Granny had not. She was talking ten to the dozen to Auntie Gertie who was seated next to her. Then she pulled the vegetables towards her, picked up the table spoon provided and started serving peas on to the table mat – not just one spoonful but several. It was not until they started rolling into her lap that she realised what she had done. 'Oh! Silly Billy,' she said. Staff and family were very amused.

*

Knipe Tarn had transformed our lives. We had a place to call home. When the boys came back from school and university holidays, everyone had space. Dorothy was true to her word and seldom came near the place. From inherent grounding, we stuck religiously to the rules. Downstairs was not used unless Pa was in residence and we were invited. The same did not apply the other way around, and although it did not matter then as he spent most of his time in London, in later years this was to become a problem. Elizabeth did not at that time voice an objection to the arrangement. Indeed we believed – genuinely – that we were company for Pa when he was around. He was a sociable chap and adored Barney and Ben.

I was also grateful to have somewhere to do serious work when I could exclude myself from day-to-day activities at Gilpin. This was seldom, but the little team had grown again with the addition of Suzi, who was to become a part of the Gilpin furniture.

In July of that year we had quite a party to celebrate Barney's twenty-first birthday. Throughout our working lives, Chris and I had been too busy to assemble much of a network of friends. There had never been time for socialising. But our stalwarts came and Harry took charge of the kitchen so that we could all have dinner together. Peter Crook, who was in fact Ben's Godfather, made a delightful speech all the more amusing because he was quite drunk.

Chris and Harry, with Jenny and Chris B part-time, made an exceptional team and their cooking had gone from strength to strength. Gilpin was becoming known for food and both resident and non-resident guests came regularly.

One evening Brian Sack and Francis Coulson from Sharrow Bay came to dine. We were all very nervous but they were charming as ever. Chris, understandably, was the most apprehensive. The menu (probably foolishly) was more challenging than usual. They both ordered hot smoked salmon soufflés to start. I was in the kitchen as the soufflés came out of the oven, ready to rush them to the table. They were perfect. Then Chris dropped the bain marie and they fell to the floor. I decided to tell Brian and Francis the truth. 'Dear boy,' Brian said, 'of all people we understand these things. Give her a glass of wine and tell her we're only human.' They were too and came quite often thereafter.

Chris's thirst for knowledge could not be quenched. She and Jenny went to a cookery school in Italy one autumn and returned inspired.

I believe that one of the worst nights of all the years at Gilpin, and my goodness there have been some, was one shortly after Barney's twenty first. Chris was cooking on her own and Richard and I were both on duty. I heard the scream from the restaurant and flew into the kitchen. She had knocked over a large pan of boiling water and it had gone over her stomach and right down her legs. She was crying with the pain and trying to get her body under the cold tap.

I wanted to take her to hospital and just tell the guests the truth, leaving Richard to organise some cold meat and salad. But Chris wouldn't hear of it. She cooked until the job was done, simpering with the pain and trying to see through tear-filled eyes. It would be inaccurate to suggest that it was as bad for me as for her. But in a sense it was. My mind was filled with pity, admiration, fear, guilt and pathos. Since Chris had decided that this was the way it was going to be played, there was no point in sharing with the guests the existence of any sort of a problem. This was difficult in the extreme. Richard was very distressed too. When we finally got to A & E at Kendal hospital it was late and fortunately quiet. The doctor was very cross with her. She had to have several days off with her legs up.

One evening shortly before service of dinner commenced, Chris shouted from the kitchen, 'John, there's a large pig in the garden. Just the other side of the drive.' I ran through to the kitchen. Yes. There was indeed. It had very heavy shoulders. I suspected it was a boar. I returned to the lounge and asked the guests to stay indoors. They were all fascinated. I called the police. Then the supposed boar started digging up a flower bed. This was not so good. Our new gardener had only planted it up the week before. Two policemen arrived soon thereafter, with a gun. They shot the boar. The guests were not so pleased about that. The fillet of pork didn't sell well that night! The policemen came by the kitchen to say that the danger was over. Apparently the boar had escaped from a nearby farm.

Our second Christmas at Gilpin was healthy. All six rooms were full with proper paying guests. Two couples who had spent the previous Christmas with us had rebooked. We have always regarded repeat business and recommendations as a sound litmus test of our success or failure.

All went well until the last day of the Christmas break when it rained cats and dogs. We had since almost day one at Gilpin been worried about the ageing oil-fired boiler which ran the hot water as well as the central heating. The cost of replacing this had proved out of the question. Additionally, we wanted to have a better idea of the future size of the building before deciding on a specification for new plant. There was a further problem. The boiler was in a small basement outside the kitchen door. Access was via a lethally steep concrete staircase with low headroom and potential for a sore forehead. The floor of this basement had been found to be wet on several occasions and it was obvious that the area was not watertight.

During that last day and evening of the Christmas break, I watched with anxiety as the water level in the basement rose. The rain showed no sign of abating. Rather than running up and down the concrete steps to the boiler, I frequently touched radiators to see if they were warm. By the end of dinner service they were not. The water level had risen above the burners which were well down on the boiler.

The next morning the house was like ice and there was no hot water. All the guests were understanding and we gave thanks that this problem had only occurred on the last night. But in the end it had spoiled Christmas. We had failed and were disappointed. During the day the water level dropped and the next morning we managed to get a plumber who got the boiler going again. But our Achilles heel had been exposed.

Chapter Seventeen

THE NEW WING

O ur second year at Gilpin had, by and large, been a success. Offering dinner had boosted residential trade as well as bringing local dining business. Analysis of the figures made me realise for the first time that the expenses of running the restaurant were really a marketing cost for filling the bedrooms, which was where the profit lay.

It was very clear indeed that we needed more bedrooms. And we had to have a bigger lounge. Our restaurant business – particularly but not solely at weekends – flourished, but not having enough lounge seats was a problem. Being a hotel, guests rightly expected to sit in comfort while they enjoyed an aperitif and studied the menu. On the occasions when lack of lounge space demanded that we took them straight to the table, apologies did not compensate for the disappointment.

We had planning permission to build more rooms in the coach houses, but we were not convinced that they would be large enough or sufficiently removed from traffic noise. And that would not solve the lounge problem.

Another lesson we had learned was that the first rooms to sell were the best and most expensive. We were attracting a reasonably sophisticated clientele who were prepared to pay for a nice room. The new rooms needed to be at least as good as people had in their own homes – if not better – was the way we came to look upon it.

The bank manager was reasonably encouraging about the prospect of a new loan. In those days, banks were prepared to consider general "prospects" as a factor in a hotel's value, unlike the present day, where only actual proven profitability and professional valuation can be taken into account. We had in our favour good careers in the industry and a massive improvement in trading in year two as compared to year one. It was also apparent that for whatever reason or reasons, people liked Gilpin.

Chris's little team in the kitchen had bonded well and were producing increasingly good food. She was able to absent herself from the kitchen to help in the planning of the extension. In the end, and after many meetings with the architect, we decided to add a two-storey extension which would provide three large, luxurious bedrooms with generous en-suite bathrooms upstairs, and downstairs a lounge seating twenty to thirty, according to the configuration of parties. Proper public toilets were also included in the plan, enabling the ladies toilet by the front door to become Reception. I produced a business plan of which the bank approved. Planning permission was sought and granted.

As with any building or conversion project in an operating hotel the process was hell. The contractors, as a generalisation, want to make as much noise as possible from early in the morning until their premature departure in the afternoon. They want to have radios blaring. They want to swear loudly, whistle and liberally distribute empty cans, bottles and cigarette ends. They turn up on a Monday then mysteriously don't on Tuesday. Thus planning for their presence is impossible. From their point of view they can keep several clients on the boil at the same time.

We were pathetically green at managing this process and the methodology they employ to hike their bills above the estimated prices. In Forte and Trusthouse Forte days, projects for which I had nominally been responsible were managed by professionals. I had no experience of these matters and received precious little advice from the architect. The dust and dirt from the building site seemed to have miraculous ability to permeate inside the building, and every afternoon demanded a clear-up operation outside and a spring clean within.

Bills arrived and I had no know-how of how to compare them with the overall expected total. We demanded additions to the original specification with no idea of the impact on the cost. No-one warned us.

We did not know then (as we do now) that a new building's footprint always looks smaller than it will when the walls are up. We felt sure that the contractor had made a mistake. He produced his tape measure and proved that the foundation he had built was in agreement with the plans. I knew how meticulously we had designed the layout of the room and was confident that all was well. Chris would have none of it and insisted that I go to Windermere and buy some chalk to draw on the concrete the outline of the sofas, coffee tables and other furnishings. It worked. But she remained unconvinced. Typical!

Chris started to apply herself zealously to decor and demonstrated a natural capacity to source and choose fabrics and furniture. She had little help with these tasks. Nor did we in the physical process of moving furniture, hanging curtains and changing plugs on lamps. And all the while we were running a hotel and attempting to calm disturbed guests. Opening day approached – a Friday of course – and we were still at it long after the guests had gone to bed on the Thursday night.

Yvonne, a friend of Richard's, had helped Chris with the decor. She had kindly agreed to come and stay for a few days and assist with the finishing touches. My job on the evening before opening was principally putting plugs on the many lamps – thirty-two to be exact. There was no time to stop for anything to eat, although the kitchen produced sandwiches at some stage in the evening. We finished at about 3 a.m. and turned in for a few hours.

On Friday morning the remaining furniture arrived. Nothing quite like leaving things to the last minute! The sofa for bedroom Heathwaite would not go through the door. The front legs were too long. After consultation with Chris and a panicked overview of options (none), I sawed the legs off the sofa and then glued them back on once in the bedroom. DIY is not my natural forte and I was of course under considerable pressure. It was not a bad job.

The project and associated workload was massive for our little team, and a few weeks before opening the new wing we decided to take a holiday.

We booked the ferry from Hull to Zeebrugge and then drove to Obergurgl in Austria for a week's skiing. It was to be our first holiday for ages and we were all excited. Except, that is, me. I knew by then that we did not have the money to finish paying for the new wing. And I didn't know what to do about it. All sources of funds had been squeezed. I made a conscious decision – in complete contrast to our stated modus operandi – not to share my anxieties with Chris. Anxieties? No. Dread. Cold fear. I put on an act for the whole holiday, thinking about nothing but money all the time. Every carafe of wine at dinner and every spag bol on the slopes seemed to exacerbate the problem. And then we got back.

The stack of mail was waiting. Among it the bills. They totalled way in excess of what the bank had agreed to loan. I think that one of the most painful meetings at Gilpin was the day when the architect, the main contractor and the sub-contractors and I sat down at table one in the restaurant to discuss what to do. Analysis of the invoices led me to believe that fault lay on both sides. There had obviously been considerable naivety on our part, with particular regard to alterations to the original specification. From the contractors' point of view there had been minimal flexibility nor warning of where we were heading. Some compromises were made and a delayed payment plan agreed. I got the very clear picture that they had visited this scenario before. A big, hard lesson learned.

The famous recession of 1989 to 1992 was, as far as we were concerned, beginning to bite. The new rooms and the lounge were a great success and opinion from guests was extremely encouraging. But money was painfully tight and we were trading below the projections agreed with the bank. My first job after checking guests out each morning was to sit down and do a manual cash flow for the next day. Online banking did not exist so there was a large element of guesswork. Dealing with screaming suppliers was a daily task. Most were small local firms like us and their concerns were understandable – which made the task harder. The bank were disinterested and frequently sent letters condemning the overspend on the overdraft facility and demanding its reduction or else.

It became apparent that we were heading for a financial crisis. I opened an account with American Express Bank, which facilitated an overdraft with them at an extortionate interest rate. It helped to pay some bills. One week I took cash from my personal credit card to pay the wages. It was a very anxious time with many sleepless nights. Both Chris and I worked ridiculous hours in order to minimise the wage costs of others.

Then, and out of the blue, and as if matters weren't bad enough Armageddon knocked on our door. Among the post was a bill from the landlord of The Hole in the Wall for £17,000 plus VAT. It was for a year's rent unpaid by the tenant. I tried to hide the problem from Chris. But she knew me too well. I hoped it was a mistake but somehow felt that it was not. I telephoned. Apparently there was (and I think still is at the behest of wealthy landowners in Parliament) a rarely employed law called Contract of Privity, under which a landlord may, if the first tenant of a new lease defaults, seek redress from the original tenant: us. Our solicitor had mentioned no such threat. What struck us as particularly unfair was that the situation had been allowed to accumulate for a year without warning us.

The solicitor who had conveyanced the lease was (not surprisingly) unwilling to help. The gist of his argument was that it was the responsibility of the client to ask questions rather than of the solicitor to advise of every conceivable problem which might arise in business. Christine recalled that she had a cousin who worked for a big law firm – in Manchester she thought. Our instinct was that this needed some big boys with clout to match that of the landlord.

We attended a meeting in Manchester. We were greeted with great charm in offices which oozed confidence and money born out of fat fees. The legal position was quite clear. But, the failure of the landlord to advise us earlier of the potential problem was unreasonable, and this might be used as a lever to fight our corner. Eventually, and after more sleepless nights, the demand was withdrawn. However, the legal bill was not insignificant. Thereafter, and for the remainder of the tenancy (some seventeen years) I contacted the landlord quarterly to assess the position.

There were no further problems and happily the lease has now expired. Bath had continued to exude poison even to the last! We never returned – and even being on the M4 still gives me the creeps.

Despite the economy we were busy, and badly needed help everywhere. Having a proper reception office made an enormous difference to the way we worked and to the experience of the guests. Suzi was a great asset on good days. Bad days were another matter. We had employed two sisters who lived in Windermere to do the bedrooms. They were from a good family and pretty too.

One day I took a call from Ben's housemaster at Ampleforth, Father Leo. Were we aware that a young lady was in the habit of collecting Ben from school on Sunday afternoons and taking him out in a car? We were not. The girls' insistence on having Sundays off was explained!

Ben left Ampleforth that July and the usual anxieties and arguments abounded about what to do next. University or gap year? What career? Chris and I were opposed to gap years and have always felt that since you have to get an education you might as well get it over with. But Ben had other thoughts.

Barney had by now finished his studies and gone to Russia on an exchange year. Communications were infrequent. Unless he needed money. We worried. This was still Iron Curtain days.

We were desperate for investment in the kitchen. When we bought Gilpin there was an ancient oil-fired Aga which was the main cooking appliance. Chris, not surprisingly, had not got on well with this cumbersome and uncontrollable appliance and we had quickly replaced it with a six-burner stove with two ovens. But everything else had remained almost as it had been when Gilpin was a private house. The refrigeration was inadequate, some of the working surfaces were wooden and the floor was concrete. We must have been teetering on illegality. It was clear that a total kitchen refit was unaffordable. But the minimum would have to be done to make our kitchen workable and legal. The still room was no better and all washing up was done by hand.

We ordered some stainless steel tabling, a commercial microwave oven, an upright refrigerator and a small commercial dishwasher. The new equipment was to be delivered early afternoon on the day in question. In anticipation of this, that morning, after breakfast, was devoted to removing some of the stuff to be replaced, including the old wooden workbench. The new gear arrived. Plonk! Thank you very much! Bye bye.

The stainless steel benches were flatpacked. Allen keys were needed to assemble them. I did not possess allen keys. It was 3 p.m. The wheels of my car almost left the road en route to Windermere to buy the necessary tools. On my return, having had to go to Kendal to get the right sized allen keys, Chris and Harry were chopping and peeling sitting on chairs.

The anxiety of the situation was exacerbated because this was (obviously) my fault. What, on removing the packaging, had seemed a simple job involving a few screws and nuts, was not. There were washers of various sizes and components which had to be assembled in a certain order like a jigsaw puzzle. Several false starts brought little encouragement. The benches were being lifted into place as the first check came in from Richard in the restaurant. The new appliances made life easier and there was a general air in the kitchen that this was on its way to becoming a professional setup.

Since day one we had used linen cloths on the restaurant tables. Two per table – one right down to the floor to cover the table legs, which were not things of beauty – and a top cloth changed with every service. We had silver cutlery which Richard kept meticulous, silver butter dishes and cruets and always a candle on each table in a low candlestick so as not to get in the way of guests talking to each other.

Chris arranged small posies of fresh flowers as required. The tables exuded conservative restaurant charm which was accompanied by professional service, which was in Richard's and my blood. We trained our small team of ladies in the relatively simple disciplines. We had always believed that being charming was the most important ingredient. We got to know our guests and their likes and dislikes. We pandered to the foibles of the awkward. It was good, pleasant service.

One evening, a staff member tripped after dinner service while carrying a just-extinguished candle. Molten wax was distributed liberally over a small area. I had it in my head that the way to remove this from a carpet was to cover it with brown paper and apply a hot iron. I tried this. Lifting the scorched brown paper revealed a perfect burn mark on the carpet in the shape of the iron, which was itself caked with wax.

Neither Chris nor Richard were impressed. A rug covered this area by table three for several years. Apparently the trick is to use blotting paper.

*

Barney returned from Russia to our great relief, bringing his friend from university, Vladi, to stay with us. Barney had been staying with Vladimir and his parents in Moscow doing goodness knows what. The idea had been to learn Russian. I have never to this day experienced this linguistic feat in action. Chris and I suspected that vodka and Muscovite maidens had been higher up the priority ladder. Vladimir, conversely, spoke excellent English. Something was afoot in the USSR and Boris Yeltsin was behind it.

Barney had returned with a heightened sense of independence which was difficult to get on with, particularly since he was living with us at Knipe Tarn. Ideas for the foreseeable future varied from opening a chicken farm in Russia to sailing a Dutch barge across the English Channel from Holland and mooring it at Camden Lock while converting it into a London home.

Imagination is a wonderful attribute and Barney has never been short of it. He did however come up with one very clever idea, and but for some bad luck he might have become a millionaire and deprived Gilpin of his presence. He was certainly not a computer geek. He has always been too outgoing for that. But he was beginning to believe that computers had a major role to play in the world order. And of course he was right – and some believe that we are only looking at the tip of that particular iceberg. Robots are already with us and are starting to play an important part in some hotels. Artificial intelligence exists.

Barney devised some software aimed at gyms. The computer in a club would store all the data about a member, their vital statistics, health and physical achievements. It would then recommend the next series of activities. He teamed up with a techy able to write the programme and it worked. Unfortunately, all of us were very naive about patents and associated matters, and the idea was stolen by a big company, having been displayed at a gym exhibition at the NEC in Birmingham.

Then there it was on the television. The tanks rolling into Moscow. Vladimir sat with eyes agog and tears running down his cheeks. All communications were down. There was no way of knowing what had happened or was happening to his family.

Chris did her best to be "Mum" but Vladimir was inconsolable. After a few days a phone call came through. They were alright. However, Vladimir was anxious to return home and his stay with us was curtailed.

This was not an easy time to get a job, as Barney discovered. He had a good education behind him, a degree in Business Studies, a Masters in Tourism and bags of charm (Ampleforth was very good at that), but little experience except in helping out. Meanwhile he was a huge asset at Gilpin and threw himself into helping to make life a little easier for all of us.

He was particularly good in the kitchen but particularly bad at getting on with Chris. To an extent this tribulation, although packaged in a great love, has persisted. He declined to follow the instructions of his mother and was always finding different ways of doing things. This created some difficulties with the other members of the team, who were used to obeying Chris's directions.

On one particular day when he was washing up in the kitchen, he cut his hand on a knife which Chris had discarded in the sink. True – she was particularly bad at doing that – and perceived kitchen wisdom is that knives are never left submerged in sinks. That and (as a complete aside to kitchen practices) leaving shoes abandoned at the top of staircases.

Around about this time, Zoë came on the scene. She was the sister of Brent, who had been at university with Barney. This pretty, extrovert, fun-loving, intelligent, crazy, kind girl pitched up with Barney one day and this was to be the start of a romance which would lead some years later to a wedding, our first grandchild and the team at Gilpin being what it is today.

Barney eventually landed a job with Marriott in London and Ben left on an adventure in Kenya. Chris and I had Knipe Tarn to ourselves again. Except that was for the frequent visits of my father, who although he "lived" downstairs, bounded up the staircase as soon as he heard either of us come through the door. It was indeed his house – and we recognised that – but privacy was a rare treat.

And then there was Chris's dad Reg, and Ada. Reg liked to visit people – often without much notice. 'We'll be arriving this evening just for a day or two. Don't go to any trouble.' But he went into a great strop if tea wasn't ready by six. A week later they'd leave.

Reg's intransigent regime and trying to run a hotel did not run on parallel tracks at all. I knew then and still do that Reg was a thoroughly decent human being who loved Chris to bits. But he just didn't think the same way as I did and his dyed-in-the-wool Yorkshire approach to life was very different to mine. He started at this stage (an attitude which got much worse as time went on) to complain about how hard we (Chris in particular) worked, and although he had once had his own business in agricultural contracting, he seemed to have no comprehension of the difficulties of starting up a business and of the need for total commitment. Whether this was genuine concern for his daughter or annoyance at not having her at his beck and call, I never did manage to fathom out.

He was also very uncompromising. We only had one bathroom in the flat upstairs, and Chris and I had to get to work. But Reg was not prepared to have his regime subjugated to our needs. Very annoying.

Although Gilpin was quite busy at this time, costs always seemed to run ahead of increased sales. This is to an extent an endemic problem of the hotel business, which is why so many privately run hotels have failed and so many corporate ones are like graveyards. Thus money continued to be in short supply and Chris and I worked very hard to try to keep standards up and costs down.

We took little time off and although we were relieved to have escaped the precarious situation of Bath and were happy to be pursuing a dream, we were short of stimuli other than work. I had quite a lot of time when my brain did not really need to be in a high gear. Laying tables and dusting is pretty egghead stuff. But my brain wanted to be in demand.

Without consciously deciding to do so, I started to compose a novel in my head. Then I wanted to write it. I asked Chris if she would mind if I bought a small computer. I don't know to this day what she honestly thought. I suspect she knew that it was something I really wanted to do and didn't want to deny me. Laptops did not exist, never mind tablets. It was called a "luggable" and the description was very accurate.

We could ill afford it but I went ahead. I found writing a change from hotelkeeping and it refreshed me as well as being a challenge. My luggable also became very useful for work purposes and proved a good investment. I worked hard on my book and when the time came to send off some chapters to agents, I took it as a personal affront when rejected.

I always knew that I would come back to writing when time permitted.

Chris gave me infinite encouragement and never understood my fury at rejection.

As far as I was concerned, the early nineties were when computers started to impact on businesses. They had of course been around for years. At the Waldorf Astoria in the mid-sixties I was introduced to theirs, which only dealt with the sales ledger. It was the size of two double-decker buses glued together, with whirring wheels the size of cable drums. But clearly computers were coming into their own at this time and I determined to learn more.

Suzi and I devised a system for the Gilpin accounts. She processed the invoices, initially manually, into ledgers, then gave me a trial balance from which to prepare the monthly accounts – also manually. It was a laborious process but one which worked well because it enabled the inclusion of intelligence – a rare commodity in computers. The time came when we felt we must employ a bookkeeper to do much of this work. Mike (I shall call him) came two half-days a week and his work saved me an enormous amount of time. It also enabled me to have results much more quickly and to provide information to the bank.

Mike's arrival coincided with the invention of BACs, although it might not have been called that then. Instead of paying suppliers with individual cheques, Mike prepared a list of payments to be made by the bank direct to our suppliers. The schedule included the name of the supplier, the account details and the amount to be paid. The list had to be signed by an authorised signatory (Chris or me only) before submission.

Prior to putting the system to work, we had to collect the bank account details of the suppliers whom we were to pay in this manner. This information was held on file. There was also a significant reduction in bank charges from using this system. Mike brought this list to me weekly. I did not check the amounts payable with invoices. Why should I? That was his job. Besides, he was a charming, well-spoken, good-mannered gentleman in whose mouth butter would not melt. We regularly treated Mike and his wife to dinner in the restaurant as a thank you for his hard work.

One day, Chris phoned her order through to the butcher we used and he said he could not supply us as he had not been paid for two months. She came to me upset and angry. She rightly said that it was my responsibility to ensure payment of our suppliers. It just so happened that I remembered signing off a payment to the butcher just the week before – quite a large one. I phoned the butcher and asked him to check. Did he realise that he was no longer paid by cheque? Yes. Had he checked the bank statement? Yes. I promised him a cash payment of whatever was owing on delivery of Chris's order. Agreed. I looked in the file which should have contained the supplier payment list. It was empty.

Now thoroughly perplexed, I phoned the bank and asked if I could have copies of the payment lists for the past month. Give them half an hour and I could call round and collect this information. I did. And there it was – the previous week – XYZ Butchers: £1,427.16. But the sort code and account number did not tally with the payment made.

I phoned the butcher again. Did they only have one bank account? Yes. I phoned the bank and asked to speak to the manager. He took my call and asked for the account details for the payment of £1,427.16. The manager said he would call me back. He did. The destination account was in the name of one Mike Somethingorother – our charming gentleman bookkeeper. The payments were apparently made entirely on the basis of the sort code and account number. Not the name of the account. So the payment that I had authorised in favour of XYZ Butchers had gone to an account belonging to Mike. So had many others.

We involved the police. Mike was prosecuted and ordered to pay some minimal retribution. He had, it transpired, been playing this game with a number of his clients. Amazingly, he came to see me one day before his trial and demanded to be paid his outstanding fees. My reply was not polite.

The boiler was proving quite incapable of dealing with the three extra rooms and the lounge and demands of a busier kitchen. ABC Plumbing and Heating were brought in to spec a new boiler and gas (LPG in our case as there was no mains gas) was regarded at the time as the favoured fuel. We needed to get the new boiler installed before the next winter set in. A temporary device was connected to the system while the changeover took place. We were delighted to see the back of the ugly oil tank which had been located outside the kitchen.

It all worked fine and looked modern and efficient. It had been located in the basement where the oil boiler had been, and a drain had been installed so that any ingress of rainwater would run away and leave the boiler high and dry. Another potential problem knocked on the head. Yippee!

Then the man from CORGI (gas inspectorate) came to sign off the job as safe. No it wasn't. LPG (unlike natural gas) is heavier than air, and as such, any subterranean installation cannot run on LPG.

In fact we were sitting on a potential bomb. Any gas leakage, instead of dissipating into the air, would accumulate in the basement and could cause an explosion. We had thirty days to have the problem rectified. ABC Plumbing and Heating admitted their error. The gas boiler was removed and replaced by a modern oil-fired boiler. Back came the oil tank. At least it was new and clean! We had tons of heat and hot water.

Barney, Zoë, Brent and goodness knows who else were all now living together and working in London. Barney and Zoë visited quite frequently. It can't have been much fun. They always wound up working. Barney had been promoted in his job and was obviously doing well and learning plenty. Tales of bent bookkeepers and illegally installed boilers must have caused them to wonder what kind of idiots we were. The same question had occurred to Chris and me.

Of Ben we had heard nothing for some weeks. There was no answer from the telephone number in Kenya he had left with us – the home of the parents of a boy he had been with at Ampleforth. We managed to persuade the school to give us the English telephone number of the same people. Charming of course but no help. Ben had been fine when he had left their place in Kenya to go hiking. How naughty not to have been in touch. But public call boxes in Kenya were few and far between and those that did exist rarely worked. We shouldn't worry unduly. Boys will be boys. The police in Kendal were neither helpful nor hopeful. They thought it was extraordinary to allow a teenager to be wandering around Kenya alone. Very irresponsible of his parents. We might try ringing the Foreign Office. They agreed to report the matter to the High Commission in Nairobi. They said much the same as the Kendal police.

Then we got a telephone call from Ben. Reverse charge. He had had his passport and all his money stolen and did not have the wherewithal to pay his fare home. Oh yes – sorry he had not been in touch. Public call boxes in Kenya were few and far between and those that did exist rarely worked! The one he was on at the moment was pure luck. It had suddenly descended from a tree in the jungle! The name of the place where he was now? It didn't have one! So how could we deal with the passport and where should the money be sent? As soon as he knew where he was he would let us know. He did. He was somewhere near Arusha in Tanzania. He would stay in this guesthouse until everything was sorted out. How would he pay for the guesthouse? With the money we were going to send him. Of course! How silly of us!

I spent hours on the telephone with the Foreign Office. This was going to be very difficult. Could Ben get to Dodoma or Dar Es Salaam? Almost certainly not. He had no money. How was he going to get back to England then? With the money that the Foreign Office were going to send him. And passport. Yes indeed. Of course. Eventually he did arrive back. We felt sorry for the other passengers on the flight. He had grubs growing in his feet!

My relationship with my sister Elizabeth had always been questionable. She was not very kind to me when I was a little boy and once put a slow worm down my neck. I attribute to this my absolute terror of snakes. I know I loved her but I never knew quite where I stood. At the time to which I refer, her partner was Bernard. One night when it so happened that Barney, Zoë and Ben were with us, I got a phone call from Bernard. It was late to be making phone calls and we all assembled in our upstairs sitting room to find out what was going on.

Bernard wanted me to know, in no uncertain terms, that Elizabeth and he were furious at what was going on at Knipe Tarn. By taking over the upstairs flat, we were denying use of the house to Elizabeth and him, as well as to Melanie (Elizabeth and Roger's daughter) and all the other members of the family and their friends.

We had also caused Dorothy so much grief that she had had to cut off ties with Knipe Tarn (which she loved) and stopped going, thereby leaving our father to fester in Dorothy's horrible little flat in London, alternating with being very lonely on his visits to Knipe, which was resulting in his becoming a depressed alcoholic.

I think Bernard must have been pissed, although he seemed lucid. But I could not get a word in. I asked if I could speak to Elizabeth. He wouldn't let me. I suppose we should have seen this coming, and in a way what Bernard had said was true – at least as far as denying others access to Knipe was concerned. We had however believed – genuinely – that being around to keep Pa company on his visits was what everyone wanted. He was nearly eighty. As far as the rest of the conversation was concerned, it was away with the fairies.

Ben went to Newcastle University that September to commence the long path to being an architect.

Suzi was turning out to be a great asset. She was a natural hotelier who could turn her hand to anything. She was also fun to have around. One day a parcel arrived. I saw from the label that it contained the "Do not Disturb" notices for the bedroom doors which I had asked Suzi to order.

I opened the package. They were very smart. Just the right size for the doorknobs. The print was the shade of green that Chris had specified. They said "Do not Distrub". We were now the proud owners of 500 Do not Distrub signs. Very useful. Thanks Suzi!

Towards the end of that year, Chris started to become very tired and irritable. She was struggling to run the kitchen morning, noon and night and although this was hardly surprising in itself, I was worried. She was referred to a specialist and we went together to Manchester.

Chapter Eighteen

THE ORCHARD WING

The specialist was large (in every dimension), old-fashioned, proper and dressed in a morning suit. He declared that it would be inappropriate for me to be present during his examination of Chris. I didn't get this at all and told him that I really needed to know about Chris's condition. I tried, unsuccessfully, to read a newspaper for what seemed like hours. Then I was admitted to the consulting room.

Chris had to have a hysterectomy. She would be off work completely for several weeks and then confined to light duties for several more weeks. Arrangements were made to perform the operation in about a month's time. He said that she was also exhausted and must start to take life easier with immediate effect. She must be fit for a serious operation.

As we drove through Manchester on the way home we were both quiet. We had changed the old Ford estate car for a second-hand BMW, which was much more comfortable and slightly sporty. 'Well! At least we know what it is,' I said.

'I've known for ages,' Chris replied. 'About the hysterectomy and the exhaustion. And the depression,' she added.

There was really no answer to this so I didn't give one.

'You'll have to find a new chef.'

I noted the "you".

I didn't think this was the right moment to say so, but privately I was relieved. We had both in our hearts known for some time that something would eventually have to give. I had never intended nor expected when we started our own business for Chris to have to work so hard. Nor myself actually. I recalled somewhat bitterly a stupid comment I had made to Chris on our first evening at The Hole in the Wall. 'Now you can take it easy,' I had said. How could one be so stupid at my age?

She fell asleep in the car. I started to compose an advertisement to put in the *Westmorland Gazette* and *The Caterer and Hotelkeeper*. We were very inexperienced at recruiting staff and had never used any method other than advertising in the local and trade press. I imagined agencies existed but we had no knowledge of them. *The Caterer* was expensive. But this was a crisis.

I knew Chris pretty well by now. We had been married for over 20 years. Normally contained when dealing with other people, unless grievously riled, she took no prisoners with me. She was scared for herself and the business. And probably for me. She didn't like change. And this situation meant serious change. Change for her personally, and for the way Gilpin was run.

It would necessitate finding a new Head Chef. We couldn't go backwards now, just as we were gaining momentum. We would have to employ someone with ability and vision. Someone who could work with us and not demand to call the shots. Someone with passion but without the egotism which often accompanies ambition. In other words someone expensive, who, unlike Chris, would expect days off and holidays. So a sous chef too?

I phoned the boys and Chris and I shared the news with Richard. Chris rallied, as she always does, and started to get excited about a new role in the front of the house, thereby easing some of the payroll costs there. She started focusing on design, and books and magazines arrived by post. This was clearly in her blood and her next port of call. She started reading relevant magazines in bed at night and the tearing out of pages became a familiar sound. She usually fell asleep with the bedside lamp on, and her glasses too. I had to go round to her side of the bed to deal with both.

People have often asked us what is the most important ingredient in running a hotel. There really is no answer. You can't have great food and dirty rooms. Superb food and poor service. The gardens must be lovely. The basis of marketing (now of course a massive discipline in its own right) is understanding people – guests and potential guests – why they do things and what they want. This necessitates some knowledge of history and geography. You must have courage, tenacity, leadership, taste, ability to communicate, and a grasp of law and accountancy. Some DIY saves a lot of money. You have to have knowledge of your business. Battersea and subsequent experiences had served Chris and me well.

A few people have succeeded in the hotel business without acquiring these attributes. Many more have failed. Perhaps the most important attribute is good judgement of situations and people. Hotels fly on the wings of people and you cannot survive without surrounding yourself with sincere, honest, professional staff: a tall order in a small concern.

Chris had long since set out her stall in terms of the ethos of hospitality and food at Gilpin. I knew that decor was the next chapter. And I was happy that it was. She has always been proactive, energetic and focused. And having a new passion was good for her and for all of us. I have never been jealous of the praise thrown at Chris for what she does, and she has always been at the forefront of those aspects of the business which get noticed. No-one has ever said to me 'that's a good insurance policy' or 'what a wonderful job description'. I don't care. I know that what I do and did is necessary, even if not exotic.

The adverts in the trade and local press brought a healthy response. I looked forward to the interviews, although I admit now as I did to myself then, that interviewing chefs was my least-favoured category.

Time was when interviews were largely conducted on the basis of truth. Truth from the employer about the real nature of the job, and truth from the potential employee about what he or she had done in the past and what they would be able to do if offered the job. This two-directional integrity had started by this time to be watered down. European employment law and a generally less acerbic interpretation of the concept of truth were responsible, coupled with restrictions on what could and could not be asked at interviews and what could and could not be set out in references. A sad and silly development. And this state of affairs applied particularly to chefs.

This is absolutely not to suggest that chefs are less truthful than other employees. It is to identify that their achievements (and aspirations) are less able to be accurately assessed, partially due to a degree of subjectivity over their performance. Food is a very subjective matter. The particular difficulty that we had over this appointment was that the successful candidate would be taking over from one of the owners – a staggeringly difficult situation, particularly since it had to be made obvious to applicants that we believed that the food we were offering to our guests was what they wanted and a major reason why our business was growing.

This angle undoubtedly disqualified several of the interviewees, either because they were unable to accept this perspective or because we were unconvinced that they would be able to live up to it. In the end we appointed Christopher Davies, whom we liked a lot and trusted to honour his promises. He was able to start at about the same time as Chris's operation, which meant a very brief handover. His appointment was a big relief. Chris was to be with us for nine years and he fulfilled his undertaking to travel on parallel tracks to us.

Chris's hospitalisation hurtled towards us and I was conscious that I was going to have to lean heavily on Richard's shoulders while I was back and forth to Manchester.

The big day came. I sat impatiently in Chris's room while the operation was performed. The consultant pronounced the procedure a complete success without complications. I sat by her bed until late into the night. She was groggy and kept falling asleep. Nurses came and went taking her temperature and blood pressure. She slurped some soup.

The histology took an agonising three weeks before the all-clear.

The preparation of our accounts was getting to me. It was slow and unpunctual. The bank wanted better information and so did I. I had read up on options for the in-house preparation of spreadsheets and decided to deal with this significant project while Chris was out of the way. I diverted from my usual route to visit Chris in hospital and called into a large computing shop in Manchester. I knew what I wanted and bought a programme called Quattro Pro. I'm not good at hospital visits, even to the one I love. You run out of things to say. And Chris gets particularly impatient and spends the visit dictating things for me to do.

I was particularly keen to get away that evening and get stuck into Quattro Pro. I'm good at accounts but have never had a minute of computer training. I did not know if I would be able to do it. My experience to date was that any instructions associated with computing were written in gobbledegook.

I got home, grabbed a sandwich and switched on my computer. As usual, the default interface was required to be downloaded onto a megabyte PDF via an intranet connection with an aggregate value stored on a cloud expanded to the sum of each menu accessed by using the browser and the inverted keyboard expressed as a percentage of the function keys on the web access. Bollocks!

By five in the morning I had programmed a basic profit and loss account. I shared my work of art with Suzi the next day. I was supremely proud of myself and our accounting function evolved quickly into an efficient and timely process. The profit and loss account soon resulted in a cash flow projection. Accounting was of course a strictly "non-exotic" function and few accolades were forthcoming from any sources except the bank, and I believe that the accuracy and speed of subsequent reporting was a major plank in the relationship with them.

Unfortunately, shortly thereafter the Windermere branch was held up at gunpoint (you'd think the hoodlums might have picked the Piccadilly Circus branch!) and the manager retired with shot-up nerves. So my achievement was forgotten. Not by me.

Back home, Chris was a nightmare patient. At least in the hospital there were doctors and nurses to help. Not so at home. The noise of pages from design magazines being torn out was thunderous!

Chris did return to work and to the kitchen, and she and Chris Davies made a compatible pair. The quality of the food was noteworthy and the level of return business, both from local people and returning resident guests was obvious. This was soon acknowledged by Gilpin being awarded a "Highly Commended" from Cumbria Tourist Board and one AA rosette for food. These were our first accolades.

It just so happened that the letter from the AA came on a day when Chris was in London on a wine course. She was staying at the Marriott in Swiss Cottage where Barney worked. I thought it would do Barney's career no harm to let his colleagues and thereby possibly his bosses know that his parents' hotel was worthy of these accolades. So I broke the news to Chris and Barney by sending them both (separately) a rather OTT fax with the letters from the CTB and AA attached.

Through the door one morning, after the last guest had checked out or gone out for the day, walked a middle-aged couple and a girl who appeared to be in her late teens. I was laying up tables after breakfast, wondering by chance if this activity really was good use of my time. I went into the hall to greet them.

'I'm Edward Redmayne,' the man said, 'and this is my wife Jean and my daughter Sarah.'

The accent was approximately local.

'Good morning to you all,' I said, shaking their hands one by one. 'What can I do for you? I'm John Cunliffe. My wife and I own the hotel.'

'Sarah has just graduated from Blackpool Catering College,' the man said. 'She wants a job. In management,' he added. 'We've done our home-work and it seems as if Gilpin would be suitable.'

'I'll fetch Christine,' I said. 'She's in the kitchen. We'll have a chat with Sarah.'

'I'd like to be present,' the man said.

'How old is Sarah, Mr Redmayne?' I asked.

'Nineteen.'

'And she wants a job in management, you said?'

'Yes.'

'How is she going to manage anything if you don't let her?' I asked.

'He's right,' Mrs Redmayne interjected.

'Yes,' I said. 'It's Sarah we're considering employing.' He looked cross. 'If you would like to have a seat here,' I waved to a sofa, 'I'll get someone to

A holiday in
Altea, Spain.
Good legs and a
pretty face...

Below:
Beckenham Place
Park. The boys in
the garden, Chris
at home

15,000 MEALS TO COOK A DAY!

FOOD, glorious food must be the motto of Christine Cunliffe who has just become the borough's number one dinner lady.

Christine, pictured, is Bromley's new senior school meals organiser and has the responsibility of getting 15,000 school meals out to hungry pupils every day.

She has worked for the council as an assistants meals organiser for more than three years and is anxious to continue providing a wide range of nutritional meals at good value for money.

Parents providing a packed lunch for their child would find it difficult to match the school meals' value, she believes. Meals cost 50 pence and are presented buffet style.

Christine or an assistant is out every weekday monitoring the 109 kitchens in the borough, and she encourages parents to look at the school meals on offer if they arrange a convenient time with the head.

The boss. A local newspaper story about Chris's appointment as head of Bromley's school meals service. I was a fan!

At The Hole in the Wall, Bath. Head chef Bernard Habert larking around

Far left: Celebrating saying goodbye to Bath

Above: Gilpin Lodge before any additions

Left: A thorough spring clean of our new hotel

The early Gilpin Lodge team. From left: Christine Barker, Richard, Jenny, Pauline, me, Chris, Alison Barker

The Head Chef and her boys

Next Head Chef Chris Davies multi-tasking; Outhouse; Chris sharing a joke with Richard Marriott

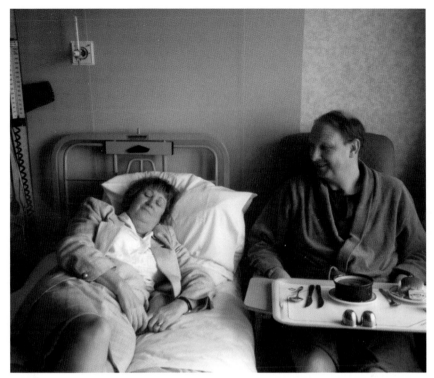

My appendectomy

Our first award: the 1993 AA Award for Best Newcomer in Northern England

Here comes the bride: an early Gilpin wedding

A sporty guest

Promoting afternoon tea

When the restaurant was in the Small Lounge

Troutbeck. Lots of pine

A serious planning meeting with Ben, Chris and Barney

Below: the (post-grad) gangster and the graduate

With dad and Barney. Above: Ben's 21st birthday party at Knipe Tarn. A good do...

Barney and Zoë married in September 2000

Xiá trying to look angelic

Alice and Freddie looking adorable

Ben and Rachel married in June 2014

In Monaco
at a Relais
& Châteaux
conference

Two generations

'Long sufferers' at Cartmel Races. From left, Richard, Gill, me, Claire, Chris, Janine, Tina, Paula, Suzi, Sarah

Winning a Johansens Most Excellent Service award

Red Stars and Rosettes from the AA

Winning AA
Hotel of the
Year, 2011-12,
with Sophie
Raworth from
BBC News

Another
Johansens
award,
presented by
Penny Junor

Accepting a
special award
for Lifetime
Achievement
from Prue
Leith at the
Cumbria Life
Food & Drink
Awards in 2017

The new Spa Lodges at Gilpin Hotel

One of the Spa Lodges, above, and Garden Suites, right, at night

The Lake House and Knipe Tarn put back together again, and left, an inquisitive llama

Gilpin Spice: another project finished. Xiá, second from right, in training

We've come a long way... a present from Antarctica

bring you coffee and Christine and I will talk to Sarah.'

They sat on the sofa, like three birds on a telegraph wire. I fetched Chris from the kitchen and introduced her to the Redmaynes. We took Sarah to the Drawing Room and talked at length. She was timid and obviously used to her father taking the lead. But somewhere in her make-up there was also determination. And charm. She asked intelligent questions. I asked Sarah to rejoin her parents and promised to get back to her in five minutes.

Chris and I talked privately. Chris doubted she would be tough enough to survive. I took the view that there was nothing to lose. I told Chris of my musings of half-an-hour before about laying tables. We shared our concerns about the escalating payroll costs but agreed that we could not operate without more help. We decided to offer Sarah a job as Assistant Manager. She and her parents seemed pleased. She would sort out accommodation and start in two weeks' time.

That was twenty-four years ago and Sarah is still at Gilpin – now as House Manager. She has, together with Richard and Suzi, been the adhesive that has held Gilpin together, and her natural professionalism has made her beloved to many guests. And of course to all of our family.

Around about this time, the ongoing subject of background music surfaced. The debate was to carry on until the present day and has become for me more of a crusade than an hotel operational issue. Unfortunately, it remains a failed crusade.

After the construction of the New Wing, which included the Drawing Room, pressure on lounge space was relieved but the shortage of dining room tables was dire. So we had extended the "little lounge" behind the fireplace and converted it into another dining room. This provided a further eight tables, giving us seventeen altogether divided between three rooms. This formula provided an intimate configuration with each table against a wall or a window. No one was stuck in a void.

In doing the electrical drawings for the new restaurant, the Courtyard Room as it was then called, the architect had advised that we should include wiring for speakers. The rationale was that even if we never needed them, it was an inexpensive addition which might at some future date prove useful. And so we did, with the wiring leading back to the main hall.

As we subsequently refurbished the Morning Room and the Main Restaurant, this facility was appended. The necessary equipment for playing CDs and for amplification was added. Initially this was only used for the chimes of Big Ben on New Year's Eve. But as time went on, demand became apparent for background music at dinner time.

To say that Gilpin was then, any more than now, run as a democracy would be inaccurate. Decisions were almost all made by Chris and me. But, in deference to encouraging our management and staff to feel involved, and in recognition of different generations and cultures, we regularly consulted the team about ideas. Chris was particularly good at doing this on a very ad hoc basis. I tended to wait for periodic meetings.

The upshot of the background music debate was that most of the front of house staff thought that it would be a good thing. Subtle, orchestral CDs were purchased – not vocal, classical nor pop. The system was only switched on at the beginning of dinner and sotto voce, with the emphasis on sotto. On this basis I remained dispassionate.

The rot had however set in. We were by this time, thanks primarily to the Cumbria Tourist Board, receiving a smattering of American and Japanese visitors, the latter drawn by their allurement to Beatrix Potter. One morning after breakfast, an American who had been particularly boring the evening before (ice tea; why no aircon? I want some 'wadder'; coffee served with dessert, etc) had sought me out.

'Jahn,' (as he pronounced my name), 'I've gotta complaint.'

'I'm sorry to hear that Mr Blumenthal,' I said. 'What's the problem?'

'You forgot to switch the music on at breakfast.'

'No I didn't Sir. We don't play music at breakfast.'

'Why not Jahn? That's when you need it most, when everyone's quiet.'

'When it's quiet. Precisely,' I said.

'Are you pissing me about?' He asked, an edge to his voice. I resented his language.

'No. I'm telling you that English people like to be quiet in the morning. It's a time when we read the newspaper, plan the day, consider the weather, discuss issues or just think.'

'You and your boring weather,' he retorted.

I walked away without saying anything more. I was off that evening and when I came in slightly late the next morning, the music was playing. Mr Blumenthal was sitting with his wife having breakfast – grinning.

'Morning Jahn.'

Sarah was beside herself. 'He threatened to make a scene if I didn't switch it on,' she whispered to me.

'Morning Mr Blumenthal.' I walked over to the amplifier and switched it off. He got up from the table and came into the hall where the controls were.

'Switch that on,' he snarled at me. By now I was furious.

He was quite a short arse. I drew myself up to my full six foot two-and-a-half inches and said to him in a very firm voice, 'You do not decide on the policies of this hotel. You do not countermand my valid instructions to my management and staff. And you do not throw your weight around and behave as if you are something more important than you are. Otherwise you can pack your bags and leave – when you have paid your bill in full.'

This creeping cancer of background noise has, over the intervening years, pervaded all our lives to what I believe is a serious degree. Many will I am sure regard my stance as old-fashioned to the point of being almost Calvinistic. I disagree. I believe that the constant and ubiquitous invasion of our senses by background music, now often so loud as to be no such thing as background, is a barrier to thought, consideration or other important emotional functions.

Chris and I once, many years later, sat at dinner on a cruise with the actors Timothy West and Prunella Scales, who were, it transpired, officials of an organisation (the name of which I forget) established to promote the suppression of background music in public places.

We got on well. Better move on!

Happily, Chris was proved wrong (yes, it can happen) about Sarah, and she quickly became a major asset to Gilpin and a great help to, particularly, Richard and I in running the restaurant. She had been well-tutored at Blackpool College and adapted quickly and comfortably to the ethos of Gilpin Lodge. Indeed, I would go further than that and say that she took over as "leader" of hospitality and guest welfare – a role she has championed ever since. She was and is particularly good at remembering guests' names and their backgrounds and preferences. She knew exactly what was going on at all the tables in the three rooms and quite soon became virtually the restaurant manager, in all but title. Guests relax with her because she has a natural northern charm which is endearing and unthreatening.

She changed my life in that I soon became comfortable to leave her, and ceased to feel obliged to be in charge at all times if Richard was not there. She also got on very well with Chris Davies, which occasioned good relationships between the kitchen and the front of house.

The additions to our staff were significant steps forward in our positioning as a professional hotel. I came to realise that guests did not like to see the owners around morning, noon and night on a daily basis. I think they felt uncomfortable relaxing when we were obviously working all the time. Even though the hotel was very busy, the payroll costs were scary. It was obvious that, yet again, we needed more bedrooms. And we were confident that we could fill them.

In the interim we started to do Sunday lunch, for which there seemed to be a healthy demand. It thrived. The good old-fashioned traditional thing. We shunned any direction which smacked, even remotely, of nouvelle cuisine, which was raising its pitiful head in some circles. It was, after all, merely a French expression for mean portions and greater profits. In addition to rich gravy on the meat (roast beef was always available) we served additional gravy in sauce boats, thereby offering the option to splurge the Yorkshire puddings. Thus at least two good things came out of Yorkshire – Chris and puddings!

Sarah's involvement was particularly fortunate in that, just as Chris was regaining full fitness, I had to have a few weeks off myself. It was Mother's Day (not Mothering Sunday as the Americans have to call it: "mother" is a noun not a verb!). The hotel was full and lunch was booked to the hilt. During the service of breakfast I felt profoundly ill with a piercing pain in my abdomen. I told Chris I had to see a doctor immediately. She reminded me that it was Mother's Day. At that time we had a doctor's surgery on Sundays in Windermere. You could turn up without an appointment. The good doctor felt certain that I had acute appendicitis and phoned the hospital in Lancaster.

Nobody could be spared from Gilpin to take me and I suppose because I was going to a private hospital (we had enjoyed BUPA for years), an ambulance was not available. So I drove myself – carefully and with difficulty. I was operated on within an hour of the surgeon examining me. Chris came to see me in the afternoon and reported to my groggy self that Richard and Sarah had managed lunch with aplomb. The kitchen had also excelled. It was the biggest number we had ever done, with four tables being relaid. Then she fell asleep on the bed.

Shortly after my return to work we had two "situations" involving the RAC, which in those days still inspected and rated hotels. Their influence, though not as great as that of the AA, was important. My dad came to Knipe frequently, and without Dorothy was good company, although we would have liked the odd evening to ourselves. He liked to dine at Gilpin and understandably felt somewhat proprietorial, based both on his present status and the background of Gilpin having been his home.

On this particular occasion he was with a doctor friend who lived nearby. My dad and his friend Ian were seated at a table next to one occupied by a single gentleman. We had quite a few business guests in those days, mostly from K Shoes and Marks & Spencer, so this situation was not unusual. Chris Davies came out of the kitchen to say hello to Tony, and after a brief chat he excused himself and came to find me.

'The man on table 4 is an RAC inspector,' he whispered. 'I recognise him.' We passed the word round.

Shortly thereafter, my dad's and Ian's main courses were served. Our policy was, after service of the main course, to give it a few minutes before enquiring of the guest if everything was satisfactory. But my dad did not give it a few minutes. He hailed Richard over and complained in a loud voice (a normality with very deaf people) that his steak was overcooked and tough.

The RAC man had his back to me while dad was facing me. I put a finger to my lips and tried everything I could think of to signal dad to be quiet. But no. He forged ahead. Dad was capable of being very – what shall we call it – forceful? 'You need to change your butcher,' he declared. I was waiting in dread of his adding 'and your chef'. He didn't. It was very naughty and he wouldn't have done it if my Chris had been in the kitchen.

I wrote him a note and slipped it in front of him while he awaited a replacement steak: 'There's an RAC inspector at the next table. Please don't make any further derogatory comments.'

He looked shocked. The matter was not discussed. It was as if it had not happened.

A few weeks later, whether as a result of the steak incident or not, we had another single gentleman come to stay. Our knowledge of inspectors was not great and we didn't recognise the man nor have him down as an inspector. I became slightly suspicious at dinner when he quizzed me over the grape varieties in a New Zealand Sauvignon Blanc. I suppose he was trying to find out if I was amateur or professional. I explained politely that it was Sauvignon Blanc!

After breakfast he announced himself and produced a business card. Unlike Michelin, who rarely introduce themselves, the AA and the RAC normally do. Chris, the RAC man and I repaired to the Drawing Room and I asked someone to bring coffee.

'I'll start with my arrival,' he said. 'The girl who checked me in was good and called me by name after I had introduced myself. But she then escorted me to my room and carried my bag.'

Chris and I waited. 'I don't like that,' he continued, 'it makes me feel uncomfortable for a girl to carry my luggage.'

'She's quite a strong girl,' I ventured.

'That's not the point,' he retorted. 'She's a girl.'

'We only have nine bedrooms,' I said. 'We can't have a dedicated male porter.'

'Understanding your problems is not part of my remit,' the man said. 'Our job is to assess quality.'

'With no regard to our size or viability?' I asked.

Chris kicked me under the table.

'In America and many parts of Asia, the girls often do the portering jobs while the men make the beds,' Chris commented with a beguiling smile. 'They usually generate more tips.'

'We're not in America or Asia,' he observed. 'This is good old-fashioned England.'

I could feel Chris starting to bristle.

'To move on,' he said, 'I thought my room was small for a Highly Commended hotel. And there's supposed to be a full-length mirror in the room.'

'There is,' Chris said.

'There's not,' he retorted. 'Tell me where it is.'

'Behind the bathroom door,' Chris said.

'That's not in the bedroom.'

There was a long pause, then Chris just said: 'Have you finished Mr Finnigan? I don't think you and I are going to see eye-to-eye over how a hotel should be run.'

Ever since the New Wing had been built we had spasmodic smoking chimneys in both the log fire in the Drawing Room and the original one in the small lounge. There seemed to be no pattern to these incidents. One day everything was fine and the next it was like a pea souper. The amount of energy devoted to finding a solution was massive. We eventually came to the conclusion that the culprit was the wind direction. How do you change that? The architects we used at that time suggested that we needed to extend the chimneys so that the down draft from north-easterly winds didn't push the smoke back down the chimneys into the rooms.

It sounded sensible. Builders were employed. Scaffolding was erected. Stacks were extended. Hopes were as high as the chimneys. Five thousand pounds worse off – and no difference whatsoever. The furnishings were suffering and a constant smell of smoke was present. Log suppliers were changed. Coal was tried instead of logs. Coke was tried instead of coal. No change. Then a guest who was not even an engineer solved the problem, which he had had in his own home.

Apparently there is a critical ratio between the size of the grate and the diameter of the chimney flu. A simple baffle was made and installed to reduce the size of the grate. Instant result in the Drawing Room. Problem solved overnight for a hundred pounds. Bless him. But the same solution could not be applied in the small lounge as the fireplace was too small. A whole new fire and grate was needed. A fireplace specialist was called in. A new fire was chosen and fitted. Instant success.

Or was it? The guests in Cleabarrow, the bedroom above the small lounge, complained of a constant burning smell. We extinguished the fire below. The next day the smell in Cleabarrow was worse. The fire below had not been lit. We moved the guests to another room. The fireplace in the small lounge, despite not having a fire in it for twenty-four hours, was almost too hot to touch. I had the inspiration (well, some would say it was common sense) to go outside and check the chimney. Smoke was billowing out as well as sparks. Thus we proved the adage that there's no smoke without fire!

Guests were just beginning to assemble for drinks before dinner. Chris and I concluded that we could not rule out the prospect of the building catching fire, even though the source of the smoke was a mystery. I dialled 999 and asked for the Fire Brigade. They arrived ten minutes later. Two appliances and a platoon of men. They were as mystified and worried as we were. They suggested we should evacuate the hotel. How can you do this with twenty or so guests anticipating dinner? How could you explain such an action when there is no fire?

The firemen took a hose onto the roof and poured water down. It came out in the fireplace as you would expect – together with steam and soot which collected on the carpet. The place began to smell like a steam train. Hoses were brought in through the front door and across the floor of the small lounge. The guests stepped over them as they were escorted to their tables. Water was squirted up the chimney. More steam and soot. Not surprisingly, gravity being what it is, the water came down again and flooded onto the carpet. The fireman in charge concluded that there was a secondary fire behind the fireplace. He assessed the risk of the chimney catching fire as very serious. The whole fireplace including the beautiful Arts and Crafts surround must be broken open. Chris pleaded and burst into tears. So we had two floods!

The senior officer agreed to try to save the surround but was adamant that the fireplace itself must be jemmied out. The guests carried on eating, drinking and being merry. Axes, crowbars and sledgehammers were fetched. Our new fireplace was smashed out and behind it was voilà – a burning fire, rubble, soot and dry plaster blazing away. It took some time for the dust to settle.

Looking back on this scenario it seems unlikely. But it happened – just as I have described it. Today, political correctness and the sanctity of health and safety would demand the evacuation of the hotel, and guests would in all probability demand to be evacuated. And reimbursed! But then common sense existed and the spirit of Dunkirk lingered on.

To say that the place looked as if a terrorist attack had taken place would be an understatement. The guests left their dinners to survey the source of the problem. The fire was quickly extinguished. The boss fireman said that someone must stay up all night, fire extinguisher at the ready, in case of further combustion. The surrounding area was so hot. Richard and I tossed a coin for the job. He lost and went to change into some comfortable clothes. We rewarded the firemen with steak and chips. Chris dried her eyes. The next day the insurers authorised a new carpet. At last the evidence of my attempt to lift molten wax with a hot iron would be permanently removed. A bitter row ensued with the fireplace installer but the firemen's report left little room for manoeuvre. A new fire was installed.

We had a mixed relationship with the fire brigade. In those days, unlike now with in-house risk assessments being the name of the game (in other words, no-one except the hotelier can be blamed in the event of a fire, even though clearly we are not experts), we were told what we had to do. It was a much better arrangement in that professionals assessed the risks and remedies. Thus, while incidents such as that with the fireplace gave rise to extreme gratitude on our part, some of the requirements of the fire brigade were impractical and often hugely expensive and unattractive.

Inspections were without warning and often inconvenient. One such resulted in a requirement that the door to the morning room and the door to the main restaurant must be kept closed except when a person was either entering one of these rooms or leaving. We protested that a waiter or member of staff carrying plates, trays or other items did not have free hands with which to open doors. The inspector was adamant that fire precaution was his sole remit. How we used the rooms and operated was our problem. He suggested automated doors. We protested that this would be dangerous in such a small area – doors could open and cause injury. Not his problem. The use of door stops to keep the doors open must cease. We appointed fire precaution experts to plead our case. Fat fees of course. But we continued to keep these doors open.

Other inspectors (apart from the AA, the RAC and the tourist board) came unannounced to check the kitchen for hygiene and the bar for tampering with drinks. Watering down spirits is a common trick of the trade (at Ring & Brymer on the racecourse bars we had optics which required a key to remove them from the bottle). The hygiene people also had draconian powers which could require unaffordable alterations and changes to procedures.

I don't disparage these powers which along with others became increasingly onerous as the European Economic Community changed silently and unbidden into the European Union. Intelligent interpretations of legal requirements changed over time as gravy train-borne bureaucrats in Brussels and elsewhere, charged with making laws and laying down regulations, happily applied themselves to these tasks. Obligations which in theory should be applied across the EU were applied to the letter in the UK while they were, by and large, ignored in other member countries. And still are. This is of course partly why we are such a great country.

As our trust in Chris Davies and his small team became cemented, so Chris's diminution of kitchen responsibilities accelerated. As 1995 glided into 1996, it became obvious that several more rooms were both essential and sensible. Gilpin was thriving, held back only by lack of capacity. Yet another man was in charge at the bank and initial noises about five more rooms were favourably received.

The architects felt that the "mood" of the Planning Board was right for an expansion at Gilpin, and although the attitude of the board was still senescent, an acceptance by younger members was at last creeping in that quality tourism might actually be a part of the Lake District's future. Plans were submitted to build five more rooms on the same level as Heathwaite, Troutbeck and Kentmere, which had been built in 1991.

Chris moved into "design" top gear and her humble and obedient chauffeur and gofer complied, along with undertaking many other semi-invisible roles.

My father and Dorothy had by now bought two apartments in Altea in Spain: one for their own use and one for use by friends and family. In early 1996 we were invited to use the visitors' flat for a couple of weeks. We accepted with gratitude. Dates were synchronised with Barney and Ben and girlfriends and we set off for the first real holiday in ten years.

We had a memorable family time. Dad and Dorothy were not in residence so we did not have to mind our Ps and Qs too much, although threats were in place that bad behaviour would be relayed back by the concierge in charge of the small development. He was, it later transpired, heavily in Dorothy's pay!

Chris and I relaxed like we had not done for some time, and we enjoyed discussing the Orchard Wing as we had decided to call the new rooms. It had become very clear to us ever since we had been at Gilpin that we had struck upon a formula that our guests liked and were prepared to pay for, within reason. We discussed, while sitting round the pool, the application of these tenets to the Orchard Wing and made many decisions, nearly all slanting towards bigger and better rooms, excellent but unpretentious food and ever greater hospitality.

The latter, as a concept, was growing in importance in our minds, although it had always been a cornerstone of Gilpin. You can feel it when you walk into a hotel or you can feel the lack of it. All hotels are in business to try to make money. The art of hospitality is not to show this.

American corporate hotels are particularly bad at delivering hospitality and no amount of smartly dressed attendants offering "welcomes" or "have a nice days" at the front door can disguise the blatant commercialism of the enterprise.

It is, of course, partially about making time for hospitality. And time is a cost. It's a hidden cost. You never see it listed on a profit and loss account. Neither do you see "maintenance of standards". Management time achieves both concepts. In larger hotels, guests now don't expect to see senior management, who spend their time in meetings and sending emails.

Shortly after our return from Spain we received news that the planning application had been approved and so had the bank loan. The architects for the Orchard Wing project strongly recommended the appointment of an on-site project manager.

Our inexperience in this field was exposed by our belief that this was the job of the architect. The fee was considerable but we took their advice. Probably one of the best decisions we ever made. Meetings were attended, contractors were appointed and decisions were minuted.

Chris was struggling with the design process. It soon became apparent that DIY interior designing was not what the industry wanted. Attempts to obtain information and samples were blocked. If you wanted help you needed to employ and pay a professional. Trade terms (being as much as half the price of retail) were otherwise by and large unavailable. We were frankly out of our depth but Chris felt passionately that she had the talent to design our rooms to the requirements and liking of our guests.

The build process commenced in the autumn of 1996. Almost within days, we hit a problem. The problem was rock. The structure of the rock meant that dynamite would be necessary to remove some of it. This would be extremely expensive and involve the employment of specialist engineers. The soundness of the existing building could even be affected. The alternative was to alter the footprint of the new building and incorporate some steps and a ramp. It was not a very difficult decision to make.

As usual during a project, running a hotel and keeping the guests happy is tricky. To some extent this is due to an attitude of mind of most (but not all I must add) people in the construction business. To be fair, tranquility, tidiness, beauty and geniality are bad bedfellows with diggers, dumpers, drills, mud, swearing, smoking and all the associated nastiness of a building site.

Compromises had to be made over working hours, stoppages impacting on costs and many associated matters. Some guests are understanding and some check out before they have checked in. We fully understood this and have done with subsequent projects. Extreme diplomacy is required and readiness to make recompense for inconvenience. The one thing we could not under any circumstances afford to do was to close the hotel while the noisy, dirty part of the job was done. Hell.

One rainy morning, a new bank manager appeared. He had apparently replaced the one we had been dealing with. He seemed surprised that we had started the project. He told me that the proper paperwork for the additional borrowing had not been completed. I suggested, but don't recall the exact words, that that was the bank's failing. This was perhaps tactless, but I disliked this man on sight and resented the fact that we had to once again educate a new bank manager as to what we were all about.

As the conversation progressed in an increasingly unhelpful direction, it became apparent that this man had done very little homework. He advised me as his parting shot that we must stop the work as the funds would not be forthcoming to pay the bills.

Chris and I decided that at this stage that was out of the question, as considerable expenditure had already been incurred. It was also essential that if we were to meet our cash-flow projections, the new rooms must be open for Easter 1997.

I told the man from the bank that I did not accept his decision nor the basis on which it had been made. I asked him for the name and address of his area manager and this he reluctantly supplied. I wrote to the area manager and drove that afternoon to the area office in Preston to hand deliver the letter, which I kept professional and civil. I protested about the events of the morning, the attitude of the bank manager and the lack of consistency which resulted from the frequent changes of manager. As a welcome surprise, the area manager telephoned the next day and said that he would be in our area the day after that. Could he call and see me?

He agreed, when we met, that my observations were "partially" accurate and conceded that the way in which matters had been handled was not up to the bank's standards. He promised to arrange to have the necessary paperwork sent off to me by mail the next day. I stipulated that I could not agree to an early repayment penalty. I did not like nor trust him and decided to seek other banking arrangements, but in the meantime to get on with the project. The contract, when it arrived, was not based on the figures I had agreed with the previous manager. The stipulated expectations for the new rooms were unachievable. My instincts had been right. We signed, continued with the project and set about finding a different bank.

The new rooms were called Rydal, Grasmere, Patterdale, Thirlmere and Buttermere. They did not open for Easter but in May. Under the external entrance to the Orchard Wing, we sealed a time capsule not to be opened for a hundred years. I recall some of its contents: a mobile telephone the size of a shoe box, a Spice Girls CD, a copy of that week's *Westmorland Gazette* and a bottle of port – vintage 1997. We won't be around in 2097 to see the capsule opened, and I doubt the kids will. The grandchildren probably will be. I hope Gilpin is still going strong then.

We had a grand opening party and the weather was kind as the time capsule was cemented in. I made a speech and the chairman of the Cumbria Tourist Board replied and cut a ribbon placed across the entrance. She included in her speech an observation that Gilpin was gaining a reputation for trailblazing as a hotel in the Lake District.

On 17th May 1997 we became a grown-up hotel. We had fourteen rooms. We did all meals and room service. We had a proper management team. We were set to be profitable. We had by then three AA rosettes for food. Beautiful landscaping had replaced the scars of the building site. The drive had been resurfaced. New signage had been erected. Suzi, Gill, Sarah, Paula, Richard and Chris the chef were in fine fettle and a brilliant business case had been agreed with Midland Bank, which was to become HSBC. I delivered it personally to the regional office in Blackpool.

Our new bank manager came round as I was hanging the six pictures in the hallway outside Rydal, Grasmere and Patterdale. It was the hardest DIY job I have ever undertaken. Each picture was identical in size, about a metre square and they had to be equidistant from each other, the floor and the ceiling. Since then I became (and still am) Gilpin's official picture hanger.

The new bank manager was very impressed that we were such a practical and hands-on outfit.

Chapter Nineteen

PLANT, LABOUR AND MATERIALS

We slipped into operating with fourteen rooms very easily. All of us except Sarah that is. We have a longstanding joke (a kind one) about her. She simply does not like change and as we are as a business rather prone to change, she struggles when it happens. Five more rooms meant ten more guests for dinner, so we decided that for the first time we must allocate times for guests to come down for dinner.

'It'll never work,' Sarah said. 'Can you imagine telling Mr and Mrs X that they've GOT to eat at eight? They always have dinner at seven.'

We were having one of our by then quite regular meetings with Richard, Sarah, Paula, Suzi and Chris the chef. Chris Davies of course welcomed the move. Spreading out dinner times is a huge help to the kitchen as well as the restaurant. In fairness to Sarah she was thinking of the guests – not herself.

'It's all about how it's done,' my Chris stated. 'We will initially have to educate the regulars.'

'Fifty- and sixty-year-olds are not easy to educate,' Sarah maintained.

'Oh yes they are,' continued Chris. 'You have to explain to them that it's for their own good. That if, say forty guests – assuming ten non-residents

– all come down to dinner at the same time, chaos will ensue and no-one will have a good evening.'

'We'll see,' Sarah sighed with resignation.

Needless to say, our regulars did accept the rationale and new guests perceived no change. We had always applied an arrival time to non-resident guests.

The only major problem which the new rooms brought was that the septic tank arrangement could not cope. It's not a charming subject so I don't intend to dwell on it, but as it turned out it was a major issue in the history of Gilpin, and one that nearly brought us to our knees.

We discovered at this time that, a bit like smoking chimneys, architects (at least the ones we used at that time) are not experts on these matters. At least they did not pretend to be and suggested the engagement of a specialist engineer. They introduced us to a rather eccentric and slightly morbid man (you would be wouldn't you?), who operated from Windermere so was familiar with the problem of dealing with effluent in very rocky areas. All sorts of tests were undertaken and they revealed that the area around us was about as bad as it can be. More tests were conducted and the prognosis went from bad to worse.

As we headed into the summer and got busier, the problem got worse. It was eventually decided at a terse meeting, also attended by the architects, that the only solution was a fully fledged treatment plant, which as the name suggests, processes the waste rather than just letting it sink into the ground. Contractors were sought and prohibitive sums of money were discussed. It was not an option to do nothing. A sum was agreed with a firm whose name I will not reveal, the price being subject to installation. They could start the following week.

The written quotation which followed stated that the price quoted included 'all plant, labour and materials'. The new bank manager was sympathetic and gave the go-ahead. In order to get the job done as quickly as possible we reluctantly decided to abandon any attempts to avoid disruption. We apologised profusely to our guests and agreed that work could start at dawn using the most efficient diggers and dumpers available – however noisy they might be.

The job was done, quickly, efficiently and indeed noisily. Many guests were fascinated by what was going on, particularly as Crook Road had to be closed for half a day while the enormous "plant" (which is in inverted commas for a purpose which will be revealed) was craned over the wall into the pit which had been dug. Everything was connected, switched on and we waited with bated breath. It worked. It was completely quiet. The smells disappeared. The pit was filled in and everything looked good again. Life returned to normal. Or so we thought.

The question of offices had been dire for some time. Chris and I didn't have one. We conducted meetings in restaurants and did paperwork wherever we could find a chair and a flat surface. Most of the time we needed three people in reception to deal with incoming telephone calls, reservations and all the jobs that needed doing. We had taken on as a receptionist an old friend who had been in our lives since she had done secretarial work for me many years before. Michelle (not her real name) was from the Lake District and we liked to employ local people. They tended not to turn round after a few weeks and say 'oh I don't like it here. There aren't enough nightclubs,' or some such. Her husband was an accountant and he was moving to a firm in Kendal. It seemed a good idea. Only Suzi was suspicious. In those days we tried to avoid hierarchies and no discussions took place over who was senior to whom.

I'm not very good at working without my own office. I like quietness, privacy and an atmosphere in which I can consider matters, particularly if they concern people. I'm also tidy to a fault. That is probably an understatement. I cannot work surrounded by other people's chaos. I tried working from Knipe but quickly realised that this was not fair to Chris. If I wasn't available, she had to deal with all the problems.

Absence also meant failure to meet and greet guests and to check what was going on. My little rule had always been to have a wander around the public areas of the hotel at hourly intervals – irrespective of what I was doing. I couldn't do that from home.

It was a very different operation then to now when we have heads of department and responsible people around all the time. I think guests' expectations were also very different. We still have a healthy percentage of repeat guests but so many book online from all over the world that they really don't know (or care) who the owner or manager is as long as their expectations are met.

In those earlier days they did know and care, and if Chris and I were not apparent most of the time, we got it in the neck. Sarah, Suzi, Richard and others all did a good job. But as far as the guests were concerned, they had to see Chris and John.

I'm not quite sure, to this day, why that was. I have thought about it often and I think it related to a perception, as opposed to a fact, that if we were around, things were done better. I write 'as opposed to a fact', but was it? I have the advantage of having worked for a long time employed by others as well as at Gilpin, and there is no doubt whatsoever that survival and the achievement of something approaching perfection are good goals. Let's face it, even then, in the absence of the sort of employment legislation we have now, you had to do something fairly bad to get fired. By contrast, you probably had to do rather more to be noticed and promoted. It was certainly the norm, in employment, to take days off. There's no doubt that for most of my life, within and without Gilpin, I worked many more hours than people do now. At Gilpin, in the early days, seventy to eighty hours a week does not seem exaggerated. We just expected to be there.

The first and most obvious reason for this was that for years and years we just could not afford to employ enough people to get the job done properly. In the hotel business, ever since I joined the game, labour costs have always been the "killer". And few banks have understood this, although I don't intend to diversify into the question of banks at this stage. But if you open your office at eight in the morning and lock it up again at five in the afternoon, Monday to Friday (excluding Bank Holidays) it is I suppose hard to place yourself in a 24/7 situation. Hotels are 24/7 in fact 24/7/52.

What is the difference between standing in a queue for five minutes to cash a cheque and waiting for five minutes to get a glass of wine? I don't know. But people do it in the bank without a murmur. In a hotel they shout like hell. We could not afford to have them shout like hell. So we had to be around. Before minimum wage and living wage and stuff we used to think we were doing really well if payroll costs were less than 35% of net turnover. Now we're doing well to stay under 40%. In a few years' time, who knows?

The second reason why we expected to be around was that we did it better than anyone else. Now there's a boast. Conceit even. But we did. And if there was a shortfall in delivery of service for whatever reason, we apologised the most profusely and made amends the most genuinely. With the exception of Suzi, who could sell ice to an Eskimo, Chris and I regarded it as a real failure if we answered the telephone and it was a reservation enquiry which did not result in a booking. Why? Survival.

And the third reason was this funny word which is in the title of this book: perfection. A belief that if you are going to bother to do it, you may as well do it well. Or better still perfectly. I know that when I worked for other people, I strived for perfection, but knew it was not achievable. However, at Gilpin we strive for perfection, know it's not achievable but castigate ourselves from here to kingdom come if everything is not perfect.

Tied in with all of this is the age-old dilemma which presents itself almost every day. Should we keep an inadequate employee or not? There is of course no standard formula for answering this question. Legality comes into it – are we entitled to dismiss him or her? Morality plays its role. What are the person's circumstances? Might they improve with encouragement or a good rollicking? How bad is their badness? Is their attitude or failure infectious? Perhaps sadly above all considerations, who is going to do the work they did if we part company? Will the business suffer even more if there is no-one to answer the phone, cook the dinner or make the beds?

So back to the question of offices. Working from home didn't work. We didn't have enough office space. So we rented a Portakabin for me and plonked it down in front of the outhouses – exactly where the copper tree outside Gilpin Spice is now. Telephone and electricity were connected. I had my own filing cabinet and computer. And I have mistrusted the concept of working from home since then. If you are selling widgets to eejits by telephone (and being paid commission accordingly), then I can see the sense. Otherwise it's another term for avoiding responsibility to your colleagues. Human beings are social animals and they need human contact, and above all direction and checking upon. Otherwise standards slip.

And then the invoice came in for the treatment plant. It seemed in order. It was payable within thirty days so I filed it accordingly. Then about a week later another invoice came in for the installation of the treatment plant. Much the same sum as the first one. It must be a mistake.

I checked the written quotation: 'including plant, labour and materials'. Quite clear. Nonetheless, I felt a shiver physically run down my spine. I knew it was a mistake. But something told me it was not.

Should I share this with Chris? The total, if correct, was double that agreed with the bank. It was Saturday of course. So no-one to telephone. I tried without success to put it behind me throughout the rest of Saturday and Sunday. I didn't tell Chris.

First thing Monday I made a number of telephone calls. The company who had quoted for the job was adamant that two invoices was correct: one for the supply of the plant and one for the installation.

Many meetings followed with everyone who had been involved in the decision to accept the quotation. All seemed to think that the wording of the quotation was perfectly clear. I wrote to the company stating our case. The reply, by return, was brief: if payment was not received within the specified time, they would start legal proceedings to recover the entire sum.

Rightly or wrongly, I suspect the latter, we decided that we could not afford the solicitors in Manchester who had dealt with the Contract of Privity case. We approached a local firm who also thought that our position was clear. But they needed to consult a barrister. And so the matter escalated and the attendant workload started to seriously divert me from trying to run a hotel. Although everyone seemed confident, Chris and I were worried sick.

Three days had been set aside for the case to be heard at Liverpool County Court. We collected our solicitor at 6 a.m. on the first day. He wanted to spend time with the barrister before the case opened. It was a grim, foggy January morning and progress was slow. And then all traffic stopped on the M6. The signs said there had been an accident and there would be a long delay. The solicitor telephoned the court. The clerk said she would tell the judge.

We were an hour late. In view of our telephone call, the judge had started another case, a question of child protection. It should only take an hour. It took the rest of the morning so our case did not even get under way until after lunch – which seemed to be as sacred an institution as with cricket matches! We were off to a bad start. The judge addressed the barristers and merely asked, 'What can I do for you two gentlemen today?'

Was this really how it worked? Did the judge really not know what the case was all about?

I found giving testimony unchallenging. I just told the truth. Naive fool! We knew we had lost by lunchtime on the third day. Chris had overheard the two barristers discussing costs and agreeing that Mr and Mrs Cunliffe would have to pay them all.

When the moment arrived for the judge to deliver his judgement he was at pains to sympathise with us. He felt that it was understandable how the situation had come about. But unfortunately, as had been established by the barrister representing the plaintiff company, in the case of So and So versus Such and Such, the term "plant, labour and materials" had been established as having a legal definition involving the plant, labour and materials involved in the installation only, which did not therefore include the treatment plant itself. The two invoices and costs came to just over £82,000, payable within fourteen days. We didn't have it. Nothing like.

Chris and I were due to fly to India in a month's time. Some guests who had stayed at Gilpin owned a tour operator based in Delhi. A special itinerary had been prepared for us. They were far from pleased when we cancelled and they declined to refund the deposit we had paid. Another expense. The bank agreed to fund the debt and costs, but it would have to be a separate loan repayable over just five years. With a fair wind behind us it was just possible. But belts would have to be tightened.

To make matters worse, Chris and I fell out spectacularly over the outcome. She blamed me. I felt that all actions taken had been done so in good faith and with appropriate professional advice and consultation between her and I. I even quoted the judge as having admitted (to all intents and purposes) that the result was bad luck.

We were both of course very upset, disappointed and depressed. The future seemed to have significant question marks over it – again. And if another economic downturn were to occur, it seemed very possible that we would struggle to repay the bank.

Chapter Twenty

A FAMILY AFFAIR

Barney was at home for a few days waiting to start a new job in London. He was incredibly understanding and supportive and was instrumental in persuading Chris that the treatment plant situation was indeed unfortunate, but not due to negligence or fault on my part. I think the biggest anxiety was that Chris and I wanted, in the wake of building and opening the Orchard Wing, to continue to develop Gilpin in an increasingly qualitative direction. Part of this process was to employ more professional people. The affordability of this intention was now in question.

This aim of increasing quality was reinforced by several visits from John Donnithorne (of Grosvenor House days) and his wife Pat. They had sold their hotel in Bath and were enjoying retirement. John loved Gilpin and told Chris and me that we were definitely Relais & Châteaux standard. He was constructively critical of some issues and confirmed that we must employ a few more people to deliver consistent quality. Independently of our own thoughts, he felt that it was wrong to be around morning, noon and night. It suggested lack of confidence, even miserliness. But how could we afford to employ more people with this crippling debt to the bank?

In the short time that Barney was at home, he helped at Gilpin in many ways and started to show interest in what was going on. He refused, however, to be drawn on whether or not he wanted to join Chris and me. But the subject was out in the open and at least there was not a straight refusal. I could sometimes hear his mind ticking! I felt sorry for his dilemma and understood that it was perhaps too early to make that decision. But as the millennium approached, so did Chris and I hitting sixty. Chris and I were beginning, just beginning, to find it increasingly hard to put in the hours needed to do the job properly. Barney knew this too and later on told me that he could feel this even then. The treatment plant debacle had come at exactly the worst time, when we needed to be employing more people to share the burden.

To add to our woes, Suzi arrived one morning and announced that she was pregnant. It was early days and she would still be able to work for some months. But it was another anxiety. I depended on her for help in many important parts of the business.

Problems at Gilpin always seemed to come like London buses! Particularly the 137. One day I received a bill from our accountants. Charming people who helped and advised me at every turn. But the invoice was for double the expected amount. I telephoned the partner with whom I dealt. Oh yes. Sorry about that, we forgot to invoice you last year so this is for two years. Forgot? I was furious. If the accountants can't do their paperwork properly, how can I expect small local outfits to do theirs? People who write invoices after a day's work baking or butchering or fishmongering. Or was it my responsibility to remember who had invoiced us and who had not? I thought not. I had no choice but to pay up. But I did not shut up. I changed accountants to a local firm.

I recall two stories about the boys round about this time, both involving cars. Chris's and my cars to be precise. One evening off while Chris and I were preparing dinner, Ben came into the kitchen and said, very casually 'the car's in a tree'. It was a strange turn of phrase and I had this ridiculous mental picture of our Mercedes stuck in the air supported by the branches of a tree – green leaves sticking through the spokes of the wheels and out of the sunroof. I recall responding (ridiculously) that cars don't fly. He suggested that I come with him. The car was indeed well embedded into a sturdy oak in the drive – at ground level.

On another occasion, Barney was helping to ferry our Christmas guests to Bowness pier for our Boxing Day boat lunch, which had become a firm favourite as a part of our Christmas package – and still is. Richard and Sarah have presided over this activity for years. The new guests expect that they are going to be served cold meat and salad (or some such) and have to buy their drinks. Instead they are delightfully surprised to find Richard in a morning suit and Sarah dressed to kill, serving a three-course hot meal with a flight of fine wines. As *Miss Windermere* or one of the similar craft operating from Bowness heads towards Ambleside, often into a swirling December mist, pale sunshine rises from behind Coniston Old Man. The champagne begins to work its midday wonders as only champers at noon can. You get the picture?

A more mundane task altogether, my job that year was to shepherd the guests from the Drawing Room into the cars as they came back from the last run to Bowness. To this end I was standing with my back to the front door of Gilpin, somewhat anxiously awaiting Barney's return – anxious because some of the guests were getting impatient. Then the car came into sight, moving very slowly, which was not surprising because the bonnet was fully open. Actually more than fully open – it was vertical. And at a slightly squiffy angle. It turned into the drive and proceeded in a stately manner towards the front door. I have to record that had I been Barney, I would have parked in front of the outhouses. But no. Not Barney.

'I delivered the passengers to the boat,' he declared proudly, 'but because I knew there were more guests to collect, I took a short cut back up Windy Hall Lane.' I said nothing. 'It turned out to be a bit icy and well, this wall got in the way.'

Wall got in the way. Like Ben's tree!

Michelle was not working out and we were learning another lesson: don't employ friends. Although capable of good hospitality skills, she also had a side which was more akin to the worst kind of doctor's receptionist. No amount of coaching and gentle hints would eradicate this disposition. Indeed, as was soon to become apparent, Christine's and my attempts to reform this failing were creating a wall of resentment. This, and its effects was made worse by the fact that she unashamedly used her previous status as our friend to pull rank on colleagues. This caused overt frictions. Our happy business was becoming tainted.

It came to a head one breakfast service. Sarah and I were on duty in the restaurant. Michelle was in reception. As sometimes happens (you simply cannot allocate times for people to come to breakfast) all the guests came down at the same time. And everyone wanted tea not coffee. So we ran out of teapots. We have always put a tea and coffee tray in the bedrooms (to charge for room service to deliver tea in the morning is the worst kind of hospitality – who wants to have to open the door to waiting staff when you've just got out of bed?) so while rushing past reception I asked Michelle to run to a few bedrooms, get the teapots off the trays and wash them if need be. She did. I thought no more of it. Breakfast passed. I went into one of the offices to open the mail. Michelle came in wearing a face like thunder and closed the door behind her.

'How dare you talk to me like that,' she shouted.

'Like what?' I asked, genuinely puzzled.

'Demanding that I go and find teapots. Not even a "please". And I'm not a waitress.'

'It was a crisis, Michelle,' I said. 'I needed teapots urgently. The guests on table 14 had been waiting at least ten minutes for tea. They were getting quite belligerent. And what do you mean you're not a waitress? We all do everything at Gilpin, as you know full well. I'm not a waiter either. I own the hotel, but that doesn't mean I won't do anything that needs doing for our guests. What do you think I've been doing all morning if not running around serving tea and coffee and breakfasts and clearing tables and taking orders?'

'I'm a receptionist,' she said. 'In fact I am reception manager. I don't run around carrying teapots.'

She was still standing, wagging her finger at me.

'I think you had better sit down,' I said. 'The time has come for you and me to have a chat, because your attitude doesn't suit the hotel business.'

'I don't want to sit down and I don't want to chat with you or anyone else,' she shouted. 'I don't know who you think you are but you seem to believe that you can talk to people any way you want.'

'I know exactly who I am. As I just said to you, I own Gilpin. And I don't think I talk to anyone in an inappropriate manner. And while we're at it, you should be aware, which you are, that Christine and I have owned Gilpin for over ten years, many of our staff have been here all that time, which is I think testimony as to how they are treated and spoken to, and we most certainly set the tone of how the hotel is run,' I stated.

'You by contrast have been here just a few weeks, you behave as if you own the hotel, you don't actually, from what I see, like looking after guests and treating them as such, and you are constantly trying to make trouble with other staff by claiming that you are a protected species because you have known Chris and I for twenty years or so.'

She stormed out of the office, slamming the door behind her.

Chris had been out shopping for the hotel. She was incredulous when I told her what had happened. We agreed that Michelle could not really carry on working at Gilpin, particularly under the circumstances.

That afternoon we received a hand-delivered letter from a firm of solicitors stating that they were representing Michelle who was claiming constructive dismissal. This we had not expected. We were obliged to advise our insurers of the position, which we did. As usual in these situations, not that we had had much experience of fallouts with employees, the insurers' main concern was to avoid the cost of litigation so we were obliged to undertake all sorts of politically correct actions which were time-consuming and upsetting.

The case continued for just short of two years, during which Michelle attempted by various devious means to persuade many of our staff that I in particular, but by extension Chris too, were bad employers, nasty people, dishonest and inadequate at what we did at Gilpin. It even transpired later that she had made a list, in anticipation of a showdown, of a few guests with whom we had had problems for one reason or another, and had written to them asking if they would supply character references supporting her, and at the same time denigrating Chris and me.

For whatever strange reason, she was determined to have her moment in court and eventually a date was set. Chris collected the barrister whom the insurers had instructed from Oxenholme station and we met all afternoon preparing for the hearing in Carlisle the next day. It transpired that when Michelle's solicitor's firm found out that we were represented by a barrister they had also, at the last minute, instructed one. As we all sat in the courtroom waiting for the adjudicators, Michelle's barrister came over to us and spoke to our man.

'This is a farce,' he said. 'She's got no case at all and I've told her so. She won't tell me who is going to pay my fees but I don't come cheap and I have suggested to her that she drops the case before it even gets started. She is very reluctant to do so. I don't really know the lady but I get the feeling that it's a matter of pride. A token offer would probably do it. Are you agreeable to that?'

Chris and I voiced the opinion that if we were to offer anything at all, she would claim to have won and make a meal of it. Unlike her barrister we did know the lady – very well. Our barrister said he would have to take instructions from the insurers. He left the room to make a phone call and returned a few minutes later to advise us that the insurers had instructed him to offer £1,000. We said we weren't happy. He said that as they were paying him he had no choice but to take their instructions.

She did make a meal of it. Before we even got back from Carlisle, everyone knew Michelle had won and been offered "substantial" compensation.

Paying the bank was a constant anxiety and while watching every penny was essential, the other objective was to maximise occupancy. I was conscious that our main tool in doing this was through trying to run a good hotel and thereby generate repeat business. But the thought nagged at me, were we doing enough to generate new business? Filling fourteen bedrooms was quite a different game to filling nine.

I was mindful of John Donnithorne's advice to apply to join Relais & Châteaux, but Chris and I thought we were not polished nor grand enough to do that at this time. We were conscious that we did not have a view of Lake Windermere. Our main competitors did. We considered it a major disadvantage. We felt that once we had got potential guests through the front door we could capture their hearts. But getting them onto that coconut doormat was the hard part. We had almost no overseas business and yet other hoteliers whom I met mainly through Cumbria Tourist Board meetings seemed to have good business from the USA and Japan.

Josephine Barr's "Selected British Hotels" was at that time a household name in our industry for American business and I wrote to Jo, as we came to know her, and asked if she would consider taking us on. She replied that she had heard good things about Gilpin, and as she was going to be in the UK in a few weeks' time, could she come and meet us and have a look around. We had decided, in putting our marketing efforts under the microscope, that having just a brochure to send out to enquirers was inadequate, particularly since we could not feature a lake view. So we commissioned a local man who worked for Border Television to make a video for us.

The World Wide Web was in its infancy, and DVDs were not yet commonplace. In order to keep costs down, I wrote the script and did the voiceover. Jim, who was producing the video, did all the photography and added suitable music. We were very proud of it. On a trip to London, we bought a portable video player so that we could tout the video round as appropriate.

I was particularly pleased to be able to use this machine to play the video to Jo Barr. She was incredibly impressed and suggested that we should use it in presentations to travel agents in the USA. She also agreed to take us on and include Gilpin in the "Selected British Hotels" brochure. Through membership of this "club" I also got to know George Goring, who was the chairman of Pride of Britain Hotels. I wrote to George and asked if we could join. After an inspection by relevant members we were accepted. This was an exclusive group of hotels, and due to very generous mutual visiting rules, Chris and I were able, relatively inexpensively, to familiarise ourselves with what other hotels were doing.

This became a valuable tool. It was also pleasant and sociable. We attended our first AGM and I was extremely nervous at having to introduce ourselves and Gilpin to the prestigious members. Our affiliation with Jo Barr and Pride Of Britain exposed us to many friendships and opportunities. Our sense of being all alone in our endeavours was replaced by a feeling of fraternity.

Several hoteliers, albeit owners and managers of bigger properties with larger management teams, regarded filling their rooms as almost their principal responsibility. Chris and I rather envied their ability to jet around the world and leave the operation of their businesses to other people. We never felt we could do this, and I feel comfortable that for Gilpin that was the right decision. But nonetheless, our newfound associations persuaded us that this aspect of our job probably needed greater focus than we had given it.

One notable expedition under the auspices of this attitude was a trip with fellow Jo Barr hoteliers to Atlanta, Chicago and Washington. It was good experience for novice hotel marketeers, good camaraderie, very hard work and great fun. The video and player was an excellent tool and impressed travel agents much more than just brochures and slide presentations. Chris and I had a spectacular row when she got herself lost at Atlanta airport. She claimed not to know our destination, airline, gate or flight number and had not taken her boarding card with her. Our colleagues found it very amusing. She did not and I was in a panic. She did eventually find us, having had to take a train from another terminal. The dangers of retail therapy!

We did not have a great deal of time for socialising with other hoteliers but Pride of Britain brought us into contact with David and Patricia Nicholson at Holbeck Ghyll Hotel, a charming property just south of Ambleside. We coveted their lake view. David and I established an informal whinge society and we spoke several times a week about all the bad things going on. It was nice to have someone to talk to. Mike and Jean Bevans from Linthwaite House just down the road also became friends. We envied their lake view as well. Led by Mike, we tried to set up a consortium of privately owned hotels in the north of England with a view primarily to referring business among ourselves.

Mike was the chairman, Terry Parkinson from Borrowdale Gates Hotel near Keswick was the treasurer (and Terry and his wife Christine became good friends of ours), and I foolishly volunteered to be secretary. The main lesson I learned from this exercise was how difficult and argumentative people can be – even decent like-minded people. Compromise seemed to be impossible. I was glad that I did not have to work with them on the day job. Mike did a spectacular job of trying to broker peace between members. I cannot recall who they all were. Craig Bancroft and Nigel Haworth from Northcote Manor were members as was Clive Wilson from Lakeside

Hotel at Newby Bridge. The board met frequently in the early stages and we took it all very seriously, and I think spent a lot of time on a doomed enterprise which could have been better spent managing our own hotels.

One of the hardest and one of the first decisions was what to call ourselves. We played with a tiresomely long list of words and always came up with a brand name which was too long. Eventually we settled for "Fine Individual Hotels". I was never happy with this. I spent hours doing the minutes of all the meetings. Chris was brilliantly supportive even though FIH took me away from Gilpin work for hours on end.

I eventually came to the conclusion that a democratic organisation such as FIH could not work. It had to be such because the board had no powers and the consortium had no clout with which to demand compliance with its policies. Furthermore, I could see little return from my efforts in terms of business to Gilpin. Consequently, I resigned as secretary and as a member. I am not sure what happened to FIH.

Between Pride of Britain and Fine Individual Hotels, we had quite a network of properties to visit, and as and when time could be found, we spent the odd night in sister hotels. It was always good to draw comparisons and to keep in touch with colleagues. Sometimes one came away jealous. They did things so well. On other occasions you felt proud of Gilpin.

One evening Chris and I were staying in a hotel which shall definitely be nameless, particularly as the rather awful incident was not the fault of the hotel. We decided to have a drink from the minibar before proceeding downstairs for dinner. I poured Chris a whisky – her usual tipple. Then I opened a small bottle of white wine for myself. I was surprised how easily the screw top came off, but gave it no further thought. Not until I started to pour the wine into a glass. It had a very strange smell. Then it clicked what it was. Urine. Yes. Someone had actually drunk the wine and then filled the bottle with urine. Supposing I had not sniffed before drinking? What will human beings not do?

One of the, I suppose with hindsight rather obvious, requisites of a good hotel, which we identified from other hotels we visited, was to have an accurate and informative guest information booklet in the bedrooms. We had rather shied away from doing this as keeping it up to date is very time consuming. However, I determined to make myself do the job.

As it turned out, fate accelerated the process. A single lady arrived at Gilpin and checked in. Suzi recognised her as a Cumbria Tourist Board inspector. I knew they expected a guest information folder. I sat down to deal immediately with this substantial task, even if I was able only to get one copy into this lady's room. Progress was slow. There was so much detail. I felt I had to be around at dinner, so had to leave the chore. I thought I might just be able to get it done by the time she went to bed. But she turned in early. Now what? I carried on till four in the morning and put the finished product on the coffee table in her room while she was at breakfast. At our meeting later that morning she just smiled and observed that the guest information folder was good. 'A pity it wasn't there yesterday afternoon,' she added. Busted!

One sunny afternoon, the peace of the Lake District was shattered by the arrival of not one but five helicopters. We didn't have a helipad as such in those days, and this small flotilla zapped around the estate for quite some minutes looking for a suitable place to land. It must have been springtime because Chris was protesting about damage from the downdraft to the blossoms and the camellias. We did indeed have a booking for afternoon tea for ten persons, but no-one had told us how the party were arriving. They had flown in convoy from Hamburg. A long way to go for tea. The men were all the pilots but the ladies tucked into wine as well as tea. It crossed my mind that having a pee in a small helicopter on the return journey might be a bit of a problem. As if to answer my question, they queued up to use the toilets before departing. They particularly liked the buttered dropped scones with homemade raspberry jam – a speciality of Gilpin's at the time.

Chris and I were still living in hope that Barney and Zoë would ask if they could join us at Gilpin. The workload had not diminished and we still had to be very careful with money. The bank loans put us under severe pressure. We needed help – professional, dedicated help. The one thing about which we were determined was that Gilpin would not be allowed to slip in standards.

One evening when Barney and Zoë and Chris and I were in our living room at Knipe, I broached the subject. 'Now onto a serious matter,' I said. Chris and I had planned more or less what needed to be said and had decided not to mince words.

'Your mother, Barney, and I, are going to have to make a difficult decision within a few years.'

I looked towards Barney. He knew what was coming.

'We're just the right side of sixty and Gilpin is getting busier and busier and marketing is becoming more and more complex. Neither Richard nor Sarah are cut out to be Gilpin's GM and we're finding it harder and harder to cope. We're still paying off two bank loans and we don't have the means to buy our way out of this problem.

'To be absolutely frank, you two are going to have to join us and shoulder some of the load or we're going to have to think about selling. If we did that, I don't think we would walk away with a fortune. The loans are too big in relation to the profitability.

'If I may continue to be honest, while I will most certainly not pretend that a hotelier's life is easy, I do believe that the hardest part is over. The hundred-hour weeks which I don't think you really believe but it was and still sometimes is the case, are I hope a thing of the past. But put two more family members into the team and the workload in theory should be halved.

'We don't want to retire. We love Gilpin. We would work with you. We would work together.'

The silence was pregnant, so I pressed on.

'Barney. You've had a sound exposure to hotelkeeping both in practical terms and from your degrees in business studies and tourism. You know what it's all about.

'Obviously Zoë, we know your attributes less well. But you both have bags of charm and intelligence. The staff know you. You won't earn a fortune, but my calculations suggest that your input would pay for itself and more. In other words, Gilpin can afford you. In a few years, the smaller loan will be paid off and things will get easier. Then we can consider further borrowings to put on more rooms which is what we obviously need.

'And in the longer term? I think that would be up to you. You know my views on family businesses. If they work badly – disaster. If they work well, the sky's the limit. I envisage an ideal size of thirty rooms that could generate sales of four or five million. And you can certainly generate profitability out of that. But that's another sixteen rooms from where we are now. Chris and I can't deal with that on our own. But together we can do it. I've finished!'

Zoë looked at Barney. Barney was silent. He stood up and paced around the room twice (a bit like Vincent Franzini at the Café Royal used to do) and then sat down again.

'Do you really think that Zoë and I haven't discussed this?' he asked eventually.

'I would be amazed if you hadn't,' I replied. 'But you have never discussed your thoughts with us. Which is why we needed to ask you.'

'Get on with it Barney,' Zoë said.

'OK,' Barney continued. 'We were going to tell you before we went back to London. We would love to join Gilpin and make your lives easier. We propose to give notice for our jobs so as to finish with London just before the wedding. So we can start work after our year off.'

'What wedding? What year off?' Chris asked. 'We haven't discussed a wedding or a year off. You're not teenagers.'

'We'd like to get married.' Zoë said.

'To each other may I ask?' Chris quipped.

'May I have your son please?' Zoë asked.

'I have a strong feeling that you've already had him,' I added.

'Is this a flavour of how life is going to be, mother-in-law-to-be and father-in-law-to-be?' Zoë asked.

'You'd better believe it daughter-in-law-to-be,' Chris said. 'Six months.'

I fetched a bottle of champagne from the fridge. We toasted each other and Gilpin.

We discussed with my dad having a marquee on the lawn at Knipe Tarn. He thought it would be great fun. We agreed that each family would draw up an "ideal" guest list – as a starting point. Then we combined them. They totalled 317! Clearly this was out of the question. We were still paying back the treatment plant loan to the bank and austerity was the watchword.

How do you cut out two-thirds of your guest list? We all agreed that

100 guests was about right and probably all that the Gilpin team could cope with. They were not experienced at weddings and banquets.

We had done a few weddings at Gilpin and each, for various reasons, had been a mistake. We learned the hard way that you could not mix a wedding with other guests staying in the hotel. The disruption to normal services for non-wedding guests was unacceptable. Additionally our average stay of three nights became disrupted as wedding organisers did not want three nights. And the wear and tear on the building, the staff and us was disproportionate to the financial gain.

Only a day later my dad had cooled on the idea of a wedding at Knipe. No! He had frozen on it! There wouldn't be enough toilets; what if someone drowned in the swimming pool? The kitchen was inadequate; we didn't have enough cutlery or crockery; car parking would be a nightmare. All rather spurious objections, which could have been overcome. But clearly he didn't want to do it or maybe Dorothy didn't want it. That was it. Dorothy. Of course. In either event, we decided that if that were the case it would be best not to tempt fate and wind up with family unpleasantness. We would do the wedding at Gilpin. We had wanted to avoid this as it would cause us to lose much-needed revenue.

It was therefore under the new circumstances even more important to cut the number of guests to 100. By having the event on a Sunday, at least we only had to close to the public for one night. Drastic and unwelcome surgery was undertaken on the guest list and we got it down to 130. The casualties were mostly Barney and Zoë's friends, of whom there were legions. The window in the corridor outside bedroom Patterdale had to be turned into a door in order to give the guests access to the croquet lawn where the marquee was to be.

The date was set for 10th September 2000.

On the night of the millennium, all the preparations were in place. I was particularly proud of the menu which (composed by me) followed a musical theme about concertos, symphonies and sonatas. It sounds a bit corny now but we had spent hours on its creation. Then just as we were putting the finishing touches to the tables, Richard received a phone call to say that his stepmother was in hospital and seriously ill. He came to consult Chris and me, distraught with indecision. We told him he must go immediately, and with heartwarming reluctance he did.

The pressure was on. It all went well. There were few dry eyes as the strains of Auld Lang Syne struck up. One could not do other than contemplate the horrors of the 20th century, albeit two world wars had barely touched my generation.

To our astonishment, and indeed delight, my dad was with us that night. What a strange marriage. He had been born in 1912 so had been affected by both wars, including the premature death of his father after the first and his own involvement in the second. He had followed in his father's footsteps and been commissioned into the Royal Army Medical Corps where he was involved in life-changing work on sterilisation of medical equipment. And my poor uncle Jim, my mother's brother, had been a prisoner of war in Hong Kong under the Japanese.

But that's another story, and a long one which had significant ramifications for my family.

And so an exciting new year, century and millennium began.

Chapter Twenty-One

A WEDDING

W e had decided that after so much hard work and effort over Christmas and at New Year, by every member of the team, we must do something special for our annual staff party. We had one of these jollies every January because it is a quieter time than December. Usually it was a dinner in a nearby hotel. Inevitably they turned into somewhat rowdy affairs with far too much booze being consumed. We never stinted on the cost of these events. They became an expectation and were good for team building.

Whereas these days Barney is clever enough to say a few words early on in the evening when people are still relatively sober and respectful, I was too naive and possibly too old-fashioned to do that and felt that the right time for speeches was over coffee at the end of dinner. So invariably I was heckled, shouted down, cheered, booed and roistered. I could write a separate book about Gilpin staff parties, but it would probably get me into serious trouble.

The most notorious of these was at the Burneside Hotel in Bowness, where my speech was marred by two completely separate events. I had decided to prove my modernity and had purchased a new computer capable of doing a Powerpoint presentation with which to illustrate my speech. I had taken a couple of dozen photographs for the purpose. The first picture was of a toilet with a red cross through it indicating that use of the toilets was not allowed during my speech. All of the other pictures were equally infantile but appropriate for entertaining the troops when half cut.

However, during the drinks reception, my father (a guest at the party) had accidentally poured a pint of ale into my new computer. The computer did not like this and protested by giving off a fizzing noise and switching itself off. Nothing would persuade it to be switched on again. I'm not sure whether I was more annoyed about the new computer or the fact that my carefully prepared speech was now useless.

I am not good at improvisation. I fretted throughout the meal and between mouthfuls did my best to make notes for a new speech. After the service of coffee, I stood to deliver my hurriedly prepared oration. I was greeted as usual by applause, bravos, cat calls and assorted ribaldry. After a short time, and just as my confidence was returning, a loud, drunken and slurred voice from the back of the room piped up: 'Why don't you pay your staff decent bloody wages?' I was not prepared for this (nor would I have been, even had a slide to cover this eventuality been available and my computer not blown up), and nor did I recognise the man, so I replied (with hindsight rather feebly): 'I think we should discuss wages tomorrow.'

My assailant continued: 'I want to discuss fucking wages now.' The head housekeeper's husband, Dick – a big man – put his arms around the man's neck and sought to shut him up. But, strengthened perhaps by alcohol, the guy ducked out of the hold and punched Dick in the face.

All hell now broke out and it seemed to me that continuation of my speech was out of the question. Some people were shouting at the barracker, who was, I was told, called Sam and was the boyfriend of one of the room assistants, to shut up, and others were shouting that they also wanted more fucking wages.

Then the police arrived – summoned by the hotel's management. Sam was still proving unexpectedly lusty and it took three coppers to cart him away. Things became even worse after that. Suzi had persuaded the bar staff that because she was sort of management, she could order unlimited quantities of Bollinger on the Gilpin account. Suzi, who was a loveable but naughty girl, was very persuasive when on Bollinger. She had had a good upbringing and was quite a connoisseur of champagne. The house champagne simply would not cut the mustard. But I am afraid that I cannot tell the rest of this story! Altogether a less-than-successful staff party.

The Christmas parties were only rivalled in their complexity, hilarity, popularity and naughtiness by the "Long Sufferers" parties, as these events became known. They were not an annual event but a periodic one sparked off probably by the hotel winning a special award, or maybe the achievement of a good result for the year – the latter an irregular event!

We took the staff who had been with us for a long time (an indeterminate and subjective qualification) on a treat. Although others got added in later years, the really Long Sufferers always included Richard, Sarah, Gill, Paula and Suzi. We included the Head Chef. Barney, Zoë and Ben (and the current girlfriend) came more latterly. It became a competition (led by Sarah of course) to be the most glamorous, and this included wearing the shortest skirt. Sarah could get away with this! The boys made a good effort too, with Richard leading the parade in his Duke of Edinburgh guise (and attitude). We generally went to race meetings, with Cartmel being a favourite and very convenient. Also pleasantly informal and reasonably priced for a gang. We booked a table in the best restaurant.

One memorable year we went to Doncaster to the St Ledger. Chris was of course on home turf, and as such, a favourite to win. Suzi tried to get into the members' enclosure and nearly pulled it off but for the fact that she didn't have any shoes on by this time in the afternoon, and that foiled the plot. Like most tales involving Suzi, I can't finish telling the full story.

But to return to the Millennium. Chris and I decided to take all the staff to Amsterdam on a day trip. It had to be in two shifts so as to keep the hotel running. Richard was to head one and Chris and I the other. Had we known the complexity of this venture we would have thought of a simpler idea. Some staff didn't have passports. Others' passports were out of date. Some nationalities required visas to visit Holland. Some were denied boarding the flight because they did not have visas they did not know they needed. And so they were left behind.

The drivers of the minibuses (Richard and me on the two separate days) could of course not drink, so the pain of the convolution was doubled. Some wanted to see canals and some wanted to be in the red light district. One particular girl, who had better remain nameless, was casually perusing the contents of a sex shop (while I was cowering with embarrassment in a corner of the room pretending to count the boarding passes for the return flight) when she called out that she had a pair of leather knickers such as the ones she was examining but that they didn't wash very well! We got home not much before midnight and I made up for my abstinence without delay. The effort had been made. Never again.

Chris and I were determined that, even though Barney and Zoë's wedding was a family affair, it would be done utterly professionally and, functions being second nature to Richard and me, the event was planned with military precision. The family and friends' accommodation position was assisted in a fortuitous manner.

Relations with my father had not returned to normal since the disagreement over the wedding venue. This and the rumpus over selling Knipe had left a taste which none of us would allow to fester for ever, but feelings were just not quite the same. Additionally, Chris had had a further tiff with him. She wanted to have the spare bedroom in "our" upstairs flat at Knipe Tarn painted and, feeling (understandably) that this would be welcomed by everyone, made the necessary arrangements (at our expense). When the painter arrived to start work, my father charged upstairs to see what was going on and admonished Chris for making such plans in "his" house.

We really did look after my dad with extreme care and love, and Chris cooked dinner most nights, for which he joined us, never giving us a moment to ourselves, which was often very unwelcome after a long day's work. We were more than grateful to have upstairs at Knipe Tarn to live in and although we craved privacy and a front door of our own, we accepted the situation with appropriate grace.

The bedroom did not get decorated. Dad refused to give in and the painter was sent away. Chris was livid. Unlike my dad, who was not at all houseproud (Keats Grove in Hampstead did not see a paintbrush in the entire time he owned it), Chris was extremely so (as am I), and "tat" offends her.

Chris's auntie had died just before the millennium and left her a small legacy. One evening I came home at eight or thereabouts and Chris poured me a gin and tonic and said, 'John. I've got something to tell you.'

It sounded ominous, but she was smiling. I took a good slurp of my drink. 'I've bought a house for us,' she said. 'I've used Auntie Mary's money as the deposit.'

It crossed my mind that maybe I should be getting used to this by now. It was not as if it was the first time. Yet, paradoxically, I felt that she should have consulted me. It was a significant step with ramifications way beyond just where we laid our heads to rest.

'I don't quite know what to say,' I attempted.

'That's not very positive,' she replied.

'Darling. I'm not being positive or negative. I just don't know anything about it at the moment. You haven't told me a thing except that you've bought a house. It's a rather strange action without any discussion. Particularly under the circumstances.'

'What circumstances?'

'Well. Dad of course.'

She sat down on the poof and turned her back on me. 'I'm so disappointed in you,' she mumbled.

'In me?'

'Yes in you. Your Cunliffe lack of perception. I have never had a penny to call my own in all my life and the first time I do and attempt to do something that I really want to do, you put me down. I've been camping ever since we left Beckenham, first in that wretched little flat in Bath, then like a gypsy at Gilpin in any room available, then in a caravan and since then in this flat courtesy of all your family when it suits.

'I can't take your father's attitude any longer. I look after him and get barely a word of thanks. His nightly presence whatever time we get back from work is so selfish. I married you – not him. Yes, I know it's his house and all that. Don't I just know it? And now he tells me that our children's bedroom is "his" not "ours".

'We've got all these people coming to Barney and Zoë's wedding, which we have to hold at Gilpin at the expense of the business because he and Dorothy between them haven't got the generosity to let the wedding be held at this lovely place which just sits here half empty. And although there will be guests staying here – yes there bloody well will – they've got to stay in a bedroom which hasn't been decorated for over twenty years because he wants Knipe to become like Keats Grove became. A hovel in the poshest part of London. There's a bloody swimming pool downstairs. Wouldn't you like to use it? Don't you think your boys would like to use it? Oh no. That's in Tony's territory. You would have to go through his laundry room to reach it.'

She put her head in her hands and started to cry. I had known she was upset by what had happened over decorating the boys' bedroom but I had not realised the extent. She lifted her head and shook it defiantly. She explained to me that she had not gone out to buy a house without discussing it. That she had been driving down Hollins Lane on the short cut to Shap Road on the A6 outside Kendal and had seen builders' vans outside some barns nearly opposite the cricket club. She had pulled over to ask what was going on and the developer Robert Hughes just happened to be there. We knew Robert because he dined at Gilpin sometimes. He had greeted Chris with his usual friendliness and offered to show her around the small estate which consisted of one large detached house which had already been sold, three semi-detached houses and one terraced two-storey house. They had only just started work on the conversion from farm barns.

She went on: 'Robert said that there was considerable interest in the properties because of the small size of the development and the beautiful views towards the southern fells and the Pennines. Both considerations were right. He said one of the semis was under offer and he expected another to sell later that day. He showed me around all the properties. The end one really appealed to me. It had a reasonable-sized garden and a double garage. I've made an appointment to go back with you at eleven o'clock tomorrow. Robert's going to meet us. But I had to make a decision there and then. Robert said that number five would almost certainly go before the end of the day. So I wrote a cheque. But he did say that if you didn't like it tomorrow he'd give me the cheque back.'

I knelt down and put my arms around her.

'Sorry,' I said.

As the evening progressed, we chatted about this situation. We knew we could not just abandon my dad, but we agreed vehemently that it would be great to own our own place again and to have somewhere to escape to. We decided not to say a word about it to dad.

I loved it. It had all the advantages that Chris had described. The views from the dining room and kitchen were southern Lakeland at its best. It was right slap on the road but it was only a lane. We hadn't bargained, at that stage, on the lorries going into Burneside to get to the Cropper paper factory. One of the three bedrooms was downstairs and we thought this would make a good study. We confirmed the purchase and started to plan. It was the first time Chris had gone into decor mode on our own behalf. It was very exciting. We had not had a home of our own for fourteen years.

Thus, and the timing was perfect, we were able to accommodate another eight bodies for the wedding, including on two sofas. The decorating and furnishing was by no means finished, but it was good enough for kids!

Zoë's father, Peter, had died the year before the wedding. Zoë and her mother Kathy as well as the two boys, Brent and André, had been badly affected. Kathy bravely decided that she would propose the toast to the bride and groom. She graciously left most of the wedding arrangements to us.

Father Christopher at the Catholic church in Kendal was a joy to be involved with, mixing an immense sense of humour and fun with deep piety. He was to become a profound example to me personally and I believe to the rest of the family. At the rehearsal in church on the day before the wedding he charmingly made it very clear that while the wedding was to be enjoyed, it was nonetheless a solemn sacrament which should be undertaken with conviction and sobriety.

Chris and I stayed at Gilpin for the night of the wedding. Her original engagement ring bought for £80 in 1964 was worn out, so I took the opportunity of the wedding to replace it with an antique solitaire diamond ring. Not megabucks. We didn't have them. Violins OK again!

As the marquee was erected, the storm clouds gathered and on the day of the wedding, Sunday 10th September 2000, the heavens opened. Zoë looked beautiful; Barney and Ben were handsome; Chris and Kathy were lovely. My dad was proud. The church was packed. The rain poured down. Father Chris's homily was full of mirth, including reference to Zoë's very eccentric shoes.

Then the party began. What a party! Sarah and Richard ran the dinner like charmed clockwork. The food was superb. There were two bands. And a lot of champagne and wine. We had even placed Balkan Sobranie cocktail cigarettes on the tables for our guests. Oh for the pre-politically correct era! Kathy's speech was inspired and delivered with confidence. Barney's reply and Ben's toast to the bridesmaids were both captivating. That was the last time I smoked a cigarette.

A lovely, happy day. The beginning of a marriage cast in love.

Clearing up the next morning was not so much fun. The hotel was full that night and the whole place looked like a bomb had gone off. The contractors arrived promptly at eight o'clock to take down the marquee; tired and hungover family members had to be prized from their beds. It was still raining.

Barney and Zoë had left at dawn to honeymoon in India and Thailand.

Chapter Twenty-Two

MODERN, STYLISH, ROOMY, INTIMATE AND SEXY

S uzi had a little girl, Chloe. She needed the money and I needed her
help so she started work again quite soon after the birth, and on days
when she could not organise a babysitter, Chloe came too. She lay in
her carrycot under the desk at my feet while her mother went about her
business. She never cried nor made a sound. It worked very well. Guests in
the know thought it was hilarious.

Before Barney and Zoë's wedding, and in anticipation of their move
to Gilpin, we had together scoured the area for a house for them to move
to. It turned out to be quite a simple process because Cherry Tree Cottage
in the village of Crosthwaite was so obviously ideal. It was being sold by
the father-in-law of Irish Claire, who worked in the restaurant and housekeeping. She was always known as that because we had other Claires. Also
because it was accurate. She had answered an advertisement that I had
placed in an Irish newspaper. Claire and I spoke on the telephone and it
was a difficult conversation because Claire had such a strong Irish brogue.
I offered her the job and she arrived a couple of days later.

Chris, Richard and I were in the still room and Claire came in through
the back door, said hello and in the next breath promised that she would

work for us forever. She did for a long time. Anyway, the purchase of Cherry Tree Cottage was easy as it was all in the family. It was a delightful property which needed a great deal doing to it, hence the price was affordable. The paperwork fell to me while Barney and Zoë were away, and faxes burned their way to far-flung destinations in India and Thailand. The solicitors were slow and pedantic (well, fancy) and I was frustrated beyond measure. I knew they loved the house and wanted it. Chris and I needed their input to Gilpin. At last the sale was completed and Chris and I did our best to make Cherry Tree Cottage habitable and welcoming for their return.

The news of their joining us at Gilpin was met with mixed reactions among the senior staff. We were very surprised by some of the negativity. It seemed to us so obvious that the input of a young, energetic, educated couple could only be good. But there's no accounting for the reactions of human beings, some of whom regarded their arrival as a threat. Others, Sarah and Richard in particular, thought it was terrific. They knew Chris and me so well and were aware that we were beginning to struggle.

For us it was marvellous. To be able to share the responsibility and workload was a dream at last come true. They brought to the party enthusiasm, fresh ideas and above all access to technology which was way outside the ability, knowledge or comprehension of Chris, me or anyone else working at Gilpin. Emails and the web were beginning to take off. I had, with professional help, created a website of which I was extremely proud, but which would now be regarded as little short of pathetic. I did all the photography and wrote the words. But it was a newborn science and one which Zoë in particular embraced.

I recall the first meeting with Barney, Zoë, Chris, myself and the management team. I had asked Barney to prepare an informal presentation focusing on his degrees in tourism and business, and experience with Marriott and Thistle hotels, leading on to what he and Zoë could bring to Gilpin.

I had expected universal enthusiasm. It was not universal and some of those present gave him a hard time. I think we were all quite shocked.

With hindsight – although I certainly did not think about it at the time – streams for promotion had been cut off. And perhaps, cosy ways of doing things were threatened.

I had no doubt whatsoever that it was the best possible thing for Gilpin and for us as a family. Barney did not waste time getting down to business. It was quickly apparent he had huge vision on the marketing front, aided by Zoë, who proved to be a natural wordsmith.

He declared that our photography was out of date and unappealing and started making enquiries about local professional photographers. We discounted the guy who had done their wedding – one who (like so many photographers at weddings) felt that their activity was the only one that mattered. To hell with the guests and the caterers. After my patience had reached the end of its tether, I had told him that he had just five more minutes. No more. He had embarked on a massive sulk.

Barney finally selected a local photographer, Tiree, who coincidentally was rather pretty. The day when the weather was forecast to be at its best arrived. As did Tiree in a mini-skirt. The lawns had been cut. The windows had been cleaned and a cherrypicker had been hired in order to capture the all-important pictures of the hotel from the field on the opposite side of the road, and above the trees at the bottom of Gilpin's garden.

The man who delivered the cherrypicker pronounced it simple. The smoothest way of elevating the basket, or indeed lowering it, was apparently by using the battery. Should this fail due to extensive use, the petrol engine would be an alternative. His only prohibition was moving the machine while the basket was elevated. Barney decided that conditions were right to do these particular photographs early in the day. I was to act as his assistant based at ground level. A suitable location was chosen for the first elevation.

Barney and Tiree squeezed into the basket. There was barely enough room for the two of them. Turning around was a challenge. Bending down was impossible. This was certainly not an arms' length transaction! The basket rose smoothly into the air. Neither Barney nor Tiree appeared to mind. I don't do heights (they come after snakes with me), so I was a little anxious. The view was still obstructed by the tallest trees. We would have to move a little to the north-west.

Down came the basket. We moved the machine as required. Barney and Tiree were raised again. The view was still blocked and the procedure was repeated. The position was alright but the basket needed to be a little further back, which could be achieved by swivelling the arm and the basket. Barney pulled some levers. A few photographs were taken.

Bacon sandwiches and coffee arrived from the kitchen. The basket had to be lowered again in order to facilitate breakfast. Barney felt that while the basket was down, it would be sensible to move to a slightly different location in order to get a contrasting angle. The move was completed. The basket rose again. The arm and basket were duly swivelled to precisely the right point. More photographs were taken. Some grazing cows began to take an interest in the proceedings. One even decided to scratch its back on the cherrypicker, sending a violent reaction up the arm to the basket. Barney protested and instructed me to chase off the cows. Satisfied, he pressed the lever to lower the basket. There was a dull whine but little else.

Barney called down for me to start the mechanical motor. Because the battery was presumably dead, this had to be done manually by turning a ratchet. This would not budge. We eventually realised that the motor could not be started without the gear being put into neutral. The man had not told us this. Too obvious perhaps. The gear was disconnected. The arm and basket jerked violently. Barney swore. I addressed myself to the ratchet once more. The motor turned and coughed but did not start. I tried several times. Barney had a good signal from where he was and called the hire firm.

Had we put petrol in the tank? No. Well that was probably why the motor wouldn't start. But no-one told us to put petrol in the tank. Well! If you hire a car you expect to put petrol in the tank don't you? Not necessarily. Well in Cumbria you do. Thanks for nothing. I called to Barney that the latter comment was unwise. If petrol did not do the trick, the hire firm might not be too keen to help. More expletives from on high.

I went to fetch petrol. Barney and Tiree were left stranded in the air like parachutists who had fallen into a tree. Before moving off I asked Barney what sort of petrol was required. He hadn't asked. Look on the motor, he suggested. Lead-free. I returned half an hour later with the petrol, and in the absence of a funnel poured as much onto the field as into the motor. I addressed the ratchet again. Harrumph. Cough. Harrumph. Harrumph. Cough cough. Encouraging. Harrumph. Cough, cough, cough.

Barney declared that there was a lever in the basket called "emergency lower control". He decided to try it. 'What if it just drops'? I asked. My question was answered by the slow descent of the basket. Albert Einstein had got it right!

Matters at Knipe Tarn were getting harder rather than easier. The subject of Chris and my limited access to the house and lack of privacy was if anything exacerbated by Barney and Zoë's arrival. I think their possession of their own house made us jealous, which was possibly not surprising. Elizabeth took, at this time, to phoning me for long conversations about how ridiculous the situation at Knipe Tarn was, lamenting the destruction of the old Norwegian cottage and protesting about Pa's selfish use of the ground floor and refusal to do anything to soften the inevitable blow of inheritance tax.

A friend of Chris's and mine who knew of our difficulties put us in touch with a lawyer who specialised in family property matters. We attended a meeting in Carlisle and agreed to the preparation of a report setting out his recommendations, which would address the question of Knipe Tarn as well as of inheritance tax. The resultant report was as clever as the invoice was outrageous. We shared the paper with Pa who said that he thought it was excellent, addressed all the issues, and, in an unusually decisive manner, expressed the view that we should follow the recommendations. Whether he in turn shared it with Elizabeth or indeed Dorothy (or her lawyer who seemed to exert a lot of influence) we never knew. But a few days later he came upstairs and announced that he could not proceed with the plan. Another waste of money. Another disappointment. And it had to be admitted, another erosion of trust.

With Barney and Zoë on board, Chris and I started to take regular days off. This was a "first" and initially we didn't know what to do with the time. Then a friend offered to teach us to play golf and we joined the club at Windermere. In those days, there was a waiting list to join and prospective members had to be interviewed by a small committee. Chris and I were probably fast-tracked as Granny had been the first Ladies' Captain at Windermere and my aunt Barbara (dad's sister) had been a scratch golfer. But nonetheless we had to be lectured on the dreadful sin of slow play (we were always slow because I lost so many balls) and of proper dress (only a shirt with a collar) and of the importance of understanding the rules and etiquette of golf as laid down by the Royal & Ancient. We've never been good, but playing golf from time to time has been a part of our lives since then. "From time to time" is of course the problem. There is never enough. But it has proved a good distraction.

An annoyance I have had all of my adult life is varicose veins. It is a condition that is both occupational and hereditary. The latter can't be helped. Standing is a part of the hotel business: talking to people; taking orders; informal discussions with managers and staff. I had my first operation at the age of 20 and I have had nine conventional operations since – bulging veins in the legs; general anaesthetic for surgery; time off for recovery; big scars and a lot of pain. And in my case the relief only ever lasted for a couple of years. Aching, aching, aching and a resultant debilitating tiredness which is only relieved by putting your legs up for at least eight hours.

One day, I read in a newspaper about a new procedure being pioneered by The Whiteley Clinic in Guildford: sclerotherapy. Treatment under local anaesthetic; long-lasting results; no invasive surgery. I wrote to the clinic and received a date for a scan and to see a consultant. The scan was not unpleasant but messy: a lot of gunk was necessary to see what was going on inside. The technician was chatty but serious. She kept making clucking noises and muttering 'Oh Lord'.

After she had finished, the machine produced an illustrated report. 'Well John. I'm not going to even start to tell you about this lot. I'll leave it to Mr P. He's the consultant.' I was cleaned up and invited to dress. Mr P. was Barrie Price. He greeted me warmly.

'You John,' he said, 'have got the worst legs I have ever seen and I have been a vascular specialist for a very long time.'

He showed me the chart of my varicose system and explained what was going on. 'Your particular condition is made worse by conventional vein stripping which you have had done, I think you said nine times. Some of this surgery has been good – or as good as that type of procedure can be. Some has been botched. But the net result is a total mess in both legs and your groin.'

I didn't know my groin and by inference other important parts of my body were involved, although I had wondered why the scanning lady kept pushing the device quite so close to my private parts both at the front and the back.

'You are going to need hours of treatment probably spread over half a dozen visits. It can't all be done at once. Your legs wouldn't tolerate it. Nor would you.' He explained what he needed to do.

My visits to Guildford were a nuisance. It's a long way. Chris took me the first time and it was obvious that between the treatment and the bandages, it would not be possible to drive. So for subsequent appointments I went on the train, even though this involved hobbling from Euston to Waterloo and back. This treatment was a life-changer. I have to try not to stand still as much as possible and I now just ask people to excuse me, explain why and sit down. I have to have a "top up" every few years. But it works. And it has made golf much more pleasurable.

Finishing off 5 The Hollins was a huge labour of love. Chris threw her full battery of skills into it and we selected each item of furniture, each rug and each wash basin with TLC. Whenever we had the opportunity, we sneaked off for a night or two like clandestine lovers and revelled in our seclusion. There was no question of leaving my dad alone at Knipe Tarn. He was in his eighties, and apart from needing care was a very sociable animal who would have gone bonkers living on his own. Bonkers was one thing he was not!

Ben was, at this stage, the only member of our immediate family not in the Lakes, and he started to make noises about leaving his job in London and coming to join us. He was working for a medium-sized practice and he felt that his work was stereotyped. The decision was undoubtedly complicated by his girlfriend Steffi, who did not want to leave London. So they visited frequently. One New Year's Eve, Ben and Steffi invited me to join them on an excursion to Buttermere for a walk. It's my favourite lake and I couldn't refuse, as long as I was back in plenty of time for dinner. Chris insisted that I went.

After an idyllic walk around the lake, we repaired to a pub and a pint or two went down nicely. Then it began to snow – heavily. Great big flakes which quickly covered the mountains and fields and roads. Temptation wormed its way into the three of us. Was it safe to drive home over the passes in such conditions? Did I really dare to absent myself on New Year's Eve? What would everyone at home think? Could they manage so many dinners without me? But it was a fixed menu – easy. What would the guests think? Taking New Year's Eve off! What would Chris think? Say? It was of course that question which sealed the decision. We drove back – gingerly.

The following year – 2001 – was marred by the foot and mouth crisis which seriously affected business. Every agency in the land urged people not to visit the Lake District and word of course spread abroad. Like the Papal visit many years before and the injunction of the police to watch the Masses from home on television, the public obliged.

Tony Blair as Prime Minister swished in and out but that didn't achieve anything. We had many regular guests who had farms and calamity seemed to be around every corner. Not that I had ever been through a war, but it felt like we were at war. However the enemy was invisible. There was no-one to fight, to shoot at or to drop bombs on.

Sales plummeted and by Easter it was evident that the year was going to be a disaster for farmers, tourism businesses and all associated trades. I think the banks had to ease their attitude or face a severe public relations backlash. Pride of Britain managed to arrange a meeting at the Goring Hotel in London at which a minister from Defra was to be present. She addressed the meeting and succeeded in saying precisely nothing.

Question time came and David Nicholson from Holbeck Ghyll rose to his feet to ask a question. There was a long silence which became embarrassing. Then he burst into tears and sat down. We all felt like balling our eyes out. The problem appeared to be that no-one actually knew what to do. The Government said one thing; vets said another; farmers said another; Europe said another. The Lake District hoteliers knew exactly what they wanted – but the fells remained out of bounds. This was not a good first year for Barney and Zoë at Gilpin.

In the end, when the crisis was declared over and the fells reopened, the public, including our guests. flocked to the Lakes in such volumes that the year turned out well. It appeared that Lake District aficionados had to have their annual fix. And that was very good for morale.

*

The infamous storms of October 2002, caused havoc in the Lakes. On the morning in question, I awoke to the sight of trees down all over the place. Sarah was on breakfast duty with me and she phoned to say that a large tree had fallen across the drive of the little estate in Bowness in which she lived. Could I pick her up? I tried to get down the lane which connects Knipe to the Gilpin road. Blocked. I went the other way through Winster and picked up Sarah. The direct route to Gilpin was blocked. Back through Bowness and Windermere to the lane via Heathwaite. Blocked. We abandoned the car and walked.

The Gilpin drive was blocked by several fallen trees. It was going to be one hell of a job to get the drive open. No cars could get in or out. Sarah and I climbed over the trees to get to the hotel. Richard had been well and truly disturbed during the night and was already there getting breakfast under way. One of the chefs had also abandoned his car and made it in. A particularly obnoxious guest who had been in for a couple of nights phoned reception to complain that his newspaper had not arrived. I explained that he would not be charged for it!

More seriously, a guest staying with us explained to me that he was a surgeon and had been called to perform an emergency operation in Manchester. He had to get his car out. His car was in what was then the top car park. Any exit via the drive was impossible. We decided to try and get his car through the gate in the car park into the field and thence to the goods entrance. The plan was good but his rear wheel drive Mercedes (rubbish off-road) got stuck. My Land Rover was stuck on Heathwaite. I begged a neighbouring farmer to bring a tractor, which he did, bless him. Our good doctor got to Manchester.

And a few months later Ben came north. Chris and I had found a charming town house on a newly developed estate on the northern extremity of Kendal and we put down the required deposit. Initially he stayed with us at Knipe until the new house was ready. My dad quickly recruited Ben to be his carer and companion and Ben fell in with this lovingly. But he had a career to follow and a mortgage to pay.

As soon as the Helsfell Hall estate was ready, Ben set up Ben Cunliffe Architects and got to work with a vengeance. He had strong views about

Cumbrian architecture and the posture of the Lake District Special Planning Board. He was passionate about protection of the area but felt that the LDSPB needed to "get real".

Staff and retention thereof has always been the main problem at Gilpin and we purchased a nine-bedroom house just south of Gilpin on the Crook Road. I had never participated at an auction before and was very nervous about doing so. After the bidding was over, Chris and I got up to leave. We thought we had been outbid. But apparently we had bought it! I felt a plonker!

Ben's first job was to plan its conversion into a useable configuration of nine bedrooms with two sitting rooms. Ben personally managed the project in a very hands-on manner. A derelict part of the building was some years later (and unforeseen at that time) to become the offices of the newly formed Ben Cunliffe Architects. Warriner Yeat became a great help in staff retention. We have never been able to discover who or what Warriner was but yeat is Cumbrian for gate. If you have ever heard Cumbrian farmers conversing you would be able to get that. 'Shut yonder yeat!'

My aversion to shopping at IKEA was borne out of furnishing Warriners, as the house quickly became known in Gilpin circles. A couple of the would-be resident staff members, Chris and I set off to buy up IKEA in Warrington. We had hired a van as big as was permitted. I suspected that my MoD licence to drive large vehicles was no longer valid. The selection of the items of furniture should have been simple. This was a staff house. The only variant between the rooms should have been based on their size.

Oh no! Chris had other ideas. 'Room number one faces south so should have a blue wardrobe. Room number six is going to accommodate two girl chefs so should have extra wall lights in the bathroom.' And so on. The selections made and lists completed, the items had to be found and loaded onto trolleys – fourteen of them I seem to recall. Oh yes. The blue wardrobe will be found in Building 3, Area F, Row 17, Section 29. We got home at midnight. The next day a small army was needed to put the stuff together. But it did make financial sense!

History had again repeated itself at Gilpin and the fourteen rooms which we then had were deemed inadequate. We were very busy but once more the costs had caught up with the revenue and the obvious solution was more bedrooms. But where could more guests dine? We had enough lounge space but not enough dining tables. So we decided that we must add another restaurant seating at least eighteen people.

Ben's concept for the Garden Room filling the area adjacent to the small lounge and the Drawing Room won instant approval from the family and the design was imaginative and attractive, but the bank, in the form of yet another manager to whom we had been assigned, was not so keen. Could the costs be supported without additional rooms? Barney's vision was by now beginning to blossom in all sorts of ways and he expressed the view that we should stop being pushed around by dopey bankers. Barney's degree in business studies, coupled with his ample knowledge of technology and spreadsheets had given him a splendid array of tools for producing budgets and cash flow projections. He also demonstrated an ability to prepare concise and literate reports. A rare talent these days. It has stood us in good stead. We started to shop around.

Rather to our surprise, several alternative banks showed keen interest. They seemed to like our strategy and I felt sure that the feeling of permanence brought about by Barney, Zoë and Ben's arrival on the scene was an added inducement. A succession of meetings were held attended by the interested bankers, Barney and me. We were surprised by the competitiveness of the proposals discussed. They made the terms we had agreed only five or six years before when we built the Orchard Wing look silly. The deal finally struck included a compulsory interest rate hedging mechanism which was later to become important.

The Garden Room restaurant was built quickly and efficiently while plans were hatched for six new bedrooms in a detached building on the hill behind the croquet lawn. The planning of the Garden Suites (as they were to become known) was possibly the first project which leaned heavily on Barney's marketing savvy as well as Ben's architectural expertise. Barney was of the view that we needed to start appealing to a more diverse clientele if we were going to fill what would soon become twenty rooms. The design must be modern, stylish, roomy, intimate and sexy.

It was becoming obvious that we had two clever sons. Maybe the school fees had been worth the sacrifices they had occasioned!

We had for a long time known that we did actually sell sex. Well! Perhaps that we facilitated sex would be both more accurate and dignified. Each suite was to have a private walled garden containing a hot tub for the exclusive use of the occupants of the suite. Ben's design was nothing if not modern, stylish, roomy, intimate and sexy – in stark contrast to the other rather traditional buildings at Gilpin. So much so that the planning board turned it down immediately. We appealed. And eventually won. But the process caused a considerable delay which threw out the budgets. Never mind. A few clicks on the keyboard and voilà – a new budget. It was becoming very clear to me that without Barney and Ben, Chris and I would be floundering.

A part of the reason behind the rejection of the scheme by the Lake District Special Planning Board had been objections by members of the public and parish councillors. Ben had the idea to invite these people to a meeting at which we would explain our rationale from both an architectural and operational point of view. This was a stroke of genius and I think that our openness and willingness to share our vision for Gilpin stood us in good stead. We won the approval on appeal.

Both Dorothy and Elizabeth were diagnosed with cancer at almost the same time. This was terrible for Pa – indeed for all of us. He did not speak much to us about Dorothy. He was a sociable man but one who created sealed compartments. Dorothy was one such.

Barney, Zoë, Ben, Chris and I had booked to go skiing in Andorra. Dorothy was at Ebury Street, and although nothing as such was said, we got the impression that Pa had been told to stay out of the way. We asked him if he would like to come with us and he accepted. It was an awful resort and a dreadful hotel with the worst food I have ever experienced. The snow conditions were poor.

Pa was withdrawn and we tried to keep his spirits up. He spent hours every day on the telephone to Dorothy. At lunchtime one of us would take the gondola down to the resort and collect him so that he could join us at a mountain restaurant. The hotel food was so bad that this became the main meal of the day. He enjoyed these lunches wrapped up in a thick coat and warmed by the pale sunshine. Pa's withdrawal – very untypical – intensified as the week progressed. On the last skiing day it was Chris's turn to escort Pa to lunch. As they shuffled towards the restaurant where the rest of us were having a drink, she shook her head and opened her arms, palms upwards as if to say 'I don't know what's going on'.

They sat down. Chris said to us in a very low voice, 'He's not himself at all, but he won't tell me what's the matter.' Zoë poured Pa a glass of wine. He took a sip. His hand was shaking. Then he seemed to make a decision: to speak.

'The main reason why I accepted your invitation to join you on this holiday,' he said, 'was not, as you might have imagined, to get away from Dorothy's impending death, but because I feel I have to tell you something, and it is very difficult for me to do so. I wanted to do it away from Knipe Tarn. I don't really know why.'

He squinted into the sun and took another sip of wine. I wondered what on earth he was going to say. Something about my mother? About Elizabeth? Was I illegitimate?

'Dorothy and I never did get married,' he finally said. 'She changed her name to Cunliffe by deed poll. The quiet register office marriage before our wedding reception in London was a lie.'

He took another sip of wine and replaced the glass on the table.

'It was all something to do with her husband and French law about inheritances after divorce. I won't bore you with the details. I'm sorry. It was wrong to deceive you all.'

He pulled a large handkerchief from his coat pocket and dabbed his eyes.

I cannot pretend that I was other than very upset. All the chatelaine of Knipe Tarn business. I must have been – indeed I know I was – very, very shocked. I have no recollection of who then said what. I don't think there was a big discussion. What was there to discuss?

Elizabeth's condition was a very different matter. She was his daughter and he had never disguised his adoration of her – mixed with a touch of fear. She was very forthright and somewhat uncompromising. She was also only sixty-four years old. As far as I was concerned, all past differences were forgotten and I tried my best to support her and her daughter Melanie. I drove to London most weeks to spend some time with her.

One day, late in the afternoon, I received a telephone call from the Middlesex Hospital to say that Elizabeth had to have an emergency operation that evening. They felt that her father and I should be on hand. We both hurriedly packed a bag while Chris made us a picnic. I wanted Chris to come too but she said that this was a time for Pa and me to be together and to support each other.

We set off. Pa was worried but talkative. We had been told a while ago that Elizabeth's condition was terminal. It was not a question of whether she would die but when. As we were driving along, he suddenly asked me out of the blue: 'Do you really believe in a God?'

'Yes,' I replied simply.

'Have you always?' he asked.

'You sent me to a Catholic school. They did rather a good job on that front.'

'I rather envy you,' Pa said.

'Do you definitely not?' I asked.

There was a pause and then, while not exactly answering the question, he said, 'What's definite? How can anything be definite? Like you, I went to a school. Not a Catholic school but one in which Christianity was upheld and taught. Rugby, as you know. I went through the motions. Do you know, I don't think I really thought about it much. Not seriously anyway.

'I was influenced to an extent by my mother. She played the organ in Crook church. But I never really knew whether she was a real believer or just a person who did the right thing – as people did in those days. And then I became a doctor. Not just a doctor but a pathologist. Dealing with death every day in a professional way. There really wasn't space for emotion or a spiritual side. It was just businesslike. I came to the conclusion that science and religion were incompatible.

'I thought about it a lot when my mother died. I didn't know my father. I thought about it when your mother died. I'm thinking about it now.'

I took my left hand off the steering wheel and touched his right hand in the dark.

'Pray for your sister,' he said. 'It can't do any harm. Maybe I've been missing out on something all my long life.'

I heard him sob and then he fell asleep.

We got to the hospital just as Elizabeth was being returned from the operating theatre to the ward. The surgeon came to see us and shook both our hands. 'She'll be more comfortable now,' he said. 'But that was all the operation was for. So don't get your hopes up.' One forthright medic to another.

He was of course right. Soon after, she was moved to a hospice in Wedderburn Road in Belsize Park. It was bang next door to the first school that Elizabeth and I had attended – St Christopher's.

I came down from the Lakes every week to spend a few hours with her. I had never really known her position on God, but at this time she became a devout Catholic and she told me that her final days were greatly enriched by her faith. I was with her on the night that she died. Melanie and I spent the next morning arranging the funeral. I was anxious to get back to Pa and Chris.

Chapter Twenty-Three

DAD

The process of joining Relais & Châteaux had been a long, arduous and expensive process, and once embarked upon, an ominously one-way street. It was, at that time, a requirement to resign from other consortia before applying. So Pride of Britain had to go. Cheques (large ones) were written. Forms were filled. Anonymous inspections took place. Reports were filed. I was in the car on my own driving to Kendal when I got a call from Barney at Gilpin. The membership secretary of the British chapter of Relais & Châteaux wanted to speak to me. He wouldn't talk to anyone else. I pulled over into the petrol station at Ings and rang the number Barney had given me.

We had been accepted. Everyone at Gilpin was on tenterhooks and had gathered in reception. I rang to pass on the news. A great cheer went up. Our membership was to commence at the beginning of the following year.

After Elizabeth's death, Pa aged almost overnight. He became in need of more care than Chris and I could offer and at his request we found a carer who lived in. This virtually obliterated what little privacy there was. We were able to spend more time at Hollins but it was only right to be at Knipe for much of the time. Then one day he telephoned me and said that he wanted to see Chris and me. 'I don't like this carer business,' he said. 'The house is too big and there are too many stairs. And I'm lonely. I want to move into one of the rooms at the Abbeyfield home in Windermere,' to which Pa felt an attachment because it was in the grounds of Nine Oaks, which had been Auntie Gertie's home before it was pulled down.

Pa and indeed Elizabeth and I had spent many hours at Nine Oaks during Gertie's lifetime. Chris and I had had lunch there with Gertie the day after our wedding. Somehow it felt to all of us more like sanctuary than an old people's home. Nonetheless, I was surprised by his decision, and not entirely happy that it was the right thing to do. Had we brought this about by not looking after him adequately? Had the purchase of our house in Burneside made him feel that we didn't want to be with him anymore? Deep questions. No simple answers.

There was a vacancy and he could come whenever he wanted. A date was fixed. As the time drew near, I became more and more anxious. Was this what should happen to such an intelligent and successful man in the last years of his life when he should be enjoying the rewards of his endeavours? It didn't seem right. Chris particularly ensured that his room was decorated tastefully and equipped with everything which Pa might need. It was pleasant enough. But...

We took him down to Windermere with a modest amount of luggage. As we approached Nine Oaks Pa became nervous. He knew no-one there. He was warmly greeted and asked if he wanted to be called Tony or Professor. He replied Tony. The sun was shining through the window of his room. Chris had placed a beautiful arrangement of flowers on the coffee table. We helped him to unpack.

I felt the most profound guilt that I had ever experienced. I don't know why. I hadn't caused this state of affairs. I suppose it was because we were going to live in *his* house. After Dorothy's and Elizabeth's deaths he had volunteered to tidy up his affairs and had left Knipe to Christine and I jointly. I suppose this was the cause of my intense feelings. We would have preferred it all to be otherwise.

I knew he would find "tea" at 5.30 difficult. He had always liked to eat dinner late after several glasses of wine. Just before 5.30 he stood up. 'Well. Here goes,' he said stoically. 'Don't wait for me. I have to get used to this.'

He kissed us both and strode through his new front door.

As was later to be revealed, Pa and Doris "clocked each other" (as they put it) that very afternoon and almost immediately became close friends. So it wasn't too bad after all. But Chris and I weren't to know that that afternoon, and we both cried as we drove back to Gilpin.

Knipe had not seen the stroke of a paintbrush (nor a huge amount of cleaning to be honest) in nearly 30 years. Everything needed to be done. Chris and I decided to move to Hollins while the place was gutted. Pa and Doris came to dinner often, and it was apparent that he was happy and no longer lonely. Drinks had become their habit after tea.

Just before Christmas in 2005, Chris and I were driving home from Manchester Airport after an exciting cruise from Rio de Janeiro to Ushuaia in South America. It had been a long and extremely uncomfortable flight. As we came off the M6 my mobile rang. It was the warden at the Abbeyfield. Pa had fallen and she had called an ambulance. I put my foot down hard. He was being loaded onto the ambulance as we arrived.

He was obviously in great pain. Doris was looking on anxiously. 'I know I've broken my hip,' Pa said. 'It's a very dangerous operation at my time of life you know.' We muttered something encouraging. 'I may very well not survive it,' he added. Doris heard this and burst into floods of tears. Meanwhile he was directing the ambulance men what to do!

We followed the ambulance all the way to Lancaster Royal Infirmary. Parking there is not easy and this was visiting time, which made it worse. By the time Chris and I had got rid of the car, Pa had been taken to a ward. The rows of beds in a vast room devoid of character were depressing. It felt like a Victorian sanatorium. Nobody could tell us whether surgery would be undertaken that night or the next day.

Pa had been pumped full of painkiller and wandered in and out of consciousness. His periodic mumblings were mostly incoherent. At one point he seemed, for no apparent reason, to become lucid. He pulled an arm from under the sheet and beckoned to me. I was one side of the bed and Chris the other. He whispered to us both, 'I don't like it here. Can you see if you can get me moved to the private hospital over the road? I think it's called the Nuffield isn't it?'

'I'll try,' I promised. Then he dozed off again.

I pulled my uncomfortable chair next to Chris. 'I can see why he wants to get out of here,' I said to her. 'But I don't think this is the right moment. I somehow feel he should have the surgery here however grim the place is.'

'I agree completely,' she said.

Not long after that a nurse approached and whispered, 'Tony won't be going to theatre tonight. It'll be first thing in the morning. We'll be keeping him fairly sedated. If you want to grab a few hours' sleep, that'll be fine. We'll look after him. I promise.' I felt satisfied with our decision not to have him moved elsewhere.

Because we had our suitcases with us, we decided to stay in Lancaster and we checked into the Holiday Inn. I hadn't been there since Forte days. It had been a Posthouse then and was the very latest property in the brand. It was right on a bend on the river Kent as it headed to the Irish Sea. Chris and I had a couple of whiskies from the minibar and ordered a sandwich from room service. Chris called Barney and I telephoned Ben. Both wondered what on earth had happened to us and were alarmed at the news of Pa. We told them that there was no point in charging down to Lancaster at this hour.

When we got back to the hospital in the morning, we were scared to see Pa's bed empty. I rushed to the nurses' station and they told me he was already in theatre. We waited until his return some time later. He was very unconscious and looked like a big rag doll. I asked a nurse if it would be possible to see his surgeon or one of the doctors. She told me that the surgeon who had operated on Pa would be coming onto the ward soon. She said she would tell him that I wanted a word. I think Chris and I dozed a bit. We hadn't slept well. Presently, the same nurse asked me to follow her and I was shown into a small office.

The surgeon introduced himself and I explained that I was Tony's son. He told me briefly what procedure he had undertaken. 'You must be aware Mr Cunliffe,' he continued, 'that this is a very serious operation for a man of your father's age. On top of a long period of general anaesthesia, he has sustained a considerable loss of blood. I would say that the chances of a full recovery are no more than fifty-fifty.'

I was stunned.

'So the fact that he has survived the operation doesn't mean it's all over?'

'By no means.' He was obviously a man of few words.

'He asked me last night before he fell asleep about moving to a private hospital. He was the Professor of Microbiology at Kings College Hospital in London.' I felt myself seeking words. I imagined he was thinking 'so what?' 'My dad's not really used to wards,' I said rather feebly.

He smiled kindly. 'I know what you're saying. The ward is ghastly. But I most strongly urge you not to pursue that course of action. Your dad is medically in the right place with all the very best facilities to hand. If anything goes wrong, we have here clinical staff in every medical discipline and we have specialist nurses within paces of your dad. A medium-sized private hospital is not the place for a man of your father's age and in his condition. Please take my advice.'

I said I would and thanked him. I appraised Chris. She said it was what she had expected. A nurse suggested that we go and get some rest. She doubted Pa would become lucid soon. In fact he never did. We made many trips to the hospital including on Christmas Day. Barney and Zoë and Ben did too. Early in the New Year, Pa was moved to Westmorland General in Kendal. The staff on the ward were very kind and let us come more or less whenever we wanted.

As the weeks passed, it became obvious that Pa would not recover. I suppose it was a blessing to have time to get used to the inevitability of his death. I felt inexplicably close to him. Perhaps more so than when he had been truly alive. I got into the habit of calling into the hospital in the evenings after the noise of official visiting times had passed. I always knew I would find no change. The time for that had passed. I hoped he might be aware in some way of my presence and know that he had not been abandoned. I didn't think it was likely.

I usually prayed for him and inevitably started with the prayer for the dying: 'Go forth, Christian soul, out of this world, in the name of God the Father Almighty who created you, in the name of Jesus Christ the son of the living God who suffered for you, in the name of the Holy Spirit who was poured out upon you; in the name of the glorious Virgin Mary, Mother of God; in the name of all the angels and saints of God; may peace be yours this day and your home in holy Zion, through the same Christ our Lord.' It always seemed to me that this fairly concise prayer invoked the help of the important people up there without going through a whole litany.

One morning the inevitable phone call came. I was shocked to be told that Chris and I had to come to the hospital to report to the police. What on earth had they got to do with it? I was told that because my dad had died as a direct result of trauma, the death had to be signed off by the police. We went to the ward where dad had been and were advised on the telephone by a policeman to 'remain at the scene'. I found this quite extraordinarily insensitive.

I told Chris that I wanted to talk to Father Chris about a funeral. I also consulted the boys. I phoned the church and Father Chris answered.

'It's John Cunliffe, Father. My dad died this morning in hospital. He didn't recover from an operation.'

'I'm sorry John,' he said. 'I remember your dad from Barney and Zoë's wedding. A fine gentleman. He wasn't a Catholic was he?'

'No. That's the problem. He wasn't really anything. But my family would like him to have a Christian funeral and wondered if you could do it. Or does not being a Catholic rule that out?'

'Oh no.' He said. 'Far from it. We try and get our hands on a soul of any persuasion or none.' Then to my surprise he added that he had actually discovered that dad was in hospital while visiting one of his parishioners. He had given him the Last Rights without knowing his actual religious status. I thanked him profoundly.

We all wanted it be a very special send off, but I felt that a full-blown requiem Mass would be over the top for a non-Catholic. Gill from Gilpin, whose family were musical, found us a superb soprano to sing *Requiem Eternam* from Faure's *Requiem*. My dad had been very fond of sacred music. In fact when I bought my first gramophone when I was probably sixteen or so I had wanted to buy for my first LP disc *Salad Days* – a musical that was running in London. My dad wanted me to buy Faure's *Requiem*. He won.

Life was never quite the same again. We all missed the old bugger terribly and still do. Whenever I have an injection I think of dad, who was a major contributor to the medical research which led to the universal (I hope) use of disposable syringes.

Chapter Twenty-Four

RELAIS & CHATEAUX

C hris and I attended our first Relais & Châteaux conference in Geneva at the end of 2005 in preparation for our first year of membership in 2006. We had no idea what to expect and were very nervous. I suspected that if it was anything like the Pride of Britain initiation, I might have to make a speech. But this would be to over 1,000 people not just a hundred or so. Men and women speaking many different languages. As it turned out, we were warmly welcomed by the chairman of the English chapter and introduced to hoteliers we did not already know – of which there were many.

We were surprised that the conference was held in a Crowne Plaza hotel, not a Relais & Châteaux. I asked one of the organisers why this was. The explanation turned out to be that one of the rules of the organisation is that a Relais & Châteaux hotel cannot have more than 100 bedrooms. The conference was for approximately 1,000 delegates. Thus all annual international conferences have to be in other brand hotels.

Everything was arranged with precision. Most business sessions were conducted in English or French. Simultaneous translation was available. One evening, the delegates were divided into groups to be wined and dined in Relais & Chateaux hotels and restaurants. Our dinner took for ever. Restaurant chefs rarely understand banqueting.

There was to be a workshop the following February in the USA where we would have the opportunity to present to top travel agents in New York and Chicago. We also needed to visit Winnipeg in Canada to assess the suitability of Canadian cedar hot tubs for the new garden suites. On the basis of showing willingness, as the new boys, to participate, we put our names down, even though the price was prohibitive – like everything in Relais.

After my father's funeral I decided to go to the US and Canada on my own. Chris was not very pleased. There were two reasons for my decision. The Garden Suites were due to open later that year and the design process, headed by Chris, was in full flow. I didn't think she could be away at that stage. We had just started working with a new designer, Sarah Jane Nielsen. Chris had to work very closely with her until she got her feet under the table. Chris knew this really. Secondly, I wanted to be alone for a bit to grieve for my dad. Chris knew this too. Yes, I would have to socialise and do all the usual stuff. But I would have time on my own. She had loved my dad to bits and cared for him like no other. But he had been my dad.

We felt that it would be a good idea for me to take a gift to leave with the travel agents. Something very Lake District. Something that would hopefully stay on their desks and remind them of Gilpin. We came up with a Lakeland slate ruler. They were relatively small and very local and pretty. What we failed to take into account was that 300 of them weighed a ton.

I cursed our stupidity as I checked in at Manchester Airport for the flight to New York, shouldering a rucksack full of slate rulers which I pretended was as light as a feather. I got away with it. On arrival in New York, I was immediately singled out by the customs people for a comprehensive search. Perhaps it was the lopsided manner in which I was walking, weighed down by the rulers. I managed to get rid of half of them at the presentations in New York but had to take the rest with me to Winnipeg, as I was flying thereafter to Chicago.

I was impressed with the hot tubs and the assurances given about delivery and other details. I emailed Barney to confirm the order. Customs clearance for the USA was conducted after check-in at Winnipeg. I was once again escorted into a cell and taken apart. I was beginning to get something of a complex. I was after all (or so I thought) a reasonably normal looking sixty-something-year-old without the perceived hallmarks of a hardened criminal. Although very comfortably ensconced in the Four Seasons hotel in Chicago, I was lonely and wished that I had asked Chris to come with me. But soon the "business" began and there was no time for anything but attempting to persuade professional travel agents that Gilpin was the only place for their clients.

I was very glad when it was time to fly home – without any slate rulers. Chris met me and we stayed at a hotel near Heathrow. The next day, only one of us was invited to a luncheon at Le Gavroche to introduce new Relais & Châteaux members to the press. I woke up feeling dreadful. Chris insisted that it was just jet lag and that I must go. I said I was ill and asked her to go. She said she couldn't as she had to visit The Design Centre at Chelsea Harbour to research fabrics for the garden suites.

I joined the reception at Le Gavroche and it is I am sure living proof of my state of health that I accepted a glass of fizzy water when Dom Perignon was on offer. Within five minutes I knew I was not going to make it. I mumbled to the Relais & Châteaux hostess that she must excuse me and grabbed a chair before I fell over. Everyone was too busy being busy to take much notice of me, but I just wanted to get out of the place before I made a fool of myself.

Grosvenor House was around the corner and I wondered whether the doctor who had practised there when I was in charge of the apartments might still have a surgery in the hotel. I dragged myself through the revolving door and grabbed a seat by the Hall Porters' desk.

The man on duty gave me a snooty look – he probably thought I was drunk. I couldn't stand up. I beckoned to him to come over which he did. I asked if Dr Evans still had a practice there. He didn't. I explained that I was not well and needed a doctor. They could not have been more solicitous and before I knew what was happening I had been shown to a bedroom and helped by an obliging young manager to get into bed.

I phoned Chris but (of course) she didn't answer her mobile. I phoned Zoë at Gilpin and explained what had happened and asked her to track down Chris. Before I knew it a doctor was with me. I have no recollection of what he said, just of being given an injection. Then I passed out.

Much later, Chris arrived, frightened, flustered and not sure if I was seriously ill or not. I have no recollection of getting to the car or participating in a decision to go home. I have no recollection of the journey home including (Chris later told me) some sort of a seizure which necessitated Chris turning into a service area. I have no idea to this day what was wrong with me.

The rest of the year was hard. The weather was appalling. No-one was able to commit to a date for the Garden Suites to be ready for handover, so in the end we just had to make an intelligent guess and use the chosen date as a target to work to. Discussions took place then, and have done with subsequent projects, about bonuses, penalty clauses and other forms of incentives to meet a timetable. Contractors, architects and project managers take the view that all such tactics are unworkable in the Lake District due to the unpredictability of the weather.

We worked like demons to get there on time. As had become the norm, this involved towards the end total abandonment of usual responsibilities and all hands to the pumps for the lawns, gardens, cleaning, picture hanging, window cleaning, electric plug changing and (in this instance) dealing with a new animal: the hot tubs.

We did it. The result was spectacular in every sense. Ben's designs were just the ticket – a metamorphosis in Lakeland architecture.

In the intervening years we have shared out attendance at Relais & Châteaux conferences. They are absurdly expensive so only two of us go – usually. Prior to the 2006 conference, which was to be in Monaco, we had been advised that we really should attend – meaning you are up for some citation or other. We were told that our food had come in for recognition. So we decided to go in force, particularly since only Chris and I had met our Relais & Châteaux colleagues the previous year. So as well as Chris and I, Barney and Zoë went, Ben with the current girlfriend, and the new Head Chef. What absurd extravagance! Chris Davies had moved on after nine years with us – but only to Kendal so we were able to stay in touch.

Our new Head Chef was indeed cited and was presented with a trophy for Rising Chef of the Year by Princess Stephanie herself. We were very proud. And the following year we got a Michelin star – which we lost the year after.

This was a very sad debacle which should never have happened. We learned (and so did the Head Chef) that you must never, never, never forget who you are cooking for – your guests: not yourself. The Head Chef, Barney and Chris all crying in reception is not a sight I want to revisit.

This event prefaced six years in chef wilderness. We seemed unable to find or be able to keep someone whom we could make happy or who could make us content. We hoped that Barney as a younger man would be able to relate more readily with another less entrenched person. And my God he tried. We all tried. We paid good money. We gave them as much rope as we dared without allowing them to wreck the business. They knew how to cook. They knew to some extent how to manage a kitchen. They did not know what our clientele wanted on the menu and they did not know how to become a member of a team. It is undoubtedly a hard job requiring great skill, leadership, resilience and hard work. We had good days and bad and in the end we were lucky enough to appoint Hrishikesh, who is with us as I write. But that story comes later.

Chris and I also went to the Relais & Châteaux conference in Washington DC, in late 2007. We crossed the Atlantic with our friends Lloyd and Iris – neighbours from Jamaica days – on some enormous and ghastly ship. We had to share our table (I hate sharing tables on cruises), and on the night before we docked in Fort Lauderdale had to present our waiter, wine waiter and head waiter with "their envelopes" containing recommended sums. What appallingly bad taste! As if in protest at the crummy ethos of the ship, Chris caught pneumonia and was confined to the cabin for half the voyage. We stayed with Lloyd and Iris for a few days at their home near Miami and then headed for Washington in a hired car.

It was a splendid adventure and we saw a good deal of that part of the States. Our favourite hotel was Blackberry Farm in Kentucky, but our stay nearly brought about the end of Chris's life. She had had a few anaphylactic fits since her first one when she was in her thirties. She had been stung by a wasp when I was away at work. She was at our house in Beckenham Place Park and started to feel ill and then very ill. She had the presence of mind to telephone a friend who was a nurse, who knew exactly what was going on and told her to get to the hospital fast. Chris had realised after a few streets that she was incapable of driving and pulled over to seek help from pedestrians. Those were probably kinder and more trusting days. Today, help might be less forthcoming. But a man just getting into his parked car took her to Beckenham General Hospital with no time to spare. She was given adrenalin which as we now know (but didn't then) is the number one first aid essential for anaphylaxis. I was overseeing the catering at a golf tournament in Surrey and was paged to return home at once as my wife was seriously ill. What a shock that was.

Ever since then, I carry all the requisite medicines with me at all times and Chris carries a duplicate set in her handbag. This is why she always has a large handbag and can consequently never find her phone!

And so we carried on (with her being extremely brave and refusing to let this condition alter her life), believing that it was only wasp stings which would trigger this condition. But at dinner at Blackberry Farm we had just enjoyed a dry Martini cocktail and were feeling good. Chris had a terrine as a first course. It contained pecan nuts. We had no reason to see that as a problem.

Within a minute she said she felt ill. We both knew what was coming. I had not brought the medical kit with me to dinner, nor had she brought her handbag. Who expects to meet a wasp in November?

I raced to our bedroom which was in a separate wing of the hotel some way away. On my return her face, lips and eyelids were bloated and she could scarcely breathe. She managed to tell me that she had asked staff to get a doctor urgently but that they had said that that would take time and it might not be possible until the next day. She had told them that she would be dead by then. By now I was getting the EpiPen out of its packaging. I knew how to administer this. Easy. But I was terrified of the second and third stages of treatment which involved an injection by syringe into a vein in the arm. I had never done this. But I had all the kit and knew what I had to do. Then a man at the next table came over and said to Chris and me 'let me take over. I'm a doctor'.

I don't think I have ever been so relieved in my life. I had really been thinking I might lose her. They say that if you are dying, your life flashes past you. Chris later told me that that did not happen to her but that she felt very calm. Even serene. I certainly did not. I was terrified for her and for myself. I could not imagine life without her and I realised how much I loved her. The doctor administered all the injections and stayed with her for most of the night. So there is a God! As well as decent human beings. I dread to think what might have happened to the doctor if his treatment of Chris had gone wrong.

She was fine, if tired, the next day, which happened to be Thanksgiving. This seemed very appropriate. Consequently Blackberry Farm was fully booked and we could not stay another night. I was keen to get to the destination we had planned for that evening and rather overlooked the speed limit. On one particular stretch of dual carriageway I heard the sirens just before the police car flagged us down.

'Anything the matter officer?' I asked stupidly. I can't do the drawl – never mind write it – but the gist of the conversation was that I had been doing 90mph which was very unacceptable. I pulled a sob story about Chris's anaphylactic fit the evening before and needing to get her to bed. I think the two officers decided that the hassle of prosecuting a foreigner wasn't worth it. Amazingly, the restaurant and bar in the Marriott hotel in which we stayed was closed. So we ate in an Italian diner on the other side of the road. Food like Mamma does it. And Chianti.

We made it to Washington and listened to a spellbinding address by Colin Powell. He talked for over an hour without looking at a single note. There was no autocue. I do admire people who can do that. He was particularly amusing in talking about Condoleezza Rice, who had replaced him as Secretary of State. He missed having his own aeroplane! He particularly disliked fancy alarm clocks in hotels. Being woken at the right time was, he observed, very important to him and he didn't want to have to study an instruction manual on how to set the alarm. Or how to turn on the shower.

We had booked to stay at the hotel in Washington for an additional day and night after the final dinner of the conference and were able to join an exclusive tour of the White House, including the Oval Office. We were disappointed not to meet the President! However, this tour, coupled with a visit to the space museum gave us an inspirational overview of the USA of the time.

Chapter Twenty-Five

KNIPE TARN

A great deal of my time in 2006 had been taken up with dealing with my father's affairs and uppermost in our minds was what exactly to do with Knipe. Barney and Zoë were happily ensconced in their cottage, now known as Bumblebee Cottage – well it would be wouldn't it? Cherry Tree Cottage is just too mundane! Ben was settled into Helsfell in Kendal and Chris and I were very happy at 5 The Hollins. But the refurbishment of Knipe Tarn was nearing completion and we knew how very lucky we were to have inherited such a wonderful place.

With not a little sadness, we concluded that we had to sell The Hollins. The accountants said that any other course of action could cost the family dear. The prospect of living at Knipe without being confined to the upstairs flat was exciting and we had many plans, the implementation of which were only curtailed by money.

The Garden Suites at Gilpin were very popular, and in the light of opening the Garden Room restaurant, absorbing another twelve dinners and breakfasts was not a problem. Barney and Zoë had by now got their feet well and truly under the table and I could feel Barney itching to take more control. He was like a thoroughbred under starter's orders. And I was well over sixty. Neither Chris nor I had any desire to retire. There was still so much to do. Chris, I have to be honest, was more indispensable than me. No-one else could handle decor. And no-one else had the beady eye for detail which she focused on housekeeping, flower arranging, overstaffed departments and the gardens. My jobs were less exciting. We all made ourselves in charge of ensuring that guests were happy and looked after.

One of the debates we had had when planning the Garden Suites was whether to have a wall at the end of the private gardens with hot tubs or not. We felt that it was obvious that given the lovely views onto the South Lakeland hills and fells you would not want to exclude them and be boxed in. This led to a few issues with guests about the definition of the word "private". Does it mean "exclusive" (in other words excluding others) or does it mean "concealed"? We were very clear about the answer to this question – exclusive. How does one ensure exclusivity? A barbed-wire fence? Mines? A wall (thereby excluding the views)? We felt that a low wall, a bamboo hedge and a stream was probably adequate. And that's what we provided. Some guests were (and continue to be) oblivious to the lack of total concealment, and some embarrassing moments have been experienced by occupants of the suites, as well as by guests taking a stroll in that part of the gardens.

At an appropriate moment, Chris and I invited Barney and Zoë to a meeting in the privacy of Knipe. Having somewhere to meet became a big advantage to us as a family, particularly in the light of the palpable shortage of office space at Gilpin. I asked Barney if he would like to assume the title of Managing Director and ultimate responsibility for the running of Gilpin. I don't think he was expecting the question and to my surprise he said that he would like to sleep on it. Could we meet again the next morning? We did. He said that he would like to accept the invitation. I asked why he had hesitated. He replied that it had nothing to do with his willingness or ability to do the job. He was just blisteringly conscious that Gilpin had been our baby and he was not sure if we would be able to let go of any of the important decision-making. He foresaw stormy seas ahead if we did not let him get on with the job. We all knew that this was potentially a real danger. We promised to try very hard.

One of his first major decisions was to appoint London agency Ann

Scott Associates to handle our PR. Barney and Zoë were far more PR conscious than Chris and I had ever been and they believed that PR potential was a major factor in decisions and projects. They turned out to be absolutely right, and over the years since, this firm has done a fantastic job for Gilpin and been highly instrumental in putting us on the map.

Then Zoë was pregnant. This was a big thrill. A baby for them and a grandchild for us. Illogically, and with hindsight probably rather stupidly, they decided to book a holiday sailing a catamaran in the Caribbean. They asked us and Ben if we would like to come. Chris immediately accepted before even waiting for my answer. She told me later that her reaction was based entirely on looking after Zoë. The concept of all being away from Gilpin together for any length of time was a first, and worrying. But in the light of a larger team we decided that the risk had to be taken. We could not cut ourselves off from family holidays forever.

The airline, which will remain anonymous, had a scheme, operating at Manchester Airport anyway, whereby if you had an early flight the next morning, you could deposit your bags the evening before. We had a very early flight so this seemed a good idea. At check-in the next morning, we were advised that the direct flight to Barbados had been cancelled and we had to take a later flight to Gatwick to connect with another flight to Barbados on a different carrier. Yes the bags would be transferred.

The flight to Gatwick was delayed. The connecting flight to Barbados had left when we arrived at Gatwick. The next flight was not till the next day. The bags were not on the flight we had taken. The ongoing carrier's staff knew nothing of an arrangement for us to fly with them the next day. Zoë was being sick. We were all tired, worried and upset. Chris was fretting about Zoë. We were put into a thoroughly third-rate hotel and told to watch this space. In the fullness of time, a representative of the original carrier arrived and we were told that we would be on a flight the next morning.

Eventually we made it to Barbados and connected to yet another flight from Barbados to St Vincent. By the time we boarded our catamaran it was too late to sail that afternoon, so we slept on the boat after a poor dinner ashore.

And so we finally set off. The wind was blowing a gale and we were a bit nervous – Chris and I in particular as novice sailors. Nor did the boat's movements help Zoë's condition. At anchor that afternoon the wind was still strong and the boat was pitching.

Chris and I retired early but slept badly. Judging from the noises during the night we had slept better than Zoë. We got up very early. The cockpit and surrounding area was a mess and very wet and slippery. The wind and movement of the boat was, if anything, worse than the day before. We set about cleaning up. Chris lowered a bucket attached to a rope into the water to fill the bucket. A particularly strong wave struck the boat side on and the vessel tilted violently. Chris lost her balance and fell hard onto the deck. We both heard the crack. She screamed in pain. We both knew what had happened.

Chris's scream woke the others and the boys came running. Maps, charts and directories were consulted to ascertain which was the nearest land with a doctor. It was apparently Mustique – the small private island made famous by Princess Margaret. Barney decided that motoring would be quicker and more stable that sailing, so the anchor was hauled up and we set off. Chris had been made as comfortable as possible but she was whimpering with pain and any jolt obviously caused her agony. I decided that my best role was to hold her hand and give her encouragement. She blacked out several times.

On arrival at Mustique the problem was how to transfer her from the boat into the dingy and then onto land. Fortunately she was not conscious for much of this manoeuvre. A taxi took us to the doctor's surgery and mercifully he was in. A nicer and more compassionate man could not have been hoped for, and within seconds she was pumped full of painkillers and receiving the best care that a small island practice could offer. An X-ray confirmed that her leg was broken. The doctor did not have the facilities nor the qualifications to undertake surgery. She would have to be taken to the mainland.

The doctor spent ages on the telephone to our insurance company who wanted to send her to the United States. None of us could see the logic in this since it would be a far more expensive alternative for the insurance company than being returned to the UK. There was not a flight to anywhere that day, so the doctor arranged for Chris and I to be taken to The Cotton House hotel where we were accommodated in a very comfortable room. Chris slept for 24 hours without batting an eyelid.

I sat by my mobile phone. And waited. And waited. The next morning I phoned the insurers and had to wait so long to be put through to the department handling Chris's case that the phone died, restricting my movements even further until the battery was recharged. I then set off to see the doctor to ask if he could, on medical grounds, demand action. He did his best. But in the end we spent three nights in The Cotton House. I was totally unable to enjoy the facilities of this charming hotel. I was worried about getting Chris home and she was a terrible patient. For some time I had lived with the nickname "Eeyore". Now additionally I became "Fetch".

The rest of our family would not leave until our arrangements were settled, so their holiday was severely curtailed. They visited us frequently, having moved the boat nearer to the hotel. The local flight to Barbados to connect with the flight home was on a tiny aircraft in which Chris could not keep her leg stretched out. She was again in agony, but by now at least armed with painkillers.

Neither the airport authorities at Barbados nor the airline would let us check in early so we had to sit in stifling and uncomfortable conditions with our luggage for three hours. At boarding time there appeared to be no means of getting Chris onto the plane. She was invited to walk up twenty or so steps. Eventually she was hoisted into the cabin on a device designed for luggage. The promised flatbed seat did not exist.

By the time she had been admitted to hospital at Barrow-in-Furness, the leg had set at the wrong angle and had to be broken again before being re-set. Fortunately this procedure was under a general anaesthetic. Everything went well and Chris was soon back home. But just as she had been when we were at The Cotton House, she was a dreadful patient, and because she was hampered by a plaster pot on her leg she became an impatient patient – bad tempered and demanding. She wasn't able to undertake her normal activities either at Gilpin or at home.

The kids eventually arrived home. The holiday hadn't been a great success. But Zoë had survived the journey and the baby was due in December.

I had a massive row with the insurance company over the handling of our repatriation. They felt that staying at The Cotton House had been an unnecessary extravagance. It seemed to me so obvious that since there was no other hotel on the island, there had been no choice. I also pointed out that had they flown us home sooner instead of mucking about trying to find a cheap flight, our stay at The Cotton House could have been curtailed. I also protested that the delay had complicated the surgery – a fact that the doctors confirmed. We finally agreed on a figure but it left a nasty taste in my mouth and I have rather distrusted insurers ever since.

Clearly the sailing holiday had been an unmitigated disaster. I doubted we would do it again. But Chris and I are active people. We can't just sit on a beach. We love to travel and see new places. I suggested buying a caravan and a suitable car to tow it. She looked at me as a snake might regard a mongoose. 'How do you know you would be able to tow it?' she demanded.

'I had a military HGV licence from when I was in the Territorial Army,' I retorted.

'It would have to be a new caravan. I couldn't sleep in someone else's bed.'

'We've been married for more than forty years' I said. 'You think you need to tell me that?'

'It would be so boring if the weather was bad.'

'I contemplate mainly being abroad in the sunshine.'

'You'd have to drive on the wrong side of the road.'

'I've been doing that since I was seventeen.'

'Not towing a caravan.'

'No. But towing a field gun.'

'Abroad?'

'Yes. We went to a camp in Germany.'

'You've got all the answers, haven't you?'

'I have given it a lot of thought and prepared my case. Yes.'

There was a long pause.

'There's no harm in having a look,' she conceded.

It was still early, so we got into the car. I had researched dealers. She hobbled around a large dealership. We neither of us liked the idea of camper vans, so that was easy. Several makes of caravans had terrible decor so they were discounted. Many were too small with inadequate kitchens. We moved on to larger twin-axle units. The salesman detected that there was interest. He stuck nearby. We discussed the merits of twin-axle caravans. The advantages seemed indisputable. Then she pulled herself up the steps of a particular unit. She sat. She stood. She examined the cooker, the shower and the toilet. She sat on the sofa. She lay on the bed. We enquired about the price and availability.

'I like this one,' she said. 'Shall we get it John?' Without exaggeration, I had not been so surprised since she told me about 20 years earlier that she was going to be the head chef at Gilpin.

'Yes please', I said.

We did the paperwork and paid a deposit. The caravan would be ready with the necessary extras fitted in two weeks. I asked the salesman whether our car would be suitable for towing it. He felt not – something to do with torque – whatever that is. He suggested that you could not beat a Land Rover Discovery to tow a large twin-axle caravan. We passed a Land Rover dealer on the way home. They had an ex-demo available at the sort of price we had in mind. We took it on a test drive and agreed to have it.

What an extraordinary morning! And so we embarked on what was to become a passion. We acquired plates and glasses and cutlery and sheets and duvets and pillows and chemicals and water carriers and electric cables and spare fuses and a portable television and steps and heaven knows what else. We joined clubs and bought campsite guides for the UK and all around Europe. We arranged insurance. We booked a ferry crossing from Plymouth to Santander in Spain and made a reservation at a site near Plymouth for a week's "practice". We asked Chris's sister Jane, recently widowed, if she would like to come with us. She said she would.

The plaster at last came off. The surgeon was happy. Chris was still in some pain and her leg looked a mess. But she could walk again.

We set off to collect the car and the caravan. Both were ready. It took most of a morning to be instructed in the use of the various caravan components and how to hitch up safely. I drove out of the dealership onto the road with some trepidation. The caravan was much longer than a field gun! My main anxiety was getting the caravan up the steep narrow lane from the village of Winster to Knipe. Zoë had asked if she could come with us to collect the caravan. She was nearly as excited for us as we were.

As we turned up the lane leading to Knipe, people sitting on the terrace of the Brown Horse pub looked in amazement at the lunatics taking such an enormous caravan up this tiny, winding road. I rather shared their sentiment but tried to look confident. Fortunately, traffic on the lane is light and we did not meet any other vehicles. A farmer with a trailer would have been difficult. Reversing was a trick yet to be mastered. The next obstacle was entering Knipe. The gateway was narrow. We made it with six inches to spare either side. Many far more hazardous adventures were to befall us in the months and years ahead.

Our move to Knipe and the sale of Hollins had been accomplished. Our friends Lloyd and Iris, whose permanent home was in Florida, had bought The Hollins so we did not really have to say goodbye to the house. The view from the master bedroom at Knipe, previously my dad's room, more previously still my dad's and Dorothy's room, was exquisite. Chris's decorative schemes were a great success and the new kitchen was a cook's paradise. I had a whole room for an office, complete with a large walk-in wardrobe in which to hide a filing cabinet and box files. This for me is very important. I loved it.

Preparing to leave for Plymouth was a combination of nervousness and excitement. This was the first time I had hitched up the caravan after the fairly brief demonstration at the dealership. I also had to turn the caravan around. Chris demonstrated (well, I suppose I should have expected it) a remarkable proficiency in the caravan housekeeping area.

Not having to have suitcases was from the start a major attraction of caravanning. Chris is a terrible packer, and on previous holidays of all sorts the bane of my life had been having to handle an enormous quantity of luggage. While this was annoying and frequently the source of a good laugh, I did understand the rationale behind this behaviour. It's all a part of her perfectionism.

Taking the right stuff on holiday is not all that different to equipping a kitchen or a hotel bedroom. It needs to be right. Apart from the vagaries of the weather (it could be cold in the Bay of Biscay), one needs to look half decent in the restaurant on the ferry. We have hardly ever been on a holiday when we have not met people who have stayed at Gilpin. It would be hot in France and Spain. On the other hand our journey might coincide with the Mistral. And who knows? One might bump into the Queen or the President of France. We might decide to go for dinner at a Relais & Châteaux restaurant where smart clothes would be de rigeur.

Chris had to be prepared for all these eventualities. And not just Chris: if she was to look the part, I had to also. But the joy of caravanning is that it doesn't matter. You fill the wardrobes and ample lockers with anything you might possibly need and the contents either get used or they don't. All the shelves had been prepared with lining paper and I had fitted the two small wardrobes with the sort of clothes hangers that you get in cheap hotels – ones which you can't steal, or which in this case don't fall down when the caravan is bumping along the road. The dinner jacket was secure. (Only joking!) Under the bed was a cave in which all clobber not needed on a daily basis was stored.

I won't claim that our first caravan pack was perfect, but it was pretty adept. I checked the hitch-up, the safety cable, the handbrake, the electrical connection, the window locks, the roof hatches, the gas, the fridge and finally the door lock.

We departed for Plymouth having beseeched Zoë to look after herself. We had to pick up Jane from Doncaster on the way. Towing the caravan came naturally to me and we arrived at our site in Plymouth in good spirits. Preparing for our first "sleepover" was complicated by the fact that Jane was in competition with Chris for the Maximum Luggage of the Year Award. Chris had filled most of the lockers with her stuff. Where was Jane's to go? Much compromise was required.

Boarding the ferry was worrying. The bottom of the caravan scraped the ramp. Jane complained of feeling seasick before we had even cast off. During dinner she wanted to fetch her phone from the cabin to ring Kate, her daughter. She was gone for ages. She had got lost and eventually arrived back at the table in floods of tears.

The temperature warmed as we sailed south and we drove off the ferry in Santander in balmy sunshine. We drove eastwards through northern Spain. A major hurdle was experienced at our first campsite, which was delightful. Our pitch had a view out to the Atlantic Ocean. This was the life, I thought. Confidently going to connect the electrics, I discovered that whereas in England we use a 16-amp plug which connects into a socket with three holes, the socket here had two holes and one pin. So you needed a plug with two pins and one hole. You really would think that what with all the EU standardisation overindulgence, they would have taken care of this. But they hadn't. I had no adaptor. The little shop on the site had no adaptors. The lady in the shop spoke no English.

'Problema,' I said in my very inadequate Spanish. I had brought with me a cable to facilitate the conversation. 'Inglaterra tres,' I said as I held up the plug and pointed to the three pins. She understood immediately and smiled sadly. She beckoned to me to go outside where she pointed along the road to the right and said, 'Camping San Jose'.

I reported back to the girls. Chris was becoming agitated because the fridge was defrosting. I found Camping San Jose and as luck would have it there was a charming old man in a tatty workshop who disconnected my plug and connected a Spanish one. Back at the caravan I plugged in and everything came to life: the fridge, the lights, the toilet flush, the cooker, the microwave. Life was good again.

The next day we drove into France and quickly learned that picking campsites was not straightforward. They varied from superb to appalling; from neat and organised to chaotic; from helpful to rude; from clean to dog poo-ridden; from an adequate electric supply to ones which blew a fuse if you boil a kettle; from cheap to expensive; from huge pitches to tiny; from ones dominated by Spanish, French, Dutch, German or English. A big learning curve had begun. We had a good adventure but Jane did not like the food, the climate, the currency, the language, driving on the wrong side of the road or the foreigners.

On 20th December 2007 our first granddaughter was born in Lancaster Royal Infirmary. Chris and I visited the day after the birth. For some reason, which I could not explain, I was very nervous. She was tiny, with a mass of spiky black hair.

They called her Xiá, which apparently is Chinese for "glow of the sunrise". How you can condense four words into three letters I know not. She was smiling then at one day old. She has smiled ever since.

A few weeks later, Father Chris baptised Xiá at the church in Kendal. He was somewhat taken aback by the attendance of six Godparents. Barney and Zoë do nothing by halves!

What should have been a decorous, semi-religious lunch afterwards at Knipe Tarn, turned into a rip-roaring party which went on far into the evening. I recall dancing on a table. And I don't dance!

Chapter Twenty-Six

THE LAKE HOUSE

Living at Knipe Tarn was all very well, and we considered it a great privilege. But it was an expensive place to run for two people. The gardens and grounds were extensive. The heating (LPG) was prohibitive. The council tax was probably right for such a large property – but a lot of money. And we began to understand why my dad had been lonely. Perhaps even a little nervous. We had become used, at The Hollins, to living in a small community. The neighbours had not always been perfect, but they had been neighbours; people next door. At Knipe, we had no next door. We also felt that it was rather a shame that such a beautiful place was only enjoyed by two people. We wondered if we should do bed and breakfast. But how would we find the time on top of everything else? We were busy enough as it was. Then the jetty started crumbling and we felt sure it wasn't safe. It needed replacing. Big money. We decided we needed electric gates for security. Big money. The boat was leaking badly and needed a major repair job. And so on.

Both boys loved Knipe and we thought it only right to have discussions with them. Chris and I were determined that we would do better than my dad had in dealing with wills and inheritance issues. An honest assessment of the situation took place and the conclusion was that on balance, two busy people in their sixties living at Knipe on their own was probably not sensible. We decided to apply for planning permission for a new much smaller house for us and to modestly extend the existing house to make it suitable for hotel use. Ben initiated enquiries with the planners.

Then we were distracted by Reg's death. He had followed my dad into the Abbeyfield, although they had not overlapped each other. Reg had been happy there as he was a very sociable man, and the majority of the residents were women. He was treated like a talisman. And he was happy to have "tea" served at 5.30. Chris had worked her magic on his room, just as she had on Tony's, and it was a cheerful spot overlooking the playing fields.

Chris and I had started having Xiá every Saturday, and we took her often to see Reg. He treasured these visits. Then one morning Chris took a telephone call from the warden. They had become suspicious when he didn't emerge for his morning walk and checked his room. He had passed away during the night. Chris was distraught, particularly because she had not seen her dad within the preceding few days. Another strand of our lives had come to the buffers.

That summer we took Jane with us to a campsite in Provence for two weeks, and Barney and Zoë wanted to come for a week with Xiá. We booked a chalet for them. On arrival it was a terrible disappointment. The pitches were small and the place heaved with children noisily bouncing footballs throughout the evening and in the early mornings. A further disappointment was that we were advised that for the last four days we would have to move to a different pitch in another part of the site. This was hassle. Barney helped us to pack up and move.

I knew we weren't going onto the road, just up a hill to the other part of the site, and I was sloppy about hitching up and checking. As we started to ascend to the higher part of the site, I felt the car shoot forward and looked in the rear view mirror to see the caravan accelerating backwards down the hill. It had become detached from the car. It was one of the worst moments of my life. Thanks be to God in all sincerity, there were no people behind it, and it crashed through the camp entry barrier and was stopped by a wall. The bang as it broke through the barrier was deafening and within minutes a hundred or so people had assembled to see what was going on, many muttering about the stupid Anglais who had not applied the safety cable. How right they were and I felt stupid, humble and yet relieved that no-one had been hurt or killed. The site proprietors were none too pleased either. I think Chris and my family thought I was a prize prat. I certainly felt one. The caravan was badly damaged but useable and able to be towed home after application of quantities of duct tape.

While the Garden Room at Gilpin had solved the problem of dining tables, the new suites had put a strain on lounge seating before dinner. The Garden Suites had started to change the typical guest profile. A younger clientele was being attracted by the hot tubs. Barney felt that this lounge seating problem should be solved by the addition of a cocktail bar rather than more lounge space. Cocktails were at this stage starting a major comeback, emanating of course from London and the big cities. So yet another project got under way and endless meetings were convened to draw up building and operational plans. Thank God we had a "resident" architect! The new bar, being attached to the main building, had to complement its architectural style. Ben's design was exemplary.

This project was progressing well when we got back from France. The build also incorporated an accessible toilet which had been borne of a meeting with the council, to whom we had been reported for not having one. Ben had attended the meeting and there had been much measuring of doorways and simulated wheelchairs and discussions about access. The presence of a well-informed architect had flummoxed the lady from the council, whose propositions were way adrift of suitable for a classy hotel. As we were already building the bar, it seemed sensible to incorporate this facility rather than adapt one of the existing loos. We wanted the bar to be up and running well before the end of the year. This change of plan, which was obviously the right thing to do, had necessitated not inconsiderable changes to Ben's plans for the bar. He was not well pleased but agreed to apply himself to the situation with a sense of urgency.

The location of the Garden Suites had necessitated some alterations to gardens and boundaries with the fields. We decided to make the estate deer-proof. Reds and roe deer are common in the area, particularly in the winter, and a herd can munch its way through a garden overnight. Shortly after these fences had been erected, we were approached by a man who wanted to dispose of five llamas which he had kept as pets. He was prepared to give them to us as long as we promised to look after them and not to sell them. We took advice on their care, purchased a couple of sheds and took them in. They're only for decoration. We've never attempted to use their wool. But they're fun and we subsequently bought some alpacas to complete the Andean feel. Strangely, the two species, although "related", tend not to associate with each other. One evening just before service of dinner, the llamas and alpacas were spotted strolling through the gardens, whence they went on to the road. The guests witnessing this found it all highly amusing, but it was actually very dangerous as cars defy the 40mph speed limit and race along that road. Service in the hotel ground to a halt as I rounded up all the staff to help collect the animals. This was no mean feat as they can move very fast. The task was eventually completed. The next day, self-closing springs and locks were fitted to all the gates.

The cocktail bar was completed well before the end of the year and has been a great success ever since. The design is impressive and the decor sophisticated. I believe it changed the pattern of drinking at Gilpin as Barney had predicted, although it is expensive to staff, as cocktails are more labour intensive that just pouring glasses of wine. I believe two thirds of pre-dinner drinks are now either champagne or cocktails. And the shortage of seating was resolved at a stroke. This brought about a hugely relaxed feel to the pre-dinner period. We had considered putting an additional bedroom on the roof of the bar but decided against it. Access would have spoiled Troutbeck – one of our best rooms – and the view from the Garden Suites would have been interrupted. Instead, we made a small private garden patio for Troutbeck.

With all this going on, the fate of Knipe (and of Chris and me) had been put on the back burner. So as we ushered in 2009 we determined to address it once again. Attempts to budge the planners on making our new house detached had met a brick wall, so Ben put in an application for a new house attached to the existing building, and for a conservatory breakfast room for the hotel part, as well as for two new en-suite bathrooms. It was a clever design which offered our new house as much privacy as possible. Secretly, I think I hoped the application would be turned down. But it was granted. Murphy's law!

While I intensely disliked the hierarchy and behaviour of our then bank, I liked and trusted our relationship manager, who had moved to Handelsbanken. I had never heard of this bank until this man wrote to me to say goodbye and to wish us well. I made an appointment to see him and he told me about the bank, how it worked, its relationship with its Swedish headquarters and above all about its policy of local decision-making. The interpretation of "local" was pivotal to Handelsbanken's philosophy, and any further business would have to be conducted with the Carlisle branch.

Barney was adamant that the new business at Knipe must include the word "lake", so that search engines would zoom in on it. So the new "department" of Gilpin at Knipe was to be called "Gilpin Lake House". Knipe Tarn would remain the postal address and the name of our new house.

It is difficult to describe dealings with Handelsbanken. They are as different to your High Street banks as it is possible to be. Transparent; honest; sincere; thorough; risk-averse; frank; helpful; businesslike; gentlemanly (and gentlewomanly); tough – are all adjectives which come to mind, but above all hugely focused on the attributes of their clients. I loved the comprehensive change and got on very well with the managers in Carlisle, who were soon to open an office in Kendal. They were fascinated by the model we had for operating the Lake House and its relationship with Gilpin. Barney, Chris and I had spent many hours discussing exactly how this would work. It was obvious that a six-bedroom hotel at four or five-star level could not operate profitably in a standalone situation. But with administration and reservations being dealt with by existing departments at Gilpin the figures seemed to stack up. In return for these services, the Lake House would pay Gilpin a management fee.

Handelsbanken agreed to fund the Lake House project, including our house. But they were reluctant to take on Gilpin at that stage. This was their cautious face. We decided not to start the project in the winter but to leave it till the spring of the next year. Chris and I were not looking forward to this. We would have to continue to live at Knipe with all this going on. We had had enough experience of builders to know what was likely to happen.

As it turned out, it was unpleasant beyond our worst fears. Our new house was at one end of the building; the hotel conservatory was at the other and the new bathrooms were in the middle. So contractors were everywhere and dust seemed to be able to creep through whatever defences we erected. For fireproofing reasons the entire ceiling of the lounge had to be replaced. There was nowhere to put the furniture. A considerable amount of rock had to be excavated and it wouldn't budge so it had to be blasted. What impact might this have on the existing building? Ben appeared confident but was I think nervous. Blowing up your parents' house would not be good for family relations. Any attempt to salvage the gardens was abandoned. The diggers, dumpers and bulldozers swept everything away before them.

As our house started to take shape, it became obvious that it should be an upside down house with the living area on the first floor and the bedrooms downstairs. We enjoyed being involved in the layout. Ben as an architect and artist is not always easy to work with. He understandably sees things as a professional. This is not always the same view as that of the client. Compromises were necessary.

Barney the businessman yet again decided that we must set a date to start taking bookings. In fairness to him the bank was adamant that we must do this and that we should stick to the budgets and cash-flow forecasts submitted. We decided to open for business on the 10th September 2010.

Then we were approached to allow the project at Knipe to be filmed for a TV programme to be called "The Lakes". The series was to run for several weeks and be screened in the autumn. Several Lakeland enterprises were to be featured – warts and all. We certainly had some warts! The film crew were charming, courteous and discreet. But nonetheless, tensions ran high at this very difficult time for us as a family and particularly for Chris and me. Decisions had to be made almost every hour of every day and as a family we are outspoken and diverse – all wearing different hats – Ben as the architect, Barney as the MD, and Chris and I as the residents and end users of the project. We found it impossible not to be aware of the filming taking place and were conscious of our deliberations, and on occasions of our indecision.

As the opening date loomed, it became apparent that huge pressure would need to be applied in order to be ready. There was now no going back. An exclusive use filling all six rooms had been booked for arrival on 12th September, and an official opening had been scheduled for the 10th. The glitterati of the Lakes, photographers and press, The Lakes film crew, the bankers, tourist board officials, travel agents, and key Gilpin guests had been sent invitations to an elaborate champagne lunch. Then, just as we began to get rid of the contractors and started to tidy the grounds, lay lawns and plant trees, bushes and flowers, the weather set in as it can only do in the Lake District. Every inch of the Lake House needed to be spring cleaned and a significant problem arose in that our house was clearly not going to be ready to live in. While a certain degree of "making do" can be tolerated, not having a staircase is a bridge too far.

Thus August and early September 2010 must go down as some of the worst weeks ever. Unpleasant, fractious, anxious, filthy, uncomfortable and stressful.

The launch party took place. The first guests arrived. And Chris and I lived in our caravan on a local site away from both businesses until our house was habitable several weeks later. I say "habitable"... yes, we had a staircase. One toilet and one shower worked. There were no carpets nor curtains. We obtained a little privacy in our bedroom by buying some coat rails and hanging our clothes on them in front of the window – there being as yet no wardrobe. We had a kitchen and a television. The garden was a builders' yard. It wasn't much fun but we knew we were on the way. And once firmly through the front door we had that marvellous thing: privacy. But not for long. Jane telephoned to say that she had been referred by her GP to the oncology department of Doncaster Royal Infirmary. She didn't know what oncology was but thought that it might have something to do with cancer. She was frightened. Could Chris and I come with her to the hospital? We of course knew exactly what the oncology department was. Her appointment was for a few days hence. We travelled to Doncaster having booked a room at the very pleasant Premier Inn in the town centre.

Jane's appointment was early and she was subjected to a chain of tests, X-rays and examinations. We flew from department to department in this hospital the size of a village. And then we were ushered in to see the consultant. I was surprised at being allowed in. But they knew what was about to happen and presumably felt that the more help there was to hand the better. There was no beating about the bush. She had lung cancer. Chris was of course her usual brick-self and supported Jane at a time of great shock. The whole procedure had been conducted with the utmost efficiency and kindness.

It was explained exactly what would happen thereafter and she would be sent the date for surgery in Sheffield. It was explained that this would be a long and serious operation – not without dangers. Convalescence would also be prolonged. And so began weeks of journeying between Knipe, Doncaster and Sheffield for various treatments and preparations. Chris and Jane decided that it would be best if she came to live with us, at least until she was quite better. With the house in such an unfinished condition this was not easy for any of us. But the decision was undoubtedly right.

The operation was to take place just before Christmas. Chris and I were in those days very involved with Christmas at Gilpin and it was to be the first Christmas at the Lake House. So there was much to-ing and fro-ing between the Lakes and Sheffield for a few weeks after Jane's surgery. This was made no easier by deep snow for a couple of weeks which made the roads treacherous. We stayed many nights at the Premier Inn just around the corner from the hospital and it became quite a home from home. On Christmas night I think we had the place to ourselves. We were worried about being away from the Lake House but family must on occasions come first. The procedure had gone textbook perfectly and Jane was making a good recovery. She stayed with us for several weeks after her discharge. I was in charge of pills. There were thirty-four a day. Quite a responsibility. She never smoked another cigarette. And has never looked back.

It's true to say that while the Lake House is now a great success, the achievement of this state of affairs took much longer to achieve than we had expected. It was an unusual business model and the relationship between Gilpin, the Lake House management, and Chris and me led to a muddled chain of command.

As an aside to this, the lawyers and accountants had an expensive field day on the subject of what should be the legal entity of the Lake House.

The one issue on which Chris and I were very clear, was that it should be separate to Gilpin, which had considerable loans. Options appeared to be a Partnership, a Limited Liability Partnership or a Limited Company. Each had advantages, disadvantages and tax ramifications. Opinions varied among our professional advisers and we had a major falling out with our solicitors at the time when we discovered from an independent source that their advice was more about making money for themselves than offering us the best counsel. I found this very disturbing and it shook my confidence. In the end, we decided that a separate limited company was the way to go and thus Gilpin Lake House Ltd was born – but it took some time and some money.

For some reason, or more likely reasons, the recession did not seem to really affect our business until 2011. Our new bankers at the Lake House rightly wanted to see targets met and our "old" bankers at Gilpin had become critical and unhelpful. We were obliged to draw in our horns to a painful degree just when we could actually have done with some support while ramping up the Lake House. I volunteered to take over the accounting function towards the middle of the year and Chris took over direct responsibility for housekeeping both at Gilpin and the Lake House. As far as the accounting was concerned, this was a terrible, if well-intentioned mistake as I had neither the training, expertise nor time to undertake this specialist task, apart from which it caused me to take my eye off several other balls.

Fortunately, we realised the error of our ways fairly quickly and appointed a professional to take over this critical function. This situation was living proof of how very careful you have to be when making decisions under pressure. I should have realised that accounting procedures had moved on massively since Suzi and I shared the accounting workload many years before. In particular, she had processed the invoices. I was now proposing to process them myself and was astounded at the volume. It was in itself a full-time job without doing anything else, never mind all my other work, including trying to make the Lake House function. And our bankers at Gilpin were becoming seriously threatening. The Interest Rate Hedging Product which our bankers had insisted we bought when we joined them had gone the wrong way for us, as instead of interest rates rising, which we had been told was inevitable when the agreement was signed – in which event the bank would have had to pay us – interest rates had fallen, resulting in us having to pay the bank at the expense of our profitability and cash flow.

I was not to know it then, but the IRHP scandal was yet to break. But just as the results of this ill-conceived scheme made our position worse, so the bank put increasing pressure on us to reduce debt. And all this with me trying to provide competent and convincing management information.

Thus we were delighted to receive word from Handelsbanken in 2012 that they were prepared to take over Gilpin. Their approach was a breath of fresh air and enabled us to start to run a hotel again as it should be run. The paperwork involved in moving to Handelsbanken just about wiped out 2012 as a year for doing anything else, and the costs involved were considerable. But it was worth it.

One of the first decisions to be implemented was to build a spa at the Lake House. Up till then we had called in therapists "to order", and treatments had been undertaken in guests' bedrooms. We did not consider this satisfactory, and many guests voiced the same opinion. Neither Chris nor I have ever "got" spas or treatments, but we had the wisdom to realise that this was and is irrelevant. Clearly there is a strong demand for this facility, and if you are going to do it, you have to do it properly.

As far as I am concerned, and I think this goes for Chris too, a realisation that you are not an expert in every subject is an important element of success. Barney by now was very much managing the businesses and showing a quite extraordinary talent for marketing. This came partly from a highly tuned understanding of technology, which he shared with Zoë, and what it can do for an hotel, but also from an impassioned imagination. The latter can be bonkers so the trick is to segregate the brilliant from the deranged. One also has to be very careful not to allow a "people" business to be overtaken by computers. So many hotels, particularly chains, have allowed this to happen.

To tell a tale against myself, when emails became an everyday commodity, I expressed the view that I did not believe they would last. How wrong I was! And what a great invention. Unfortunately, we have now become so dependent on them that when they don't function, life almost stops. Chris is not a techie person, but she has become a most prolific emailer and user of the web, the latter helping enormously in the design process which she still heads and loves. But what have emails, mobile phones and other gadgets done to our short lives? Made them even shorter than they would otherwise have been, I suspect.

I can of course remember the days when everyone with any sort of management job had a secretary. She took shorthand (unless you were lucky enough to have one who could compose a letter – I never was), typed, addressed the envelopes, answered the telephone, made phone calls, dealt with memos, booked flights, trains and hotels, lied about your whereabouts as necessary, served tea and coffee, arranged appointments, fielded unwelcome visitors and spied on your colleagues.

A letter or memo once sent could be forgotten for at least four days before a reply could be expected. The need for a paper trail existed as much as it does now, so phone calls were not the answer to every circumstance. Evenings, early mornings, weekends and holidays certainly did not involve written correspondence. Now there is no peace for anyone at any time and there is no excuse for ignorance. You cannot blame the postman. Early risers boast of their achievements. Replies from a holidaymaker generate praise – so everyone has to do the same.

On the subject of not being an expert at everything, when I first saw Ben's proposal for the spa, I thought that he had "lost it". It was a cedar cube which I perceived as being far too modern for its sensitive location in the woods overlooking Knipe Tarn.

Ben was obviously very proud of the concept and maintained that as the cedar tempered, the building would "disappear". Chris and Barney liked it so I kept quiet.

As it turned out, they were all absolutely right. The building has "disappeared" and the view from the treatment rooms overlooking the southern end of the tarn is probably as fine as it is possible to be. The inside has been beautifully decorated and is restful and conducive as an area where peace and tranquillity are key ingredients. We decorated the entrance lobby to the spa with old Knipe Tarn family photos and these generate great interest and fond memories for me personally.

I learned from this chain of events that Ben has, in addition to the obviously necessary technical skills of an architect, something approaching reverence for the Lake District.

The year, 2012, was also a year when Gilpin won several important awards, and for various reasons it fell to Chris and me to attend the AA awards dinner and the Cateys, in both of which Gilpin was awarded "Hotel of the Year".

These were moments of great pride and very helpful in filling the hotel. We found it difficult to believe that our little Gilpin Lodge had moved into these circles.

Chapter Twenty-Seven

ANOTHER WEDDING

T he question of the management of the hotel, now that we had twenty-six rooms, was frequently visited both in theory and in practice. Although we had more managers and supervisors, there was a lot more managing and supervising to be done.

Regulation from Brussels and Whitehall had changed gear in terms of employment law, risk assessments, accountancy, company law and in a host of other areas. As a Relais & Châteaux hotel, guest expectations had increased and willingness to voice dissatisfaction should cause be found. The "blame" culture was in the making and readiness to threaten litigation in the event of loss, injury or just failure to deliver expectations, often irrespective of whether these were reasonable or not. In general, the definition of truth and honesty had changed.

One area in which I particularly liked to become involved, both because of its importance and because I felt that I had something to contribute, was in the employment of senior people. Behind the difficulty in success in this sphere lay employers' reluctance to give candid references in case of litigation, and behind this in turn lay both the increase in "no-win, no-fee" lawyers, and insurance companies' inclination to impose drastically increased premiums in the event of claims. Common sense had flown out of the window and we not infrequently discovered (normally after the mistake had been made) that CVs were far from accurate, or at least not wholly true. Spurious statements are often made at interviews. In my opinion, while I am completely in favour of sensible rights for employees (and we have always tried to uphold – even promote – such a culture at Gilpin), an employer's inability to run the business as it should be run in the face of the danger of falling foul of laws giving too much benefit of the doubt to employees, is a poor state of affairs.

At one time we had no less than three claims ongoing simultaneously. One involved a member of staff who had cut her hand while emptying a bathroom waste bin. All she had to do was tie the bag and remove it – what she had been trained to do. But no! This lady had to manually empty the contents of the bin bag. She claimed mental disturbance in case she contracted HIV. Another claim was brought by a drunken guest, who although advised not to use the hot tub after dinner, did so in snowy conditions and fell and broke a toe. Another guest damaged his Porsche on the gate stop while entering the Lake House at unreasonable speed. The question of legalities has now become so serious that we have to take invasive steps to cover ourselves.

These issues, their consequences and the paperwork all fell onto Barney, who was the only person competent to deal with them. He would have been much better employed filling the hotel or boosting staff morale.

Passing time with guests remained an important activity for all of us. In the old days, being with the guests was a necessity because we were the staff and in the restaurant. We took the orders, poured the drinks, served the dishes and cleared the plates. I miss this, although the absence of need to do it and the resultant pressure is a plus. But I'm not very good at just talking. Unlike Chris and Zoë!

I need something to do. This causes me to call to mind a very simple restaurant which Chris and I used to visit from time to time when we lived in New York – in the later stages of our life there when we could afford to go out occasionally. I could never understand why the owner – a charming and vast New Yorker – chose to undertake the relatively menial task of manning the salad trolley which was a feature of the establishment. It contained bowls of many sorts of salad leaves, several varieties of tomato, cucumber, avocado, herbs, nuts, pineapple, coconut, gherkins, radishes, olives, sliced apples, grated cheese and about a dozen dressings. You pointed at what you wanted and Mister Owner scooped them into an enormous wooden bowl, added your selected dressing, tossed the concoction with great theatrical style and then transferred the contents into a smaller bowl before passing it to you. All this took time and was of course a brilliant opportunity for him to make small talk with his customers and to prove to them that his restaurant really was the place to be. Francis Coulson at Sharrow Bay often spent an evening just serving the bread, offering second and even third portions, proffering more butter or extra virgin olive oil. I think they had the same problem as I do. Thus I frequently now clear a stack of plates – to the waiting staffs' amazement.

In the years around the time of opening the Lake House, on several occasions we employed senior people to share the burden of management responsibilities and none of these were successful for various reasons including, undoubtedly, our unwillingness as a family to "let go". This is to an extent understandable. Gilpin was Chris and my "baby", and Barney and Zoë were charged with helping to bring the baby up and see it into adulthood. Why should anyone else change the plotted course? I can also understand the frustration of other people trying to act in loco parentis and finding obstacles at the proposal of any change. So we have not to date solved this difficult dilemma, other than by employing more managers at departmental level. A couple of attempts at "sort of" general managers have not succeeded.

Ben's architecture practice had the wind in its sails. I got the feeling, with no first-hand experience, that his youthful approach to design and contract management was a breath of fresh air – which of course filled the sails. He zoomed in and out of Gilpin, checking on this or that, with never a minute to spare.

I felt that the jeans and open-neck shirt approach was too informal for a professional man. But it had become clear that I was old fashioned. Other less complimentary terms have been used (not just by Ben) to describe my approach to workplace dress. I try to move with the times, but somehow the times seem to move faster than I do. There did not seem to be a current girlfriend. Unusual!

Until Rachel was introduced – a very different prototype to previous models. Just a little younger than Ben (as opposed to the more usual totty); striking; sophisticated; charming; serious; travelled and experienced. Possibly a little determined – but is that such a bad thing? Particularly when Ben is involved. This was someone significant. Her parents were local. We had barely learned to spell her name before they became engaged. Truly significant!

The wedding was set for 7th June 2014. The bride-to-be was clearly in charge. This time the wedding *was* going to be at Knipe Tarn. As with Barney and Zoë's wedding, the numbers game had to be played with the guest list, and many names from both families got the chop. The occasion of the official tasting of the menu and wines was supremely embarrassing. Kevin and Judy, Rachel's charming parents, had donned best bibs and tuckers to join Ben and Rachel, and Christine and me, for a critique of the proposed nuptials.

We assembled in the Drawing Room at Gilpin and it felt appropriate to sample the champagne which was to accompany the reception drinks. Rachel and I had already had our first "words" over the question of speeches. She had declared that there were not to be any. This was profanation to me and I had said that there would be. Chris, smelling trouble, had opined that there might be. Ben felt that there should be, but that they should be at the reception and not after the wedding breakfast as is expected and traditional. Barney, who was to be best man, agreed with Ben. Agreement had yet to be reached by the time of the tasting.

There appeared to be no sign of Gilpin's Food and Beverage Manager, who was in charge. We drank more champagne, but far from getting merry I personally was getting embarrassed and irritable.

By mid-afternoon, lunch was served. Our man had completely forgotten about the tasting until we arrived. All credit to the chefs for a highly accelerated preparation.

At the very beginning of 2014 we closed the hotel for two weeks to completely revamp the ground floor. All the restaurant rooms needed refurbishment and several other considerations were taken into account. It was felt that the little Morning Room was too small with only four tables, and Barney was forcefully of the view that guests did not like it. Well he was the man who ran the hotel day to day and if that's what the guests were saying then so be it. But above all, Reception was a nightmare and guests checking in or out (or just seeking advice or booking a table) had to queue in the hallway as if waiting for a bus.

Endless meetings were held to work out the best configuration. Eventually it was decided that the Morning Room should become a part of the front hall and the main restaurant should be widened in order to make up for lost tables. Ben knocked on walls to ascertain their status. He loved doing this. If it was a wall which was due to come down and he suspected that it was not supporting anything, a hammer or even an axe came into play – to sort of prove the point that this wall was redundant.

Barney laid out plans for who should work where using which computers, and Chris, together with her designer friend Sarah Jane, worried over fabrics, curtains, carpets, lamps, pictures and furniture. The kitchen was also to be extended and refitted. A panic arose over whether the virtually all-electric kitchen would have enough wattage or amperage or whatever it is that electricity is measured by. Ben pulled in a favour from some grandee in North West Electricity and somehow it got sorted.

The project was complicated. All of the office work had had to be transferred to the Garden Suites while the work took place, so that the normal functions of reservations, accountancy, human resources and management could carry on. It was at times impossible to envisage how the hotel could ever open again, never mind in a few days' time. Tensions were at maximum. Some of the contractors worked round the clock, including our stalwart decorator Dave Lowis, and the carpet layers Simon Burns and his team. As usual we made it, with the doors opening five minutes before check-in time. The results were stunning and such an improvement in guest efficiency and satisfaction.

No sooner had this job finished but the biomass project began. Our utility bills had gone through the roof and many months of consulting came to fruition with the decision that a biomass plant was the only option. This was another highly complex and expensive undertaking, but it was felt that government grants for such regeneration schemes would not last forever and that we should proceed while the going was good. Our new bankers declared it a no-brainer. Fortunately this work did not interfere with the running of the hotel. It has subsequently been determined that the whole methodology of calculating biomass advantages is suspect. We will have to wait and see.

The wedding day dawned and the sky was ominously grey. As we parked our cars outside the small church in Underbarrow and ran to the porch, a Lakeland special set in and we all got pretty wet. Rachel looked lovely. Judy shone. Chris was radiant. All the boys had scrubbed up well. Family from far and wide had assembled. The vicar beamed.

Prayers must have been received because as we got back to Knipe for the reception the sun came out, the rain stopped and a June day became what a June day should be. Everyone was wondering what had happened to the bride and groom. Why was it taking so long to come a mere five miles or so? And then we heard it. The thrub-thrub-thrub of a helicopter. They roared over the trees and hovered for photographs right over the tarn. The blades churned up the water and those on the edge of the lawn got another drenching but it was a wonderful surprise and a great talking point. The speeches took place in the lounge and conservatory as the weather was threatening again. Barney proposed the toast to the bride and groom, and took the opportunity to take the piss mercilessly out of his brother. Ben replied and did the same to Barney.

The marquee was perched on the very edge of the lawn with a see-through window looking over the tarn. A beautiful setting for a beautiful occasion. Gilpin again performed with precision and professionalism. The dancing went on till the wee small hours. There was no horrible rush to clear up the next day as the Lake House was not let till the day after.

Chapter Twenty-Eight

CHEFS ON TRIAL

We were still not settled with a permanent head chef. Barney, Chris and I felt that with many of our competitors in the area having a Michelin star, we must find a person who could step up to this mark. We discussed the plan with the bank and they felt that we were right. We conferred about the likely cost of this move, not just for the chief man or woman but of running a kitchen of that calibre. Several agencies were contacted.

Chris and I were by now working from home. Precious office space could not be wasted on us. That's not to say that we weren't (and still are) frequently at Gilpin. But our base was Knipe. Barney phoned one afternoon to enquire if we were in. Could he come for a chat? Of course. This was quite a frequent occurrence and he used the same tone if it was good or bad news. So we never knew which until he arrived.

'I've had a phone call,' he began, after we had all sat down, 'from one of the agencies we are using to find a head chef. They have been approached by a company who has been commissioned by BBC2 to make a film about recruiting a Michelin star chef.

'The agency wants to know if they might put Gilpin's name forward as a hotel going through this very process. There are no guarantees that we would be selected, but if we were it would be amazing publicity for Gilpin. The filming would take place in December and we would have to close for a week.

'That's about all I know at the moment and I think it's all the agency knows. The only way to find out more is really to agree to Gilpin's name being submitted and then to meet the film company. What do you think?'

It was obvious that Barney felt it was a fantastic idea and it had potential appeal as well as possible drawbacks. We saw no harm in finding out more.

A meeting was soon arranged and Chris and I thought it was best to leave the discussions to Barney and Zoë. They were Gilpin's PR and marketing gurus. When they had been appraised of the full picture, we all sat down to talk it through. Barney and Zoë passionately wanted to do it. Chris and I, brought up to be suspicious of anything to do with the media, thought it highly risky.

We also felt that the motivation of the filmmakers and of the BBC was very different to ours. Theirs was to produce a film. Ours was to recruit a Michelin star chef, or just a thoroughly competent one with whom we could get on and who would enhance our business. Were the two compatible? Of course, none of us knew for certain. We had to make a decision. The people from Two Four, the filmmakers, had been very charming and wanted to use Gilpin. But they needed an answer.

The big drivers of the "yes" campaign were three. First, the film would be screened in April of the next year for five consecutive nights at prime time – an exposure opportunity that would be unlikely to be repeated and which might put Gilpin on the map like nothing else imaginable. Secondly, the presenter was to be Alex Polizzi. Chris and I knew Alex vaguely from Forte days. She was Charles Forte's granddaughter. We liked her. Thirdly, we would be the sole arbiters of who was to be appointed as our head chef, although the company would decide on the candidates to take part in "Chefs on Trial". This latter point was the biggest drawback. How could a filmmaking company decide on candidates for a chef's job? Unless they were using a specialist agency to select them.

We agreed to do it, subject to Barney going back to Two Four and clarifying the selection process. If necessary, we agreed, he must insist on this point. It was no good us being the ones to select a head chef from a bunch of unsuitable candidates. We must not lose sight of our main objective.

Chris and I had to cancel a golf holiday scheduled for the same time as the filming. We had made a decision at the beginning of the year (which we suspected was stupid at the time) that we were going to stop mucking around at golf, reduce our handicaps from the maximum and defeat this annoying game! We took some lessons from Simon Edwards, the lovely professional at Windermere, and enrolled in a serious golf holiday in Turkey. We felt bad cancelling, particularly as Patricia Nicholson had booked to come with us. But we had aborted so many holidays for Gilpin, what was another? It was too late to get our money back. I did claim the cost as a business expense.

The filming was now the big event on the radar, as well as the consequential appointment of our chef. The summer flew by and before we knew what had happened, the filming was upon us. Some thirty people from Two Four arrived on a bright sunny Sunday in December and took over the ground floor of Gilpin. For some reason they did not stay at Gilpin but at the Wild Boar Hotel down the road.

Furniture was rearranged. Sofas and coffee tables normally positioned with symmetry were now at odd angles. Coloured foil was placed over windows to change the colour of the light. Cables snaked out of every socket. Enormous lights were erected on gantries. The crew were charming and considerate. We were drilled in what to do and what not to do.

Arguments arose over one or two issues about which we felt strongly. We were not prepared to portray ourselves or Gilpin in a light which was not Gilpin. They wanted to restrict the number of family members present at the interviews with the chefs to just two of us. We made the point that this would not happen at Gilpin with such an important appointment. We thought the viewing public would see that.

We compromised by agreeing that just Barney and Chris would sample and comment upon the dishes prepared and cooked by the chefs. Too many Cunliffes in the tasting room would detract from the main events: the chefs and the food. This was to take place in the Garden Room. But all of us would participate in the seated interviews. These people of course knew their business and they were here to make a film. Having four interviewers as well as the candidate in the drawing room apparently posed camera angle problems.

Alex Polizzi arrived the evening before the first day of filming. She knew the Two Four people and an interesting dimension was immediately apparent. Who was really in charge? Watch this space, I thought. Alex greeted the Gilpin contingent like an old friend and put us all at ease. Preparations carried on well into the evening and gin and tonics were graciously accepted by all concerned.

We were given details of the candidates for the first day. We were almost certainly more experienced at selecting chefs than whoever had chosen these candidates, and while some were interesting, others were nowhere near what we were looking for.

It's difficult to know when Barney is nervous. He's very good at hiding it. I think he must have been, although we had the comfort of knowing that this was not live television and if any of us screwed up badly the sequence could be taken again. I can tell when Chris is nervous. And she was – big time. But she did a brilliant job of hiding it from the crew and Alex. She fretted over what to wear till I thought I would go mental. What jewellery? What colour nail polish? Above all what shoes? Shoes! The leather trousers were imperative. But what if some sauce splashed them? Oh dear!

And so the big day dawned. Chris and Barney were really the stars (from the Gilpin team), as they had to judge the food, which took all morning. The cameramen spent a lot of time in the kitchen filming the chefs cooking. Alex, Chris and Barney grilled the chefs, if you'll excuse the pun, while they were trying to work. I thought this was a bit unfair. Multitasking isn't every man's thing. On the other hand, perhaps it was a part of the plan. A senior chef has to have two heads and three hands.

I was disappointed that there were no women among the candidates. There are not, in this country, many Michelin star lady chefs. I would have loved to see a strong woman annihilate laddish behaviour from the Gilpin kitchen. Although the ethos in our kitchen was pretty good, as kitchens go, there still existed (and that has not changed) in our industry a perception that bad behaviour and foul language is not only acceptable but almost compulsory. These ingredients invariably lead to bullying – psychologically if not physically.

It was all too exciting to do other than be around. Sitting at a desk and getting on with routine work was out of the question. As the allocated time for cooking neared its end, Alex called out the number of minutes left. The pressure was tangible. And then 'time up. Stop.'

One by one the chefs were summoned to the Garden Room. Chris, Barney and Alex were behind the table facing the entrance to the room. The chefs trooped in and placed their offerings on the table. The three judges examined the presentation before messing it up by putting their forks in. The commentary was polite but frank. Many questions were asked. I was glad for Chris that we had not had time for breakfast that morning.

We didn't want to rigidly plan the interviews for the afternoon, but we wanted some form of plan so that we didn't interrupt each other. This we formulated over a snatched sandwich lunch. Needless to say, Barney, Chris and Alex did not want a sandwich. The interviewees, as they joined us, were all nervous – which was not surprising. I think those who stood a chance knew it, and those that didn't also knew.

I personally enjoyed the process, and rather to my surprise did not find it difficult to behave as if it were a normal interview. The cooking skills had already been assessed. I wanted to get into the personalities; the temperament; the leadership qualities; the commercial astuteness; the honesty; the loyalty and potential to stay at Gilpin for many years, not just until a better offer came along. We knew that as soon as a chef gets a Michelin star, the phone calls and text messages offering another position at an even bigger salary never stop. I tried to be totally objective and to ignore the cameras. This was made easier because the directors and crew were so natural and helpful.

At the end of the first day, we had to choose the candidate to go through to the finals. This was not difficult. Then we all gathered in the kitchen and Barney had to announce the winner for the day. He did it superbly, with a suitably agonising pause between 'the winner is...' and '...Simon Szymanski'. Then preparations started for day two and we were again working till late in the evening.

Day two followed the same pattern. The only difference was that one

candidate was our clear favourite. His food was excellent and he interviewed confidently and amicably. He went through to the finals. Day
three brought a surprise in that one candidate who on paper was far too
young for the job, turned out to be a quite exceptional cook and also interviewed well.

After the finals on the last day, we had to select the winner. The director
from Two Four gave a little address and told us that this was a bit like the
finals of "Strictly". There would be massive anticipation on the part of the
viewing public. The dishes to be prepared that day were to be more technical than on the previous days. The questions by the judges would be more
searching. The afternoon interviews would be razor sharp. You could feel
grown men bending in the wind of interrogation.

And then decision time. Alex absented herself and the family were
locked in the Drawing Room. No cameras. Did we have the wherewithal
to send white smoke up the chimney? Oh! It was a gas fire!

To my surprise there was genuine backing for the youngster. His food
that day had been quite exceptional. But I knew that our brigade would eat
him for breakfast and that he would not stay with us for long. He had all
the fire in his belly of youth. But it was backed up by an unrealistic degree
of self confidence. Should we offer him the position of Sous Chef? Would
he accept that? This was a possibility. But that decision could clearly not
be made until the Head Chef had been appointed. And, it had to be borne
in mind, would our chosen man accept the position? Would he (as often
happens) go back to his present employers, say he was leaving and they
offer him another wad of salary? Would the salary we had in mind be acceptable? The outcome was not yet a fait accompli.

Then back to the kitchen. The tension really was electrifying.

Three men stood in a row, hands behind their backs. Their toques tall,
starched and proud. Barney and Alex looking on. A camera on the right,
one on the left and one in front of them. Like the Charge of the Light Brigade – but cameras not cannons. There's not to reason why!

Behind them the kitchen windows, the early December night drawing
in. The glare of the bright lights in the ceiling illuminating the sweat on
the candidates' brows. Zoë, Ben and I standing in the background out of
the cameras' eyes.

Total silence apart from the dull ticking of the clock on the wall. And of heartbeats.

'And the winner is...' Barney had been instructed to pause there for thirty seconds. It seemed like half an hour. '...Hrishikesh Desai.'

Hrishikesh punched the air. The other two shook his hand with disappointed gentlemanliness. Alex gave him a kiss (well she would, wouldn't she?). Barney shook his hand. Chris gave him a kiss. Zoë, Ben and I came out of the shadows and congratulated him.

While the Two Four team started to pack up their gear, Barney sat down with Hrishikesh to do the business.

Our acting Head Chef walked out that evening. This rather marred the day's events and left us with a problem as Hrishikesh, a very honourable man, could not leave Lucknam Park Hotel to join us until April.

Chapter Twenty-Nine

THE SPA LODGES
AND GILPIN SPICE

Eighteen months or so before this, we had started discussions among ourselves, and then with the bank, about further developments at Gilpin. The question of enlarging the hotel again was in a sense somewhat déjà vu. But so what? An enshrined doctrine of business is that you cannot stand still. There is a part of me that rejects this mantra. Can you go on growing forever? Obviously not. But let's not go there today. Clearly we had not reached that point yet. But our deliberations led us unanimously to the conclusion that a country house hotel, if it was to retain its personality, could not have more than forty rooms.

But Gilpin was not, we argued, just any old country house hotel. It was Gilpin. A rather special one, which focused on knowing and loving our guests and their desires and dislikes. We left the perceived maximum as forty rooms but in our hearts knew it was probably less. But we were only at twenty-six including the Lake House, so we had some way to go. We decided that another six rooms at this juncture was right, and probably the maximum for which we could borrow.

Ben's relationship with the planning board was professional if nothing else, and he always urged caution in our demands of them. His architectural practice was well versed in planning law and procedures and we respected his advice, while being aware, at the back of our minds, of his conservative approach to this subject. Then there was the consideration of where on the estate the rooms should be, in order for them to be superb, with the best possible views, yet not spoiling the outlook of any of the existing rooms.

Barney is a matchless hotel marketing professional and an expert in the collection and use of appropriate data. How do I know this when I am neither of those things? Results, trust and acumen. When we started to discuss in detail what the new rooms should be, he had not only done his homework, but had prepared a researched and reasoned paper on who the market would be for the new rooms and therefore what these rooms should be.

Ben was entrusted with drawing up suggested plans. The proposed location for the individual units, to the east of the property, but with the key aspect facing south-west, would necessitate completely moving the car park and introducing a tranche of new logistics, including the employment of concierges for valet parking. Furthermore, another six rooms would involve another twelve guests for breakfast and dinner, thus putting further strain on our existing restaurant capacity, particularly since we had lost two tables when we scrapped the Morning Room in the ground floor revamp of 2014. We were all agreed that we could not risk losing our vitally important and beloved local dining market.

Hrishikesh came to visit and to look at housing possibilities. He brought his wife Aga and little girl Eleanor. We were delighted to meet them. We asked him to take an hour out of his busy day to join our conversation about a second eatery at Gilpin.

We had by now narrowed down the options to either Aquaponics or an Asian restaurant. Both were Barney's ideas. We had spent some money on research and designs for the aquaponic option, which Chris and I hated. The generation gap was really showing its face. We felt that it was complicated, risky, labour-intensive, untried and tested, and likely to be unpopular due to ignorance of what it was. Not everyone is a forty-something-year-old trendy smart arse, we argued. Not everyone is an old fart, Barney argued back.

On the other hand, we all felt that a top quality pan-Asian restaurant would tick most of the boxes for most age groups, nationalities, and persuasions. And we had a new chef of Indian origin – although his training had been classical to a tee – backed up by a Roux Scholarship and years of experience in some of the finest restaurants in France and England. Ben, struggling with the workload of his other clients at Ben Cunliffe Architects, was further imposed upon to survey the crumbling outhouses and adapt them into a proposed restaurant downstairs and a bar upstairs.

Countless hours were spent in meetings about the proposed Spa Suites and new restaurant. Forests of trees were felled to facilitate minutes of the meetings. Designs and layouts were drafted, redrafted, amended and argued over. Plantations of coffee were drunk. Dinners gave way to sandwiches. Coffee gave way to wine. Bad temper gave way to amelioration.

It was concluded that there was only space for five, not six Spa Suites. This skewed the business plan but gave an infinitely preferable result. The bank approved the plans. The planners gave permission. Ben sighed with resignation – 2015 was set to become a busy year.

That turned out to be somewhat of an understatement. Ben and Rachel had moved to a house in Underbarrow. They had bought a dilapidated old bungalow in a quiet road just outside the village but within walking distance of the pub – a necessity for Ben. Ben had added a first floor to the house, thus giving them four bedrooms and a large ground floor, including an office for Ben and a playroom for Alice, who had arrived on the scene – a delightful little girl who looked so like both her parents. Xiá thought Alice was the bee's knees and looking after her was better than any doll.

Barney and Zoë had in turn decided that Bumblebee Cottage was too lonely for Xiá. Either she would be deprived of friends or they would have to become taxi parents, which would not suit at all. They had bought a rundown house in Windermere which needed gutting, so had moved into Ben and Rachel's vacated house in Kendal. Altogether a convenient arrangement. Xiá had left the lovely little school in Crosthwaite and was attending a bigger school in Windermere within walking distance of what would become her home.

Chris and I stayed where we were. We loved Knipe and it felt like home in every sense. We were able to keep an eye on the Lake House. The only disadvantage was lack of privacy. Arriving guests frequently walked through our front door and asked if this was where they checked in. Some Japanese guests wandered around our garden taking photographs and then walked into the house and asked if they could have a cup of tea. We were reluctant to put up loads of signs saying "private". It seemed so obvious to us that it was private.

We can live with these small inconveniences. We are very privileged to have such a beautiful place and every brick reminds me of my childhood and of my parents and Elizabeth. Our house overlooks the lawn where Ben and Rachel had their wedding and we are reminded of that auspicious day. We have a bird table on the edge of the lawn and several pheasants have become friends. They are less trouble than a dog but don't fetch balls! Our living room has a large table which is very convenient for meetings. Chris gets mad at me because I work there and she hates me leaving papers out. I sympathise and must do better. The trouble is that it's such a delightful place to work and it seems silly to put everything away just to get it out again a few hours later or the next morning.

A part of my paperwork is this book. Chris and I still see a lot of guests, both at Gilpin and the Lake House. So many are fascinated by hotels and what goes on in them. Many have said to me that I should write a book. I didn't need telling. I have been aware for many years that Gilpin was and is an epic. So I decided, as if there wasn't enough to do, to write a book. Chris has given me enormous encouragement, if that's what you call a whip! Never having written a book before, it was a new discipline and I realised even before I started that there had to be a plan – a framework. I wish I had an office where I could stick sheets of paper all around the walls – one piece for each chapter. Ideas keep striking me and I would love to note them in a visible place and see where they fall in the overall formula. But Chris would certainly not stand for that. So a large A4 notebook has to do. I do a lot of writing on holidays. Thank goodness for my iPad. I believe some authors still write by hand. I cannot conceive of anything worse.

One day Barney had been to see a guest in the Lake House and popped in – as he does. Often at six o'clock, which is wine time if everything has been going according to plan. 'Oh good. You're both in,' he said. 'There's something I want to talk to you about.' As usual, no indication of whether the something was good or bad.

He looked a bit sheepish. 'I couldn't sleep last night and I developed this thought about incentivising our managers.' This was a subject we had touched on from time to time. By now we had well over a hundred staff, of whom a dozen or so were managers at various levels of seniority. I personally have always been a little sceptical about this rather grandiose structure, but Barney has to run Gilpin and therefore unless I have hurricane strength feelings about something, I rarely demand to have my way. I can see that a defined organisation enables managers to be aware of their responsibilities. The downside is that it is a deterrent to the flexibility which a smallish hotel needs.

'I have called it the "Village Hall",' he went on. I saw Chris put her eyes towards the ceiling. '"Another Dutch Barge" was a part of our vocabulary.

'The key word is Hall. H stands for hotelkeeping or hospitality or both; A stands for Accounts, meaning in fact profitability; the first L stands for Leadership and the second L stands for Learning, being a synonym for Training. What do you think?'

'So far so good,' I said, 'but where does the Village come in?'

'Well it's another word for team really. We work closely with our managers and staff so we are like a village. A community. I'm the Chieftain; you two are the Elders; the Heads of Department and managers are the Councillors, and everyone else is a villager.'

'I see,' said Chris in a derogatory voice.

'You obviously don't like it Mum,' said Barney.

'No. I didn't say that. I just think it's a bit... silly.'

'That's because you are an Elder. If you were just a villager you might think it was quite cool.'

'Well. I don't really do cool,' said Chris.

'Look,' I said. 'It doesn't really matter whether you call it a village, a community, a parish or a team. The concept is the same. Village Hall has the advantage of the H A L L which is good.'

'Absolutely,' Barney agreed. 'And Village adds a sense of togetherness – sameness of purpose – an aspiration towards wellbeing.'

'Wow,' Chris said.

'And we devise a bonus scheme for HoDs which will be based on the four elements. Hotelkeeping will be judged on complaints and compliments which can be either verbal or written providing that they are documented. TripAdvisor entries will be a part. Hotel guides will come into it and Relais & Châteaux quarterly reports. Percentage of repeat business will be a very important indicator and is easily measured. Accounts will be a relatively simple comparison between actual and budget, taking into account sales, payroll, purchasing and overall profitability. Leadership will be much more subjective with a degree of judgement by me. But staff turnover will be a factor and I am thinking of an element of input from the staff, although I'm not sure how that will work yet. Learning will be based on percentage passes of individual staff induction tests and Gilpin Academy engagement.'

'What's Gilpin Academy?' Chris asked.

'You know quite well what Gilpin Academy is,' Barney retorted. 'You're just trying to be Elder-like. It's our intranet communication tool. All these targets will have to be set so that achievement or failure can be accurately measured. And finally, and I'm very proud of this bit, the whole bonus scheme will be in two parts. One part will be based on an individual HoD's performance and the second part will be based on consensual performance. In other words, in order to pass the second part, everyone will have to accomplish their targets. I can't think of a better way of encouraging teamwork. Well?'

He looked a bit like a dog hoping for a bone.

'I think it's great,' I said. 'Very clever.' I think it will encourage the HoDs and give them a sense of purpose. Your mother does too. She just doesn't want to say it.'

He went off happy, tail wagging, bone gripped in his mouth.

Hrishikesh joined us at about the same time as Chefs on Trial was screened. We were all quite nervous. You never know what media people are going to do. On nights when the programme was on live, all the guests came down to dinner late. We were very pleased with it and statistics about visits to our website rocketed. Chris was frequently accosted by strangers in shops asking if she was the woman in Chefs on Trial. She basked in it.

Then the diggers and dumpers arrived and not for the first time, all hell broke loose. While the noise and disruption was reasonably removed from the existing bedrooms, disturbance was evident. The usual tranquillity was interrupted. As the car park was relocated, parking became a movable feast. Driveways had to be put in to access the new car park. Large delivery lorries came at inconvenient times. The ponds planned for the area in front of the lodges had to be dug, necessitating major excavation. Research had to be done into the most suitable hot tubs and saunas. Additional septic tanks and soakaways had to be installed. This was to go on for the rest of the year.

Round about the middle of the year I started to get emails from an organisation called Bully Banks. How they got hold of my email address I don't know. But they knew that Gilpin had been sold an "Interest Rate Hedging Product" by our bank before we moved to Handelsbanken. The communications were very detailed and there was obviously someone or some people behind Bully Banks who were well informed about the banking industry and in particular IRHPs.

The fallout from this scandal was beginning to become common knowledge due in particular to the involvement of the Financial Conduct Authority. The objective of Bully Banks was to help small and medium-sized businesses who had been cheated, or worse still gone bankrupt, to obtain redress. It was a philanthropic organisation run for the benefit of its members and they wanted Gilpin to become a member, and through its contributions help Bully Banks to carry on with its work.

I was invited, before forking out the reasonable fees proposed, to attend for a very modest sum a conference to be held in Birmingham in a couple of weeks. I felt that it all seemed very sensible and above board. I had a couple of questions that I wanted to ask and I left a message on the telephone number given of the chairman of Ordinary People in Business (the full name of Bully Banks), Jeremy Roe.

I was most impressed to get a call back even though it was a Sunday. He sounded sincere and plausible. His interest in this whole subject, and the foundation of Bully Banks, had been borne out of his own losses and the realisation that individual small businesses would never have the resources to fight the banks. For him it had become a passion – a crusade. His fury burned down the telephone line. I empathised with him. I felt that we had been cheated and lied to and I shared his resentment and anger that it had been allowed to happen.

He asked me a few questions and passed an opinion that Gilpin was typical of the membership of Bully Banks and what it had been established for. He begged me to come to the conference. He told me that there would be addresses by himself, a representative of the FCA and by other members who had been cheated. I agreed to go and he promised to meet me.

I discussed the issue with Barney, who had in fact been more involved than me in our forced participation in an IRHP when we had reached agreement with our erstwhile bankers many years before. The details had been complicated and technical and he had had several conversations with the relevant department of the bank.

I recalled that he had been very upset by a claim (by the bank) that he agreed to a detail which both he and I knew he had not, because it was over a subject which was a solid plank in our stance over the question of penalties in the event of early payment of the loan – in other words if we wanted to move to another bank. This had been what would now be called a red line in our negotiations.

All this had been done on the telephone and the bank claimed to have lost the transcript. We knew that this was so unlikely that it was a lie, and this event generated a lack of trust that never went away. Barney felt that I should go to the conference in Birmingham – in fact he wanted to go too but there was some important school thing on with Xiá. Before I went, I looked up the accounts for the relevant years and established that the IRHP had cost Gilpin about £150,000.

The hotel in Birmingham was packed. There must have been 500 people there. I said hello to Jeremy over coffee and he recalled our telephone conversation. The gist of his opening address, which took over an hour and went into great detail, was that banks had wilfully and systematically misled customers over IRHPs, and when the costs thereof had started to erode the profits of small and medium businesses, the banks had used this consequence as a reason for penalising businesses and for putting customers into special measures. Worst of all, the banks, instead of striving to help customers, had worked against their interests for the benefit of the banks, including (incredibly) manipulation downwards of valuations of customers' properties which they then used to damage those businesses.

As the morning wore on, other speakers put their points of view, including someone from the FCA who tried to defend their involvement, which Jeremy had described in his address as whitewash.

I began to realise the scale of this scandal and the depth of the evil behind it. After a terrible buffet lunch, participants were invited to ask questions or tell their own story. This was genuinely harrowing and tales were told, which must have been true, which made our relatively small loss look like petty cash.

It appeared that businesses with much larger borrowings than Gilpin's had entered into significantly larger IRHP agreements, with the consequent loss of enormous sums and in some instances bankruptcy. I recall an impassioned address by one eloquent speaker who had been chairman and principal shareholder in a business which had lost millions of pounds as a consequence of an IRHP, and he was now destitute and living on the streets. He could not, I recall him saying, afford the fee for the conference but had been invited by Jeremy providing that he told his story.

Before leaving the conference, I joined Bully Banks and paid our subscription. Within a matter of weeks we were put in touch by Bully Banks with a legal firm which specialised in seeking redress for clients of banks who had mistreated them. It was all very straightforward. Barney and I had two conference calls with lawyers, and within a relatively short period of time we received a cheque which covered the amount we had paid out but not the legal fees and other costs, which were considerable. Much better than nothing.

The greed and depravity of this scandal has never left me, nor the harrowing tales I heard that day in Birmingham. With the benefit of hindsight, I think I knew where we might have been heading had it not been for our lucky escape to another bank. These terrible things were being orchestrated and undertaken by fellow human beings in offices not just in London, but as near as Kendal.

*

Alice now had a brother, Freddie. So Chris and I now had three wonderful grandchildren. Better late than never! He was a cheeky chappy and still is. Alice didn't appear to be too delighted.

Ben, Rachel, Chris, Alice, Freddie and I had a wonderful week in a villa near Montpellier. Chris and I took the caravan and met the family at Carcassonne. We had bought a new caravan earlier in the year. The original one had travelled far and was showing its age. I was also finding some of the chores quite hard and had read that newer caravans had more mod cons. We had visited the caravan show at the NEC in Birmingham the previous autumn and been astonished at how things had moved on since 2007 when we bought the first caravan. We spent a whole day there and worked hard.

In the end, it was a decision between a Hobby and a Coachman. We both felt that we would prefer to buy British but what clinched it was that the Hobby salesman admitted that although it was legal to tow a Hobby in the UK, it was not strictly legal to do so if you were a UK resident because the caravan was wider than the maximum permitted. So we had bought the Coachman, which had lots of exciting bells and whistles. This was our first trip in the new caravan and we were excited.

Carcassonne was a small airport and I got the caravan well and truly stuck in the car park. One day we visited an ancient and beautiful abbey and had lunch in a charming little cafe in the grounds. Being a holiday, we are allowed to break the six o' clock rule and we had a bottle of the local wine. It was so good that I bought a load to take home. I filled the boot of the Land Rover. Before we set off to take the family back to Carcassonne, I stashed the wine under the caravan bed. I couldn't understand why the caravan was swaying around so badly until I remembered the wine. After dropping off the kids, it came back into the boot of the car.

On the return journey, Chris wanted to visit a design exhibition in Paris. She had been working hard on designs for the new Spa Lodges. Each one was to be totally different. In the same way that the other rooms at Gilpin had been named after Lake District villages, mountains or lakes, or in the case of the Lake House after members of my grandmother's family, we had decided to name the Spa Lodges after Roman forts in the Lake District. This did not affect the designs.

We found a campsite near Brie, not too far away from Villepinte Nord where Maison et Objet was being held. Les Quatre Vents was a real find. The pitches were enormous and marked out by mature trees and abundant bushes. There was a swimming pool (masochistically cold) and a little shop which sold baguettes and croissants and almost all the other necessities of a simple life. In the evening a little cafe offered pizzas, burgers and made-to-order salads as well as remarkably drinkable plonk. And there was a laundry – happiness personified for Chris.

The exhibition was only twenty minutes away by car. We had bought the tickets online beforehand so were able to avoid enormous queues. Enormous seemed to be the buzzword for everything about this exhibition. Eight halls – some the size of Carcassonne airport. We worked hard all day, not stopping for even a light lunch. Burdened with a suitcase full of brochures we walked the mile or so back to the car park and then home to Les Quatre Vents. For me, to sit in the early autumn sun, legs up and glass of wine in hand beats any hotel lounge or bar. Peasant, I hear you say. Eh bien!

We did this for three days until we felt we had completed the task. The brochures counterbalanced the wine in the caravan, and so home via the Zeebrugge to Hull ferry – to open the Spa Lodges. Barney had, with draconian authority, conscripted not only the whole maintenance department but waiters, housekeepers and even accountants into laying turf, planting bushes and trees (£20,000 worth) and raking paths. The wettest autumn in history made this a particularly undesirable task, and the sight of dripping and frozen humans was like a picture transplanted from Siberia. Joseph Stalin Barnaby Cunliffe was in his element – also dripping and frozen. But you did it or you got the eight grams!

On 23rd December, as the Christmas guests were ploughing into afternoon tea, I was still putting 5 amp plugs onto ones supplied with 13 amp plugs. What a farce this was. Chris was still distributing little flower arrangements and Ben was marking up fuse boxes. Zoë, helped by Xiá, was putting books in the bookshelves and Rachel was unpacking tea pots, helped by Alice. Freddie was asleep.

The guests checked in. Yet another project had been completed with no time to spare. Gilpin had moved from five to thirty-one bedrooms, with a projected turnover for 2016 of nearly £6 million, compared with £84,000 in 1988.

As soon as the traditional construction industry break was over sometime in mid-January, work began on making the outhouses into a restaurant. The pan-Asian theme had been bounced off many of our regular guests, including those staying over Christmas, which had been a particularly jolly time. The Spa Lodges had been well received, despite a few teething problems with technology. The grandchildren had all helped Santa Claus Richard hand out the presents and we had spent a delightful Christmas evening with Ben and Rachel, and Rachel's parents Kevin and Judy, as well as all the grandchildren, while Barney and Zoë looked after Gilpin.

One or two more traditional guests had not approved of the idea of an Asian restaurant, but most thought it was a lovely idea and a splendid contrast to fine dining.

Fortunately for our somewhat shattered nerves, this was a relatively quiet project – much of it internal work in the old coach houses. We had decided, in the interests of cash flow as well as practicability, to only open the ground floor that year, but the upper floor would have to be fabricated as the whole roof had to come off and be rebuilt just less than two metres higher than it was.

Chris was again on the design trail and was excited by the totally new angle of an Asian theme. Hrishikesh was researching and creating dishes and menus with strains of China, India, Japan and Malaysia. Barney was masterminding the whole project, including a trip to Bali and China to research spices and ingredients.

In February, Chris and I celebrated our fiftieth wedding anniversary and had a splendid party at the Lake House. On the night of the dinner for nearly sixty guests, it snowed heavily, and while all the guests had arrived safely, getting them home might have been a different matter. Barney and Ben both made lovely speeches – except for the sarcastic references to the miraculous nature of our marriage having lasted so long.

Then Chris and I left on a cruise to the Antarctic – a present to each other from each other. A spellbinding occasion. We met Gilpin guests on board *Seaborne Quest* and spent some happy evenings with them while looking out on blue icebergs, whales, seals and penguins.

It was a difficult year for the restaurant. The Spa Lodges were an instant success and thus we had to contend with twelve more covers a night while still only having the one restaurant. Tables had to be relaid, which is not easy when a restaurant is in full swing.

In the autumn, Hrishikesh won a coveted Michelin star. This organisation specialises in suspense. Everyone in the trade knows that an invitation to an awards ceremony does not guarantee a star. Or stars. It might be for a lesser award. Or just to say 'we think you have a foot on the ladder'. Hrishikesh didn't know. So there was no point in asking him. But he had been invited to the "do". So – in with a chance.

The team in the kitchen could barely apply themselves to their daily tasks. The atmosphere was electric. Anna, our Sales and Marketing Manager and resident techie, had rigged up all sorts of audio-visual gadgets in the kitchen so that the news could be shared quickly. She had also hidden a camera so as to record the drama as it unfolded.

Only Barney seemed utterly confident. During his time at Gilpin, he had developed a very selective palate as well as having a good knowledge of what went on in other establishments, including local ones with Michelin stars. As the news broke, the personalities of our various staff, particularly the chefs, would have been a treat for a psychologist. Some punched the air. Some wept and some just carried on working.

We were back in the club.

Gilpin Spice opened for business in November. The decor was second to nothing outside London and the food was a triumph. Everybody loved it and residents, as had been hoped, booked both restaurants during their stay, thus keeping them away from the competition and resolving our table shortage in the main restaurant – now called HRiSHi.

Chapter Thirty

A LIFETIME ACHIEVEMENT

Early in 2017, Chris and I decided that we would like to try winter caravanning. The new caravan had proper piped central heating, a vast improvement on the vented system in the old one. We felt sure that if we went to southern Spain it would be nice weather by day and we would be warm as toast at night.

I had a conversation with Barney which went something like this. 'Morning Barney. How are you today?'

'Morning dad. Good thanks.' He was looking grumpy so I decided not to play my usual card of explaining that I was enquiring about his health not his morals. This anomaly has unfortunately now become a part of the English language. 'You OK?' he asked.

'Great thank you. Actually more than great. Excited.'

'Why so?'

'Mum and I have decided to try winter caravanning. We're going to go for the whole of March. Probably Spain.' Then he really looked grumpy.

'You can't.'

'Who says?'

'Well! Aren't you coming skiing with the family?'

'We've decided to give up skiing,' I said. 'A broken leg at our age is no joke.'

'Well you can't go in March.'

'Why not?'

'Because Zoë, Xiá and I are going skiing.'

'So?'

'We can't all be away at once.'

'But if we all went skiing together, we'd all be away at once – as we have been in previous years.'

'Well you can't go in March. Rather, please go in April, or even the last week of March.'

'Why?'

'The weather will be better.'

'But the whole idea was to try winter caravanning.'

'Well it'll still be winter in April.'

'But you just said that the weather would be better in April.'

'Dad, I can't tell you, but I need you to be here in mid-March. Please don't push me. Just please don't go away before the last week in March.'

'OK,' I said, 'if it's so important to you. But I don't understand why and I think it's very odd that you won't tell me.'

'I know you do. Sorry.'

A few weeks later, among our mail were two tickets for the *Cumbria Life* Food & Drink Awards dinner to be held at Kendal College on a date in mid-March. A scribbled note in Barney's hand said: 'I think Gilpin's up for some sort of award. Zoë, Hrishikesh and I are going. You will come won't you?'

I discussed it with Chris and sent him an email to say that we would. On the appointed evening, Barney and Zoë collected us from home. Barney and I were in DJs although he drew the line at wearing a bow tie. The girls looked lovely. The reception was packed and we knew a lot of people there from the Cumbria's hotels and restaurants.

After dinner, tension grew as the host, Prue Leith, stepped up to the podium to present the awards. There were a dozen or more, and Gilpin's main HRiSHi restaurant did not win the coveted "Restaurant of the Year".

I was disappointed – though we received consolation near the end when Gilpin Spice was named "Best Newcomer".

There was only one award left listed in the programme, which was described as "A Special Award".

'And finally,' said Prue, 'we come to a Lifetime Achievement Award for a very special couple who have worked in the Cumbrian hospitality industry for just short of thirty years.'

The lights dimmed and music struck up. And there was Gilpin on the screen and in the next frame a picture of Chris and me, Chris in her chef's whites and me in a blazer standing in front of the old Gilpin Lodge porch as it had been when we bought it.

I have little remembrance of the rest of the video except some very kind words from Mike Bevans, who had just sold Linthwaite House. I'm told now that Barney was in it too, and there had obviously been secret filming taking place at Gilpin for weeks.

I have some recollection of Chris and I walking up to the stage. I recall Prue giving Chris a trophy. I recall some thunderous scraping of chairs and loud applause. I think I made a little speech but have no idea what I said.

Then Barney came around the table and kissed Chris and then me.

'And that,' he said, 'was why you couldn't go away in mid-March.'

Chapter Thirty-One

SLIGHTLY PERFECT

To say that Barney and Zoë love sailing is probably an understatement. Recently, they asked Chris and me if we would like to come with them, and Xiá of course, to the Boat Show at Southampton. I forget whether we laughed out loud at this suggestion or just sniggered discreetly.

We went. It was a glorious day. We stayed at the Novotel, which is very convenient to the show, and ate in some appalling Chinese restaurant recommended by the hotel. It was a relaxed and jolly evening. Next morning Barney was on a mission. And how! We skirted aspects of the show which might have been of interest and seemed inexorably drawn towards a stand to which he had an introduction. Lagoon catamarans. Although we did go through the process of visiting other stands and crawling around other boats, both monohulls and catamarans, there was really nothing else to compare. The vessel we inspected from the bilges to the masthead was a Lagoon 450. And it was indeed a smooth baby with wood-panelled cabins, sleek lines and a functional cockpit filled with gauges and dials sufficient to make a sailor drool. And drool Barney did.

Zoë is less droolsome, and I think Chris commented that it was a boat like any other. Fairly typical. I loved it but the money was terrifying. We were unable to sail in her because she was needed to be on display at the show. But Barney forged a solid relationship with the lady in charge of the Lagoons, and she promised to arrange a date when we could sail in her.

That evening in the hotel's restaurant we talked nothing but Lagoons and chartering and using the boat in association with the business for management bonuses and training purposes, and Barney prepared spreadsheets of possible affordability between mouthfuls of steak and copious quantities of wine. We all went to bed. We had adjoining bedrooms.

Chris said she wanted a brandy from the minibar. This was rather unusual and I didn't know what to make of it. I poured us both a brandy.

'Can't we afford it?' She asked. 'They work so hard and they're in love with that boat.'

'Yes', I replied. 'But then there won't be any money left for other things.'

'You love it too, don't you? I could see you eyeing up those dials and gadgets. Tell them we'll have it. Go on before they go to sleep.'

I opened the adjoining door. Xiá was asleep. Barney and Zoë were snuggled up to each other.

'She says to tell you we'll have it,' I said.

'Pissed old farts,' Zoë replied, in her usual respectful manner.

'But what do you think?' Barney asked. I paused in an attempt to give a viable answer.

'I want it like hell for you guys,' I said. 'Emotionally I would love it. Practically I am not sure it's sensible. Financially I'm not sure we can really afford it.'

'OK. Let's sleep on it.'

We flew from Manchester to Southampton a few weeks later, hired a car and drove to the marina. The wind was blowing a gale and the skipper was not sure it was sensible to take on Southampton Water in such conditions, particularly as there was a spring tide running which would make docking very tricky. He decided that he would go for it but explained that he would need Barney and Zoë's sailing experience to help. Chris and I were given total responsibility for Xiá, who of course perceived no danger.

It was a rip-roaring sail by any standards and exhilarating in the extreme. To my surprise, I was invited to take the wheel when we were well out in the sound. To steer a straight course in such conditions was a challenge, the accomplishment of which I found exhilarating. The simple act of pushing one button activated autopilot which was altogether easier. Indeed you did nothing other than ensure that you were not going to hit anything. The depth of water had to be watched too, even though a catamaran draws far less water than a monohull due to the absence of a keel.

I loved it and so did we all. I also realised that however much training I undertook, I would never be strong enough or confident enough to skipper a boat like this at my age, particularly if anything went wrong. This became a sobering thought in the overall consideration. Under those circumstances, could we really justify owning such a craft? The docking was indeed a formidable task involving strong winds and a vicious tide. It was undertaken with great skill.

On the way back to Manchester, we were a bit quiet. I don't think any of us knew what to do. And still don't if you want me to be totally honest. Emotionally – yes. Practically – no. And that's the way it has been left. Except that we agreed we would charter a similar boat in the Caribbean the following year and see how it went.

Normally, Barney and Zoë and Chris and I don't go abroad together unless we really need to. In the past this had been for the occasional Relais & Châteaux conference or other business-related matter. But we felt that times had changed; we had more managers now and January is a quiet time. We felt guilty as we left the Lake House after lunch on New Year's Day to catch a flight to Paris Charles de Gaulle and thence to Tortola in the British Virgin Islands, and finally to Road Town in a small aeroplane which barely took the five of us and our not inconsiderable luggage.

It was a long and tiring journey but we felt worth it as we arrived at Maria's hotel in time for dinner. A loud local New Year party was in full swing in the adjoining room and Xiá was invited to join in. The next day was spent in provisioning and on the Saturday we joined our boat and set sail in the late afternoon. Captain Barney was very much the skipper, and from my point of view I was relieved that he was. The weather was idyllic and we were all happy. Xiá behaved perfectly and with absolute responsibility. Chris and I, as absolute novices, started to learn the ropes and we became adept at cooking on a gently rocking stove.

Two or three days into our holiday, Barney and Zoë were on the bridge and Chris, Xiá and I were sitting in the cockpit. It was about midday – beer o'clock! Xiá was plotting the next day's route, having been shown the rudiments of navigation by Barney at breakfast that morning.

She nonchalantly waved a pair of dividers in the air and said, 'Pamma; Pampa. I want you to know that I am very happy.'

This is the way she talks. A combination of sophistication with the odd word thrown in with a Cumbrian accent. And such innocence.

'Wonderful!' Chris said. 'Just because you're on holiday, or because you like sailing?'

'All those things,' she said, 'but mostly because we're all together. I just wish Ben and Rachel and Alice and Freddie were here too.'

'Alice and Freddie are too little to be on a boat out at sea,' I said. 'What would happen if they fell overboard?'

'I wish we could all be together more often,' she said rather sadly. 'Everyone's always working. And I'm always at school. And I have to stay there all afternoon because Mummy's got to work.'

I felt there was a message here.

'Xiá,' I said, reflecting her touch of seriousness in my own tone, 'people do have to work hard, particularly if they're going to have enough money for holidays like this. Can you imagine what it costs for us to travel all this way and to hire a big boat like this?'

'Is it a lot?' she asked.

'Yes,' I replied. 'And it all comes from Gilpin because that's where Mummy and Daddy and Pamma and I work.'

She seemed to consider this.

I mused that she might not have really worked that out before.

'So you see,' I went on, 'we all have to work hard so that Gilpin is really nice and our guests want to come back time and time again. And you have to become really clever from being at school so that when Mummy and Daddy are as old as Pamma and me, you can look after Gilpin.'

'Gilpin is nice,' she said. 'It's perfect.'

'It's not perfect,' said Chris. 'I wish it were.'

'Then it's slightly perfect,' she said definitively.

Out of the mouths of babes...

Chapter Thirty-Three

A LITTLE EPILOGUE

As we sat in the sunshine, it only took me a few minutes to know that *Slightly Perfect* was to be the title of the book that had been rolling around in my head for some years. But in less emotional moments and as the holiday progressed, I also worried. Could "slightly perfect" applied to Gilpin be construed as complacent? Self-satisfied?

Then I argued (with myself) thus: if perfect is 100%, then almost perfect might be 75%, semi-perfect should mathematically be 50%, then slightly perfect should be 25%. Could Gilpin be less than 25% perfect? I do hope not. Like all businesses dependant largely on people, we are not anything like perfect. But we try hard.

I mused about Xiá's extraordinary incongruity and whether perfection could in fact be divided into lesser levels of such.

I refuted my own analysis of perfection and decided that yes! There certainly could be *slight* perfection.

One so young had in fact given voice to a major basis of happiness – aspiration to and achievement of some degree of perfection.

Thank you very much for reading *Slightly Perfect*. If you have reached this page then I assume you have read it all.

Unless you skipped chunks!